CHIMES OF FREEDOM

Also by Mike Marqusee

Slow Turn, a novel

Defeat from the Jaws of Victory: Inside Kinnock's Labour Party
(with Richard Heffernan)

Anyone But England: Cricket and the National Malaise

War Minus the Shooting:
A Journey through South Asia During Cricket's World Cup

Redemption Song: Muhammad Ali and the Spirit of the Sixties

CHIMES OF FREEDOM

The Politics of Bob Dylan's Art

MIKE MARQUSEE

THE NEW PRESS

NEW YORK
LONDON

Published in the United States by The New Press, New York, 2003
Distributed by W. W. Norton & Company, Inc., New York

ISBN 1-56584-825-X
CIP data available

The New Press was established in 1990 as a not-for-profit alternative to the
large, commercial publishing houses currently dominating the book
publishing industry. The New Press operates in the public interest rather
than for private gain, and is committed to publishing, in innovative ways,
works of educational, cultural, and community value that are
often deemed insufficiently profitable.

The New Press
38 Greene Street, 4th floor
New York, NY 10013
www.thenewpress.com

In the United Kingdom:
6 Salem Road
London W2 4BU

Composition by dix!

Printed in the United States of America

2   4   6   8   10   9   7   5   3   1

CONTENTS

ACKNOWLEDGMENTS

I am indebted to a number of friends who read the manuscript in various stages and offered a multitude of valuable comments: Anthony Arnove, Jane Ashworth, Terry Conway, Richard Ehrlich, Steve Faulkner, Gabriel Furshong, Alan Goode, Tony Graham, Randy Ostrow.

Thanks also to Jane Barrett, Jeremy Corbyn, John Davies, Michael Letwin, Dave Lubell, Jeff Marqusee, Martin Morand, Charles Shaar Murray, Jane Shallice, Irwin Silber, Steve Wagg for ideas, sources, and suggestions. Thanks to Roger Huddle at Redwords for first encouraging me to write about Dylan.

Big up to Steve, Jane and the Mbotyi crew—thanks for the Dylananny.

How can I thank Colin Robinson, my publisher and friend, for his ceaseless encouragement, his critical advice and his challenge to me to stretch myself? As they say on the terraces, there's only one Col . . .

Finally, for many months, Liz Davies lived with Dylan's voice wafting nonstop through our shared home. Much more difficult, she lived with my babbling about the man and his music from early morn to late at night. Without her to share the enthusiasm, the discoveries and the doubts, there wouldn't be much point. She knows too much *not* to argue or to judge.

INTRODUCTION

Where do you want this killing done?

—BOB DYLAN, 1965

WHEN BOB DYLAN performed "Masters of War" at concerts in the United States of America in the weeks after September 11, 2001, members of the audience punctuated the song with lusty shouts of "Death to Bin Laden!" It seems some of them heard the protest-era favorite as an indictment, not of America's military-industrial complex, but of its enemies in the war on terror.

It is unlikely Dylan will ever tell us what he meant in singing this song at this moment. Enigma has long been his stock-in-trade. After all, he never really told us what he thought about the Vietnam War. However, it is worth noting that Dylan also chose to play "Masters of War" at the 1991 Grammy ceremony, in the middle of the Gulf War waged by the first president Bush.

Any song or work of art that survives its historical point of origin is liable to ironic transmutations. Unanchored in an environment of shared meanings, it can even be turned into its opposite. Are there better examples of the protean power of modern capitalism to appropriate expressions of resistance than the adoption of "The Times They Are A-Changin' " as an advertising jingle by mega-accountants Coopers and Lybrand?

I can't remember when I first encountered Dylan. I know that becoming aware of him was conjoined with taking my first steps as both a political agent and a self-conscious consumer of cultural goods. By the time I was fourteen in 1967, I had heard most of the albums Dylan had released by then, was familiar with his legend and convinced that he was the cutting edge of advanced cultural consciousness, the acme of cool. I knew that he had defied critics, blazed a trail, crashed on a motorcycle, and gone into retreat. I tried to write Dylanesque poetry.

For a kid who was more comfortable with books and ideas than with social interaction, but who was nonetheless turned on by and desperately wanted to be part of the "something" that was "happening," Dylan was a talisman. I loved the visceral thrust of Dylan's music, as well as the fact that it left much to ponder over. Dylan was a bridge spanning my own contradictory impulses. On the one hand, the world was clearly riddled with injustice. Those who sought to challenge it were righteous; I wanted to be one of them. On the other hand, the world was also clearly full of beautiful, tantalizing, surprising things; I wanted to experience them. I gobbled up poetry and movies and paintings and music—and also news from an increasingly violent society and from the movement dedicated to changing it. I wanted somehow to reconcile these two spheres of existence, the personal and the public, and like others of the time performed some prodigious mental gymnastics in my efforts to do so. My sixties experience—not least listening to Dylan—set me off, perhaps too often, looking for the aesthetic in the political and the political in the aesthetic.

In the sixties, I was, however, given one immeasurable gift. I witnessed and was part of a rapid and unexpected mass radicalization. The assumptions saturating cold war America were challenged with a vigor and headlong insurgency that no one had predicted. That process opened dizzying vistas of transformation—social and personal. This was a curse as well as a blessing. To be young at such times is not always, contrary to Wordsworth, "very heaven." In the sixties in the United States of America, to be young was to be constantly challenged, frequently insecure, often frightened; it was to be torn by multiple desires, thrown into the cauldron of history ill-prepared, and often ill-guided.

In tracking Dylan's febrile motion through the decade, I've recalled my own wayward developing consciousness of those days. But I've also relied on what has come after—politically and personally. When I arrived in England in 1971, I found that Dylan, along with the counter-culture of which he seemed an integral part, provided a common frame of reference. In fact, Dylan's record sales have always been proportionately higher in Britain than in the United States.

The American sixties are part of the global sixties. Remove one from the other and the equation changes, the dynamic that made the era alters. However, the American sixties do remain distinctive. What made them so was the political culture in which they unfolded. This culture was marked by the weakness of socialist traditions, especially within the labor movement, the absence of mass parties, the centrality of racial oppression, the widespread belief in America's exceptional destiny and identity, and the reality that America had become an empire that dared not speak its name. Above all, it was in the USA that the global trends of consumerization and media-saturation were most advanced in the sixties. The association of sixties rebellions with the power of images, symbols, and cultural products emanates from this American experience. Ironically, American capital has helped disseminate dissident American culture around the world, and wherever people could get their hands on it, they made their own use of it. The music Bob Dylan made in the sixties has long outgrown its national origins, just as it has outlived its era, but to understand it, to make best use of it, you need to trace its roots in both time and place.

However you measure Dylan's subsequent achievements (and they are substantial), they do not enjoy the same umbilical relation to the turmoil of the times as the work of the sixties. This is a body of song tied to the unfolding political and cultural drama of its era in a way that the later work is not. Tracing the thread that binds Dylan's art to its rapidly shifting environment is this book's primary purpose. However, in reading the songs in their musical and political context, I don't see them as transparent reflections of the times but as expressive objects fashioned by an individual in response to those times. Dylan was not a passive lightning rod, an impersonal conductor of great historic currents. Rather, he was a navigator of those currents.

The sixties played out in miniature many of the soul-shaking extremes of other eras of upsurge and reaction—aspiration, frustration, missionary zeal, and crippling self-doubt. It's rare, however, to find so much of this historical experience compressed into the work of a single artist. Few ages of social change have been as well-served artistically as the American sixties were by Dylan. His songs give us the political/cultural moment in all its dynamic complexity.

As Dylan's lifetime record/tape/CD sales inch past the thirty-five million mark, it's well to remember than he is outsold not only by the 100-million-topping Beatles and Presley, but also by Prince, Madonna, Elton John, Michael Jackson, the Eagles, Aerosmith, and Kenny Rogers. What matters in the history of popular culture, in the end, is not merely how many people buy a product but what that product means to them, the role it plays in their lives, its shaping power over their imaginations. Popular culture is not an undifferentiated mass. Both aesthetic and political engagement with it demand that we make discriminations and judgments. One of the lessons of Dylan's art in the sixties is that under the right circumstances, the producers and consumers of popular culture engage in the most lively and contentious manner in the making of discriminations and judgments. To fail to do so is to condescend to the genre, the performer, the audience, and the era.

My aim is not to claim Dylan for a cause. I do, however, aim to examine Dylan's work in its time partly in order to serve a cause: to draw inspiration, lessons, and warnings. I wrote this book with the hard rain headed Iraq's way. Many of the young antiwar activists I've met in recent months know Dylan's work and see him as an artist of protest—despite the fact that he turned his back on political engagement nearly forty years ago. Sometimes, I think they are too daunted by the sixties. Self-indulgent celebration of our generation and of Dylan does them no favors. The legacy of the era is rich, but only if it's examined critically.

During the period covered by this book Dylan released eight albums, wrote hundreds of unreleased songs, gave countless live performances, and astounded his followers with a swift succession of stylistic, political, and personal transmutations—from folk neophyte to protest singer to rock 'n' roll poet to wise old country sage. The changes were real and hectic. But in what follows I've also emphasized the continuities. This is an integral body of work produced by a single artist, recognizable through all his adventures.

This book tells the story of an artist and a movement. It's a story that unfolds through what might be called an extended, multilayered historical moment. Looking back on the decade at the end of the sixties, Julius Lester was struck by the distance that had been traveled.

> To go from sit-in demonstrations at lunch counters in the south to the Black Panther Party, from pacifist demonstrations against nuclear testing to a mass anti-war movement, from the beat generation to a cultural revolution is a ten-year journey almost beyond comprehension. Yet, this is the journey which has been made.[1]

Lester himself covered many miles: starting the decade as a folk singer, he ended it as a black nationalist, later converted to Judaism and became a prolific writer of children's books. The journey was never even-paced or straightforward, nor did everyone start at the same point, follow the same route or end up at the same destination. There were no maps. It was easy to lose your way. Dylan offered a signpost: "To live outside the law you must be honest." But as no one knew better than Dylan, it was hard advice to follow.

The ideas, impulses, prejudices I absorbed in the sixties have determined many of the choices I've made, and many of those I've avoided. I've never succeeded in balancing the aesthetic and the political. Nonetheless, as I am a hopeless case, I suspect I'll go on trying to do so, no matter how frustrating the results. This book is part of that effort.

1

THE WHOLE WIDE WORLD IS WATCHIN'

Every honest man is a prophet. He utters his opinion on private and public matters.

—William Blake

AT NOON on August 28, 1963, the Washington, D.C., police announced that 200,000 people had gathered in the city to join the March for Jobs and Freedom. For hours after that, many more continued to stream in from all corners of the country. There were twenty-one chartered trains and hundreds of buses backed up for miles on the routes leading to the capital. Among the demonstrators were tens of thousands of whites—union stalwarts, students, intellectuals, leftists. But mostly the marchers were black, and large numbers were from the South. They poured into the streets singing the freedom songs that had kept up their strength through the last, brutal years of the frontline struggle against Jim Crow. "Woke up this mornin' with my mind set on freedom . . ." Suddenly, the spirit of the mass meetings that had inspired and coordinated the wave of direct action against American apartheid in hundreds of southern towns was being carried into the streets of the nation's capital and broadcast live on network television. Rejoicing in their numbers, revelling in the discovery that they really were part of a great movement, the marchers, of all colors, were bound together by a vital intuition: you weren't as alone as you had so often felt back in your Mississippi hamlet, your college campus, your factory, or your folkie coffeehouse.[1]

As the demonstrators assembled, they were entertained by a troupe of folksingers stationed at the foot of the Washington Monument. Joan Baez sang "Oh Freedom." Odetta sang "I'm On My Way." She was soon joined by Josh White, the smooth-voiced black folkie with a long history of left-wing connections (in the thirties, White had fronted a blues band called the Carolinians, one of whose members was march organizer Bayard Rustin).[2] Together, Odetta, White, Baez and Peter, Paul and Mary sang "Blowin' in the Wind"—the wistful anthem whose recording by the folk trio had surprised everyone by reaching number two in the pop charts earlier in the summer.

Then the twenty-two-year-old author of this unlikely hit single, tousled, slight, tense, took his turn at the microphone. He stood before the greatest mass mobilization of African Americans ever seen and, without comment, sang two songs. Both were recent compositions, unfamiliar to his audience and even to his fellow folksingers. Both were perfectly in tune with the occasion, and at the same time decidedly different from anything sung by anyone else that day.[3]

The first was "When the Ship Comes In," in which Dylan celebrates a great eruption ("the seas will split . . . the shoreline will be shaking") that will usher in the day when "the sun will respect / Every face on the deck," "the fishes will laugh" and even "the rocks on the sand / Will proudly stand." In this jaunty vision of inclusive, unqualified liberation—unfolding as "the whole wide world is watchin' "—the "ship" may serve as a metaphor for many things, but there can't be much doubt that on this day, and in this era, it symbolized that complex of insurgent social forces commonly dubbed, among participants, "the Movement."

In its promise of an egalitarian future and its use of Biblical phraseology, the song shared ground with the "dream" that Martin Luther King expounded later that afternoon in the speech that came to epitomize the March on Washington and eventually an entire epoch of African American politics and culture. However, Dylan's new song also struck a note alien to King's commitment to reconciliation and forgiveness, his belief that ultimately the civil rights movement would convert its enemies. The last two verses depict a different kind of triumph:

Oh the foes will rise
With the sleep still in their eyes
And they'll jerk from their beds and think they're dreamin'
But they'll pinch themselves and squeal
And know that it's for real,
The hour when the ship comes in.

Then they'll raise their hands,
Sayin' we'll meet all your demands,
But we'll shout from the bow, "your days are numbered."
And like Pharaoh's tribe,
They'll be drownded in the tide,
And like Goliath, they'll be conquered.

The spur for this joyously humane but also gleefully vindictive paean had been a petty snub. Weeks before the march, Dylan had been turned away by a hotel receptionist who had failed to recognize the scruffy, incommunicative folksinger. After Baez turned up and straightened out the confusion, Dylan sat down in his room, remembered Brecht and Weill's Pirate Jenny,* and wrote "When the Ship Comes In," turning petulance into poetry (not for the first or last time).

The spur for the next song he sang was also a recent one, but much graver—the assassination of NAACP leader Medgar Evers on June 12 in Jackson, Mississippi, only hours after President Kennedy had announced his intention to seek new civil rights legislation. Where "When The Ship Comes In" skipped ethereally, "Only a Pawn in Their Game" marched with harsh and funereal determination. The focus of the song is not, in fact, Medgar Evers (though justice is done to the slain leader in the majestic line, "they laid him down like a king") but the man who shot him, and above all the political system that generated the murder. With its rap-like rhyming and tautly measured explication, the song is

---

* In *The Threepenny Opera*, the scrubwoman Jenny dreams of a pirate ship that will sail into harbor, lay waste the rich and comfortable, and leave her to decide who will live or die.

driven forward by a contained rage. It insists that we feel the singer's anger, but it demands more than that.

> The South politician preaches to the poor white man,
> "You got more than the blacks, don't complain.
> You're better than them,
> You been born with white skin,"
> They explain . . .

On a day when everyone else was singing about freedom and deliverance and unity Dylan was outlining a class-based analysis of the persistence of racism—and the central weight of white-skin privilege within the American polity.

The summer of 1963 was the apogee of the folk-music craze. Dylan, Baez and Peter, Paul and Mary were its biggest names—but they still meant little to most of the marchers, whose response to the singers was merely polite. What really excited the crowd was the arrival in their midst of the movie stars (Paul Newman, Marlon Brando, Charlton Heston, Burt Lancaster) and the prospect of hearing gospel queen Mahalia Jackson sing later in the afternoon (in this Dylan seems to have agreed with them). After Dylan finished his two songs, he remained at the microphone to join the other folksingers in backing up his friend Len Chandler (one of the few black faces on the Greenwich Village scene) on "Keep Your Eyes on the Prize." The whole troupe—Peter, Paul and Mary, Baez, Dylan, Odetta, Josh White, and the SNCC Freedom Singers—finished the midday entertainment with "We Shall Overcome," the acknowledged anthem of the movement.

Meanwhile, in its exuberance, the crowd had disregarded the official marshals and surged ahead of schedule toward the Lincoln Memorial. To create the illusion for posterity that Martin Luther King and the heads of the major sponsoring organizations had led the way, the marshals waded in and wedged open a space for the designated leaders, who duly squeezed themselves in front of the enthusiastic multitude, locked arms and had their photographs taken.

Once safely backstage, the march leaders squabbled. At issue was the anguished, impatient, militant rhetoric of the speech to be given by John Lewis on behalf of the Student Nonviolent Coordinating Committee,* whose young black activists had been at the sharp end of the struggle in the South. Over the previous three and a half years, since the first sit-ins, their willingness to suffer and sacrifice had driven the movement forward. The march was a vindication of their heroism and a testament to an aroused people. But the question was: where next? The SNCC activists could not share the march's official mood of optimism (a mood partly engendered by their own heroic actions) and specifically its uncritical approach to the Kennedy administration and the federal government. Many of the young militants, freshly scarred on the battlefields of the South, feared that the demonstration and the movement were being appropriated—by the Kennedy administration, by the middle-class black leadership, by the establishment media.

The draft of Lewis's speech included not only barbed criticisms of the failures of the federal government and the inadequacies of JFK's proposed legislation ("too little, too late"), but also what seemed to the elders an incendiary pledge: "We shall pursue our own scorched earth policy and burn Jim Crow to the ground—non-violently." Walter Reuther, the UAW leader whose union had bankrolled the march, was furious. Officials at the Justice Department, who had somehow seen advance copies, proposed amendments. A Catholic archbishop threatened to walk off the platform. NAACP leader Roy Wilkins, who had offered SNCC activists in the field little support, shouted and waved his finger at Lewis, and Lewis reciprocated. King urged some changes in the speech's style that, he assured Lewis, would not be changes in substance. Lewis agreed, and SNCC secretary James Forman, whom Dylan had met and admired in Mississippi earlier in the summer, hastily retyped the speech, deleting what he himself considered its deeper truths. For the moment, the desire to preserve movement unity prevailed.

Even in its censored form, Lewis's speech went far beyond the consensual limits respected by other speakers. In its litany of arrests, bomb-

---

* SNCC, always pronounced *snick*.

ings, beatings, and killings, its description of civil rights workers and black communities living "in constant fear of a police state" and its angry refrain "what did the federal government do?," it emphasized that political institutions, and not merely "prejudice," were the key obstacles to equality. On that day, Dylan was the only other voice to stress the reality of the state's collaboration with racism as he sang: "The deputy sheriffs, the soldiers, the governors get paid / And the marshals and cops get the same." It was Lewis who spelled out what "Only a Pawn in Their Game" was hinting at:

> My friends, let us not forget that we are involved in a serious social revolution. By and large, American politics is dominated by politicians who build their careers on immoral compromises and ally themselves with open forms of political, economic and social exploitation. . . . Where is our party? Where is the political party that will make it unnecessary to march on Washington? Where is the political party that will make it unnecessary to march on the streets of Birmingham?[4]

Dylan echoed Lewis's speech in the lines addressed to James Forman in "11 Outlined Epitaphs," written in September 1963, within weeks of the march, and published as the liner notes on his third album, *The Times They Are A-Changin'*:

> Jim, Jim
> where is our party?
> where is the party that's one
> where all members're held equal
> an' vow t'infiltrate that thought
> among the people it hopes t'serve
> an' sets a respected road
> for all of those like me

In Washington, Lewis's speech was well-received, but it was Mahalia Jackson's singing "I Been Buked and I Been Scorned" that really roused the huge throng, and it was King's climactic peroration that sent them home filled with hope and purpose. In fact, King at one point seemed to be losing his way as he read from his carefully prepared text. Behind him, Mahalia Jackson called, "Tell 'em about the dream, Martin." Abandoning his script, King rose to the occasion with a vision of the society they were struggling and sacrificing to create. Behind the famous speech were many of the elements that had forged the folksingers' repertoire and infused the new music of Bob Dylan: the imagery and rhythmic syntax of the King James Bible, the call-and-response traditions of the black church, the music created by the slaves and the field hands, the sense of a collective destiny that yet also demanded an individual moral choice, the search for an idiom that could reach and move masses of modern human beings. Like the singers of the spirituals, King fashioned a durable utopian vision out of the brutality of centuries of racism. He spun gold from the mire. And as he did so, Dylan watched and listened, along with hundreds of thousands in the mall and millions more via television (and not only in America).

The stirring sounds and images of the March on Washington helped place the African American demand for legal equality at the center of American popular consciousness. But they also became the means by which the legacy of the movement came to be tamed. Today the march appears a distant and depoliticized phenomenon, an idealistic celebration of human brotherhood. Even on the day itself, the debate had begun: Was this an exercise in resistance or cooptation? Malcolm X sat contemptuously on the sidelines, mocking "the farce on Washington" and decrying the moderate leaders as the "puppets" of a white political system. Some of the young SNCC activists were almost ready to agree. In the face of an America that had, in their immediate experience, revealed ever-deeper layers of brutality, the potential America of brotherhood and freedom celebrated in folk song and in civil rights speeches was beginning to seem nothing but a cruel illusion. What was needed was much more than a few legislative reforms. At this stage, these sentiments were confined to a small minority, but there can be little doubt that Bob Dylan was among them, though as ever, for his own reasons and in his own manner.

In August 1963, at the very moment the great civil rights coalition was redefining the national consensus, its constituent elements and impulses were coming into conflict; its underlying contradictions were beginning to surface. The rhetoric of love and unity was being challenged by a more militant, hard-edged analysis. The radicals were leaving the liberals behind, but where were they going?

While the march itself received overwhelmingly favorable publicity (reading the reports now, one is struck by the patronizing note with which white reporters informed their readers that the Negro masses had behaved well), not everyone was impressed by the contribution of Dylan and the folkies. In the extensive *New York Times* coverage, Dylan was mentioned twenty-three paragraphs below a quote from waning teen idol Bobby Darin, who did not perform. "Bob Dylan, a young folksinger, rendered a lugubrious mountain song about 'the day Medgar Evers was buried from a bullet that he caught.' Mr. Lancaster, Mr. Belafonte and Mr. Heston found time dragging, stood up to stretch and chat." A commentator in the *Boston Herald* mocked:

> Though I am all for such civil rights as integrate white and colored, I am not yet convinced that white should be expected to put up with white— or rather with every other white. Fair is fair, but should anyone be made to go to school with such as, say, this Dylan? And would you want your sister to marry him? . . . Our colored brethren were actually implying that we are expected to give house room to fraudulent folk singers.[5]

As Dylan sang, Dick Gregory, the comedian-activist who had repeatedly exposed himself to arrest and beatings on visits to the South, covered his ears. "What was a white boy like Bob Dylan there for?" he asked. "Or—who else? Joan Baez? To support the cause? Wonderful—support the cause. March. Stand behind us—but not in front of us." Harry Belafonte, whose commitment to the movement was regarded by activists as second to none, took a different view. "Joan and Bob demonstrated with their participation that freedom and justice are universal concerns of import to responsible people of all colors. . . . Were they taking advantage of the movement? Or was the movement taking advantage of them?"[6]

The role of the white and (relatively) famous in a mass movement for black rights was only one aspect of broader questions that were to haunt the decade. Whose was the authentic voice of the movement? What was the relationship between the experience of oppression and the protest against it? Where was the line between selling the message and selling out? In this movement to end exploitation, who was exploiting whom? As the sixties wore on, the relationship between vanguards (or would-be vanguards) and the masses of people they claimed to speak for and aimed to mobilize, was to grow more acutely troubled— even as larger numbers were drawn into political action. No sooner did challenges from below thrust themselves into public view than their language, gestures, and cultural products were snapped up by a new mass media, packaged and sold to a new mass market. These political and cultural tensions were dramatized in Dylan's music and the public response to it. Throughout the decade, they drove his art forward at breakneck pace.

America was still very "straight," "postwar" and sort of into a gray-flannelled suit thing. McCarthy, commies, puritanical, very claustrophobic and whatever was happening of real value was happening away from that and sort of hidden from view and it would be years before the media would be able to recognize it and choke-hold it and reduce it to silliness.

—BOB DYLAN[7]

Bob Dylan arrived in Greenwich Village in February 1961, still only nineteen, with a head full of songs—pop, rock 'n' roll, gospel, blues, country, folk. The scion of a small-town, middle-class Jewish upbringing in northern Minnesota, he had already renamed himself and re-modeled himself as a latter-day Woody Guthrie, a veteran of hard times and the open road. With his strangled singing, mumbling nervous manner, tall tales of sitting at the feet of ancient bluesmen and his ersatz

Okie accent, he struck not a few as affected and preposterous. Nonetheless, he quickly won the admiration of a small coterie of dedicated folk artists and fans. The Irish singer Liam Clancy recalled the chainsmoking cherub who insinuated himself so rapidly into the hothouse Village scene: "The only thing I can compare him with is blotting paper. He soaked everything up. He had this immense curiosity; he was totally blank, and ready to suck up everything that was within his range." [8] Famously, Dylan soaked up songs—poring over his friends' record collections and raiding the repertoire of every singer in town. But along with the songs there was much more to soak up "within his range"—a living heritage of political, cultural, and personal dissent.

Greenwich Village had first become America's bohemian capital in the years before World War I, when intellectuals and artists had been drawn to the neighborhood by its cheap rents and immigrant community, which, as in so many cities and eras, offered a protective bolt-hole for dissidents and eccentrics. John Reed celebrated the joys of "living at 42 Washington Square" in a poem published in 1913: "But nobody questions your morals, / And nobody asks for the rent / There's no one to pry if we're tight, you and I / Or demand how our evenings are spent." Reed shared this Village demimonde with political activists like Emma Goldman, Dorothy Day, and Margaret Sanger, artists like John Sloan and Eugene O'Neill, and intellectuals like Max Eastman. Many contributed to The Masses, fountainhead of America's alternative press, which advertised itself as "a revolutionary and not a reform magazine; a magazine with a sense of humor and no respect for the respectable; frank, arrogant, impertinent, a magazine whose final policy is to do as it pleases, and conciliate nobody, not even its readers."

The prewar Masses-Village milieu "contained two types of revolt," Malcolm Cowley recalled, "the individual and the social—or the aesthetic and the political, or the revolt against puritanism and the revolt against capitalism—we might tag the two of them briefly as bohemianism and radicalism. In those prewar days, however, the two currents were hard to distinguish. Bohemians read Marx and all the radicals had a touch of the Bohemian. Socialism, free love, anarchism, syndicalism, free verse—all these creeds were lumped together by the public and all were physically dangerous to practice."[9]

World War I fractured these comingling currents, but they were to remain, in varying admixtures, part and parcel of the Greenwich Village scene as it mutated over the following decades. The legacy of that sometimes fruitful, sometimes frustrating search for a synthesis between individual creativity and collective political action, between vanguard modernism and popular radicalism—what might be called the evanescent *Masses* moment—is the launch point for Dylan's extraordinary journey through the sixties.

I could see men of all colors bouncing in the boxcar. The first line of *Bound for Glory,* Woody Guthrie's 1943 autobiography, sets the theme and tone for the book, a picaresque account of the adventures of a democratic-minded individual among an interracial people on the move. Dylan read a friend's copy of the first edition in Minneapolis in 1960. The impact was immediate and decisive. He adopted his Woody Guthrie persona and set about mastering Woody's songbook. He even copied Woody's vernacular orthography, scattering apostrophes across the page, using phonetic renderings like *wuz* and *sez.*

Guthrie's book exalted the working class in all its colors, accents, and moods; it raged against cops and security guards; it flashed with contempt for the rich and their stooges. It was also peppered with vivid evocations of a vast, changing landscape and a cheerfully unmoralistic approach to drink, gambling, lovemaking, and crime. Importantly for the young Dylan, it told the story of Guthrie's vocation as a maker of songs for ordinary people. The teenage Guthrie had felt a need to express himself. "Things was starting to stack up in my head and I just felt like I was going out of my wits if I didn't find some way of saying what I was thinking." After trying oil painting, he turned to the guitar. He was soon playing at square dances—and making up new words for old tunes. "There on the Texas plains right in the dead center of the dust bowl, with the oil boom over and the wheat blowed out and the hard-working people just stumbling about, bothered with mortgages, debts, bills, sickness, worries of every blowing kind, I seen there was plenty to make up songs about." [10]

The music that stirred him came from working people: "no Hollywood put-on, no fake wiggling" but songs that "say something about our hard travelling, something about our hard luck, our hard get-by." But singing such songs didn't make it easy to earn a living. He tells a passing girlfriend: "Most radio stations, they won't let ya sing th' real songs. They want ya ta sing pure ol' bull manure an' nothin' else. So I can't never git ahold of money an' stuff it'd take ta keep you an' me in a house an' home—so I been a-lyin' to my own self now fer a good long time, sayin' I didn't want no little house an' all that . . ." [11]

Nonetheless, Guthrie's brilliance as an entertainer did earn him commercial opportunities. In *Bound for Glory,* he sums up his response to these in a tale of his audition at the Rainbow Room, the elite watering hole on the 65th floor of Rockefeller Center in mid-Manhattan "where the shrimps are boiled in Standard Oil." As he approaches the microphone, he reviews the varied venues he's sung at in recent months— from the apricot orchards of California and the "tough joints around th' battery park" to CBS studios and a huge union meeting in Madison Square Garden. At the last moment, he decides to sing a song called "New York Town," with new words: "the rainbow room is up so high / that John D's* spirit comes a driftin' by."

> I took the tune to church, took it holy roller, shot in a few split notes, oozed in a fake one, come down barrel house, hit off a good old cross-country lonesome note or two, trying to get that old guitar to help me, to talk with me, talk for me, and say what I was thinking, just this one time:

> Well this Rainbow Rooms a funny place ta play
> It's a long way's from here to th'USA

The Rainbow Room bosses are delighted and offer him a job. They decide he should wear makeup (he looks too pale under the lights) and,

---

* John D. Rockefeller, founder of the dynasty.

worse yet, a costume. A gushing rich woman suggests he dress in French peasant garb, or as a Louisiana swamp dweller, or as a clownlike Pierrot figure, something to evoke "quaint simplicity." Meanwhile, Woody looks out the window at the city below, and the innumerable New Yorkers "standing up living and breathing and cussing and laughing down yonder." Telling his would-be patrons that he is going to the rest room, he hops in the elevator and says to the operator: "Quickest way down's too slow." As he walks into the polished marble foyer, he sings and strums his guitar as loud as he can: "Old John Dee he ain't no friend of mine," then wanders through the teaming city. "Thank the good Lord, everybody, everything ain't all slicked up, and starched and imitation." [12]

This hunger for authenticity was to be handed down to Guthrie's sixties disciples. Not only in his public image, but in his own mind, Woody was of the people for whom he sang. Any distinction in status between himself and his audience troubled him. When he was appearing on a Los Angeles radio station in the late thirties, he used to mail out a mimeographed songbook to listeners. It included this note:

> This song is Copyrighted in U.S., under Seal of Copyright # 154085, for a period of 28 years, and anybody caught singin it without our permission, will be mighty good friends of ourn, cause we don't give a dern. Publish it. Write it. Sing it. Swing to it. Yodel it. We wrote it, that's all we wanted to do. [13]

Woody was an unashamed political partisan. He wrote a weekly "Woody Sez" column for the *People's World*, the Communist Party's West Coast newspaper, and later contributed regularly to the *Daily Worker* in New York. His guitar was emblazoned with the motto, "This Machine Kills Fascists." He wrote hundreds of songs commenting directly on the issues of the day. He celebrated Jesus as a "socialist outlaw." In "Pretty Boy Floyd," he unmasked the real criminals—those who profit from an unjust system:

> Well, as through the world I've rambled, I've seen lots of funny men
> Some rob you with a sixgun, some with a fountain pen

Guthrie was hailed by the left as a true folk poet, a people's Steinbeck, a socialist Will Rogers. He was authentic because he came from and sang of and for the oppressed. He fulfilled the left's dreams of an indigenous radicalism, Marxist politics couched in the language of the people. Guthrie certainly had the popular touch, but he was also intellectually acute and politically sophisticated. And his artistry was always more than the sum of his public commitments. He wrote playful songs for children and unsentimental odes about VD, of which Dylan showed a keen interest in both.* Alongside the naturalism and political idealism there was a streak of fantasy and morbid wit. Here's a Dylanesque verse from "So Long It's Been Good to Know You," Guthrie's macabre vision of an all-engulfing Midwest dust storm:

Now, the telephone rang, an' it jumped off the wall,
That was the preacher, a-makin' his call.
He said, "Kind friend, this may be the end;
An' you got your last chance of salvation of sin!"
So long it's been good to know you . . .

Guthrie's songs could be scabrous and profane, or reflectively melancholy. He enjoyed hating and baiting his class enemies, and reveled in their discomforts ("There's one less Philadelphia lawyer / In old Philadelphia tonight."). He was a master in the concise use of concrete detail. And he was a champion of the language of the people, however coarse:

The honest and hungry prophets raving and snorting and ripping into the bellies of the rich and powerful rulers and lying priests who beat their people into slavery and dope them with superstitions and false ceremonies and dictate to them what to do, where to go, what to read, who to

---

* In his early sets, Dylan included a zestfully silly rendition of Guthrie's "Car, Car," replete with onomatopoeic noises. In March 2003, in Baghdad, the same song was performed for Iraqi children by the seventy-two-year-old Yorkshire folksinger Karl Dallas, who had stationed himself in the city as a "human shield" to witness against the impending U.S.-British bombardment. "Not only do they join the *brr-brr* chorus," Dallas noted, "they also sing 'riding in my car' with impeccable American accents."

love, what to eat, what to drink, what to wear, when to work, when to rest and where to bring your money. . . . [They] cussed and they raved plenty. Because they was out there in the hills and hollers yelling and echoing the real voice of the real people, the poor working class and the farmers and the down and out.[14]

Guthrie's indifference to hierarchy of any kind troubled some of his Communist Party allies, and it's said that when he applied for party membership in 1943 he was rejected because of what was seen as his personal unreliability.[15] Irwin Silber recalled that "the puritanical, near-sighted left . . . didn't quite know what to make of this strange, be-mused poet who drank and bummed and chased after women and spoke in syllables dreadful strange . . . they never really accepted the man himself."[16]

Dylan took more from Guthrie than an image and an accent. In Guthrie's work, Dylan found a creative fusion of humor and rage, a wanderlust that was both individualist and populist, and, most impor-tant, an alternative to the conventions of the entertainment industry, a folksinging model of honesty and commitment. Guthrie offered an identity that was more genuinely Dylan's own than the one his society had saddled him with. Ultimately, however, neither the model nor the identity were to prove unproblematic.

———————————

Soon after his arrival in New York, Dylan made a pilgrimage to Guthrie's bedside in Brooklyn State Hospital. How much communica-tion actually transpired between the severely disabled older man and his young acolyte is a matter of debate. The importance of the meeting for Dylan is not. Within months, he made Guthrie the subject of his first serious effort at songwriting, "Song to Woody:"

Hey, hey, Woody Guthrie, I wrote you a song
'Bout a funny ol' world that's a-comin' along,
Seems sick an' it's hungry, it's tired an' it's torn,
It looks like it's a-dyin' an' never been born.

In the final verse, the apprentice songwriter speaks tentatively. He seems uneasy comparing his limited experience to the older generation's.

I'm a-leaving' tomorrow, but I could leave today,
Somewhere down the road someday.
The very last thing that I'd want to do
Is to say I've been hittin' some hard travelin' too.

For Dylan, the New York folk scene was a living connection with the left-wing luminaries of the "first folk revival." He met a number of Guthrie's old comrades—notably his one-time singing partner Pete Seeger and Alan Lomax, who had made Guthrie's first studio recordings. (Lomax's secretary was Carla Rotolo, the sister of Dylan's girlfriend Suze—the woman on the *Freewheelin'* cover). In 1940, Lomax had published Guthrie's songs in his anthology, *Our Singing Country,* where he praised "the dust bowl balladeer" as "familiar with microphones and typewriters, familiar too with jails and freight trains." Lomax placed Guthrie chief among the new school of folk artists:

The people have begun to examine their problems self-consciously and comment on them with an objective vigor and irony that reach deeper than a Robert Frost and are more honest and succinct than a T.S. Eliot.[17]

As a teenager in the early thirties, Lomax had assisted his father, John (who published one of the first collections of cowboy ballads), on field trips through the rural South to the hidden sanctuaries of American folk music. On one of these, they encountered Huddie Ledbetter—better known as Leadbelly—in a Lousiana state prison. The Lomaxes brought him to the North, where he sang for left-wing intellectuals and union benefits.

The early folk music collectors were antiquarians, searching for specimens of a lost or dying way of life. In contrast, Alan Lomax saw folk music as a living organism, dynamic and diverse—stretching from work songs and spirituals to protest ballads and commercial hillbilly and race recordings. He believed recorded music had transformed our access to authentic folk song. "A piece of folklore is a living, growing and changing thing, and a folk song printed, words and tune, only symbolizes in very static fashion a myriad-voiced reality of individual songs." What we could now hear were "the songs as they actually exist on the lips of the folk singers." [18]

As the decade wore on, the energetic folklorist acquired a deepening political commitment. In 1937, at the age of twenty-one, he was appointed director of the Archive of American Folk Song at the Library of Congress. In Washington he forged connections across the New Deal administration, stretching even into the White House. He also worked closely with the leftists Charles Seeger and Ruth Crawford Seeger. Both were classically trained composers and musicologists; like other intellectuals shaped by the modernist movement, they had abandoned the avant-garde for the study of folk music under the impact of the economic disaster of the thirties. It was through Lomax that Charles's son, Pete, was later to meet Guthrie and accompany him on the road.

Even as he promoted folk as an ever-evolving genre, Lomax insisted at the same time on the goal of authenticity. In performance style, that meant the painstaking mastery of the skills displayed by the little-known geniuses on his Library of Congress recordings. But it also implied a level of commitment, an emotional investment. He liked to quote Leadbelly: "It take a man that have the blues to sing the blues." For Lomax, the blues remained "a negro music, and no one else can sing it with the same authority. It is a direct reaction to the harsh experiences of their lives."

Where previous explorers of America's folk heritage had seen in it a spirit of fatalistic passivity, Lomax discerned an unfinished narrative of "tragedy and protest." These were the songs of a democracy struggling with and seeking to transform a hostile environment. Their proper fate was not to be preserved in museum-like isolation, but to become part of something larger. "The folklorist's job," Lomax believed, was "to link the people who were voiceless and who had no way to tell their story with the big mainstream of world culture." [19] For all his scrupulous concern for the authentic, Lomax was also a tireless and adventurous popularizer. Through radio, recordings, books, articles, and concerts—not least his own sweat-drenched performance at the White House—he proselytized for the living reality of folk music and for his own vision of the American democratic heritage.

———————————

Folk as Dylan received it in the early sixties had been shaped by this earlier political moment. His work starts from the cultural residue of the popular front, launched in the mid-thirties. During this period, the dominant organization on the American left, the Communist Party, had courted allies to its right, played down its revolutionary rhetoric, and sought to establish itself as a homegrown people's movement for social justice, not a sect of a European proletarian revolution. The slogan of the era was "Communism is twentieth-century Americanism."

All this was in keeping with the prevailing winds from Moscow, but it was much more. In emphasizing their national credentials, the Communists were part of a wider movement. The New Deal encouraged interest in American history and culture and a new regionalism in the arts. It sponsored large-scale narrative paintings in public spaces and a wide array of folkloric activities. At a time of severe social crisis and potential political polarization, various forces sought to mobilize American identity for various purposes, sometimes overlapping, sometimes conflicting. What was at stake was national self-definition, a powerful political asset. The popular front bid for this asset found its epitome in "This Land Is Your Land."

Guthrie wrote the song on February 23, 1940, in response, he said, to Kate Smith's bellicose rendition of "God Bless America," which was then blasting the airwaves. The song combines a sense of longing with a sense of belonging, and has been cursed with the soubriquet of "the alternative national anthem." But in its original form—written during the Hitler-Stalin Pact—there are two verses that give the song a different cast, and which were dropped from the version popularized in the fifties and sixties. One described "a big high wall there that tried to stop me / A sign was painted said: Private Property." The other distinctly qualified the confidence of the reclamation declared throughout the song.

> One bright sunny morning in the shadow of the steeple
> By the Relief office I saw my people—
> As they stood hungry, I stood there wondering if
> This land was made for you and me.[20]

With or without the class-struggle verses, "This Land Is Your Land" remains a concise and stirring expression of the popular front's claim on the nation. But that claim was always problematic. Some of its limitations were starkly exposed in John Lee Hooker's sixties riposte, "This Land is Nobody's Land:"

> This land, this land is no man's land
> This land is your buryin' ground
> I wonder why you're fightin' over this land.[21]

Even during his heyday as a performer, Woody was being turned into an American exemplar: "He sings the songs of a people and I suspect that he is, in a way, that people," said John Steinbeck. Guthrie himself saw his mission, partly, as a preservation of the true national culture: "The union hall is the salvation of real honest-to-god American culture."[22] And he celebrated the Grand Coulee Dam as national triumph: "Now the world holds seven wonders that the travelers always tell / Some gardens and some towers, I guess you know them well / But now the greatest wonder is in Uncle Sam's fair land / It's the big Columbia River and the big Grand Coulee dam."

Across Europe, the recovery of folk tradition had been part of secular nation-building, and for both conservatives and radicals, the music of the folk was the authentic music of the nation. Lomax was aware of the reactionary uses to which folk could be put—he could see them in Nazi Germany. But he believed that there was a democratic pulse at the heart of American folk music that could be harnessed by the left:

> The idea implicit in this great rhymed history of the American pioneer worker can be summed up in the key lines of one of the noblest of the songs: "John Henry told his captain, A man ain't nothing but a man."[23]

The desire to "Americanize" a seemingly alien movement (Marxism, socialism) was one of the missions of the popular front. Like Dylan in the early sixties, the old leftists fretted that their ethnic roots were showing, and these roots betrayed a heritage that was less than authentically American. That's one reason they had so heartily welcomed Seeger, scion of a Yankee academic, Guthrie, the dust bowl migrant, and Ledbetter, the southern black ex-con. But in adopting the rhetoric of Americanism, the left conceded dangerous ground, not so much to backward-looking nativism as to the American empire that would spread its wings after World War II. Lomax invites his readers to admire a tall tale from the old frontier:

> "The boundaries of the United States, sir?" replied the Kentuckian. "Why sir, on the north we are bounded by the aurora borealis, on the east by the rising sun, on the south by the procession of the equinoxes and on the west by the day of judgment." [24]

In 1940, Lomax supported Seeger, Guthrie, Lee Hays, Millard Lampell, and others in forming the Almanac Singers, the first urban ensemble to mix traditional and topical songs and take the package out of the concert hall. It was an inauspicious moment for the venture. With the Hitler-Stalin Pact of 1939, the broad alliance of the popular front came under severe strain. The antifascist emphasis of the previous years was replaced by a renewed antimilitarism and a stronger dose of class politics. The Almanacs' first LP, *Songs for John Doe,* was ferociously anti-FDR and anti-war ("It wouldn't be much thrill / to die for Dupont in Brazil").[25]

The Almanac Singers were a collective of some dozen performers, most of whom lived communally in a succession of downtown Manhattan apartments. They wore denim and jeans and their performance demeanor was casual in the extreme. What drew them together was a love of folk music and a commitment to turning that music to political ends. Lee Hays explained the group's name: "If you want to know what the weather is going to be, you have to look in your almanac. . . ." [26] (A quarter of a century later, Dylan repudiated that nostrum in "Subterranean Homesick Blues.") The Almanacs flourished, initially, because they were taken up by the left. They played union benefits and fund-raisers. It was during this time that Seeger introduced the word *hootenanny*—a long-forgotten specimen of American slang meaning something like *thingamajig*—as a label for informal (but publicly promoted) folksinging get-togethers. With the German invasion of the Soviet Union in June 1941 and the attack on Pearl Harbor in December, new opportunities opened up for the Almanac Singers. They were now urging on the working class in the crusade against Germany and Japan. It was at this moment that the audition at the Rainbow Room took place—only in reality it was an audition not for Woody alone but for the Almanac Singers as a group.

Despite the claims of red-hunters and some Dylan fans, the Almanacs were not part of a conspiracy to subjugate the variegated American folk tradition to a program dictated by the Communist Party. Some of the Almanacs and their coterie were members of the party. Most were sympathizers. Very few were active in or had contact with party structures, and the party itself evinced little interest in the musicians or the music. These people did follow the changing party line— from the people's front through the Hitler-Stalin Pact through the Nazi attack on the Soviet Union through Pearl Harbor and after—but they did not do so simply because they were told to. They were all strong-willed, independent-minded people; they followed the party line because, on balance and in context, it made sense to them. "Which side are you on?" the old song had asked, and under the circumstances of the day, they thought the answer was clear. They were not without a degree of ironic self-awareness. When the wartime "no strike" pledge rendered a great deal of the Almanac Singers' repertoire redundant, Guthrie improvised a verse:

> I started out to sing a song
> To the entire population
> But I ain't a doing a thing tonight
> On account of this "new situation." [27]

After World War II, many of those involved in the Almanacs took part in People's Songs, a more organized attempt to promote the left-wing politics of folk as they had been refined through the years of the popular front. The board of directors included Guthrie, Seeger, Lomax, and John Hammond. In the midst of the great strike wave of 1946, the organization declared, "The people are on the march and must have songs to sing" and announced that it intended to circumvent "the music monopoly of Broadway and Hollywood." But even as Lomax insisted that "the whole American folk tradition is a progressive people's tradition," the cold war began to freeze American public life and the House Un-American Activities Committee began to strut the stage. In 1948, Lomax served as the musical director of Henry Wallace's third-party presidential bid, and insisted that there was a folksinger on every platform. Seeger himself accompanied Wallace on an embattled tour of the South. It was the last hurrah of the popular front.

As the anti-Communist witch-hunt intensified, all the protestations of Americanism were for nought. People's Songs and the artists associated with it were excluded from the CIO unions. By 1950, Lomax had left for Europe and Guthrie had been crippled by Huntingdon's chorea, a degenerative disease of the nervous system inherited from his mother. Josh White and Burl Ives* gave the witch-hunters what they required— I WAS A SUCKER FOR THE COMMUNISTS ran a headline after White's HUAC testimony.

Even after its demise, People's Songs had a long-range impact on the folk revival that was to produce Bob Dylan. In May 1950 a new maga-

---

* The actor and singer Burl Ives appeared at numerous left-wing rallies and benefits in the late thirties and early forties. He recorded union songs with Pete Seeger and became a sponsor of People's Songs. White began his career in South Carolina as a blues guitarist, a follower of Blind Lemon Jefferson. In New York City in the late thirties and early forties, he transformed himself into a silky and sophisticated nightclub entertainer. During this period, he was promoted by both Lomax and Hammond, worked with the Almanacs, formed a friendship with Eleanor Roosevelt, and was ubiquitous at left-wing events. He resurfaced as a regular on the folk revival circuit of the early sixties, but many would not forgive his HUAC testimony; he was never invited to play at Newport, though he was on stage with Dylan at the March on Washington.

zine, *Sing Out!*, was launched, taking its title from "The Hammer Song," written by Seeger and Hays the previous year: "I'd sing out danger! I'd sing out a warning!" The song crept into the pop world during the next decade, and, miraculously, *Sing Out!* was to survive and to thrive during the second folk revival.

Meanwhile, four Almanac veterans—including Seeger and Lee Hays—decided to try a more commercial route. They formed the Weavers (named after a play about the peasants' revolt of 1381), spruced up their appearance, tempered their presentation, and enjoyed a succession of hit records, most notably the chart-topping "Goodnight, Irene," a Leadbelly song, and Guthrie's "So Long It's Been Good to Know You." However, the belated commercial success of the first folk revival proved brief-lived. After finding themselves on every blacklist in the industry, the Weavers disbanded in 1952. Folk music became politically tainted, rich hunting ground for the inquisitors. Country star Tex Ritter observed: "It got to the point where it was very difficult to tell where folk music ended and communism began. So that's when I quit calling myself a folk singer. It was the sting of death if you were trying to make a living." [28]

John Hammond's track record as a talent spotter was legendary long before he signed the twenty-year-old Bob Dylan to Columbia Records in 1961. In the thirties he had recorded Bessie Smith and Billie Holiday, promoted Benny Goodman and Count Basie, and fought a stubborn battle against segregation in the music industry. Hammond was a rich white kid turned on by the "race" records of the late twenties. In blues and jazz he found a spontaneity and energy absent from the concert hall music preferred by his parents. As a critic, as well as producer and promoter, Hammond championed both rhythmic drive and individual improvisation. From the beginning, he aimed to distinguish the authentic in jazz from its commercial dilution.

Like Alan Lomax, and many in the decades to come, Hammond found his way to politics through music. Jazz and blues alerted him to the brutalities of racial oppression. He became increasingly aware of the material conditions in which the music he loved was produced. In 1931, he took an active role in the defense campaign for the Scottsboro Boys, and soon joined the national board of the NAACP.

In 1938, Hammond staged the historic From Spirituals to Swing concert at Carnegie Hall, hitherto a bastion of concert music propriety. The event was sponsored by *New Masses,* a CP-controlled magazine markedly different in tone and style from its Greenwich Village predecessor. For *New Masses,* the concert was a welcome popular front initiative in which the left appeared as the champion of an authentic, multiracial American culture. The magazine promised the audience "the true, untainted, entirely original works that the American negro has created. We mean spirituals sung in their primitive majesty." [29] What Hammond presented that night was not, however, a menagerie of musical primitives but a succession of accomplished and sophisticated performers, a number of whom were far from "untainted" by modern American culture. The boogie-woogie piano of Albert Ammons and Meade Lux Lewis was followed by the gospel singing of Sister Rosetta Tharpe, the harmonica antics of Sonny Terry, the New Orleans finesse of Sidney Bechet, the wry blues of Big Bill Broonzy, and a climactic swinging set from Basie and his band.

"Forget you're in Carnegie Hall," Hammond told the audience, urging them to create the sort of "informal atmosphere" that would bring out the best in the musicians. But simply by importing these musicians into this august venue, Hammond was making a powerful statement. This wasn't just popular entertainment; it was great art and deserved recognition as such. The program, as devised and presented by Hammond, was a narrative summary of the African American musical tradition. It staked a claim for that tradition's rightful place at the heart of a modern democracy. In tracing the black genealogy that lay behind swing—then a huge craze among white American youth and a money-spinner for the industry—Hammond proclaimed and exposed the black roots of America's contemporary culture.

As later critics have noted, Hammond's package could be construed as a white appropriation of a black narrative. It was he who determined what was and was not authentic, and he was often uneasy when the musicians he patronized ventured outside the niches he had created for them. Hammond was a finicky populist. He demanded virtuosity and sophistication, but he scolded Duke Ellington for daring to write symphonic works and he had little time for the bebop vanguardists of the post–World War II era: "instead of expanding the form, they contracted it, made it their private language." He praised rock 'n' roll for "getting America's youth dancing again."

Hammond's ability to spot Dylan's talent was a remarkable leap across musical generations and genres. (When Dylan's first album proved a commercial flop, the boy singer was dubbed "Hammond's folly.") In a sense, through his earlier efforts to redefine musical boundaries—between black and white, between traditional and popular and classical—Hammond exercised far more influence over Dylan before they met than he did during their brief time together in the studio. As a producer, Hammond's method was stark and straightforward. In his view the job was to capture a live performance, not create an aural artefact. That suited Dylan, but Hammond was soon elbowed out of the young singer's career by his new manager, Albert Grossman, a hungrier and altogether less austere figure than the patrician Hammond.

———————

In 1952, at the height of the cold war clampdown, Folkways quietly issued its canon-shaping *Anthology of American Folk Music,* a collection destined to exercise a profound influence on Dylan and his folksinging contemporaries. Folkways was a small business run by Moe Asch, a nonaffiliated leftist (and son of writer Sholem Asch) who had already been involved in recording Guthrie, Seeger, and Leadbelly, and who had made it his mission to record and publish a wide range of vernacular music. The anthology itself was compiled and edited by a younger man, Harry Smith, whose worldview seemed eccentric in the extreme to the popular front veterans.[30]

Smith was an avant-garde filmmaker and painter, an amateur anthropologist who had already recorded Native American chants (and taken part in a peyote ritual), a marijuana-smoking bohemian with a fascination for the occult. After visiting Berkeley in 1944 to hear a Woody Guthrie concert, he was drawn into the Bay Area's experimental arts scene, and became associated with the poets of the San Francisco Renaissance. Smith was also a compulsive collector of old 78s. Out of this collection, he selected his anthology, eighty-four songs on six LPs. There were no field recordings and no art-form renditions by classically trained performers. Instead, these were "race" and "hillbilly" records, released on commercial labels, and recorded between 1927, when new technology boosted the quality of musical reproduction, and 1932, when the depression finished off the regional markets. The performers were anything but anonymous members of a folk tribe; they included a host of distinctive stylists—Clarence Ashley, Buell Kazee, Blind Lemon Jefferson, Charley Patton (disguised as the Masked Marvel), the Carter Family, Mississippi John Hurt, Doc Boggs, Blind Willie Johnson. Neither Folkways nor Smith bothered to license the recordings from the original labels or the performers (many of whom were still working). They treated this hoard of song as a common treasure.

Smith saw the 1927–32 interval as unique. During those years, "American music still retained some of the regional qualities evident in the days before the phonograph, radio and talking picture had tended to integrate local types." But it was also a period in which, for the first time, commercially distributed records made "available to each other the rhythmically and verbally specialized musics of groups living in mutual social and cultural isolation."[31] It was the beginning of a long-running process, consciously stimulated by Smith's own anthology, of interchange among musical modes, a process that created rock 'n' roll in general and specifically the work of Bob Dylan, not to mention reggae and punk and Afro-beat and the myriad varieties of drum-and-bass and acid house.

Enclosed with the LPs were Smith's extraordinary notes. For each song, he provided what he called a "condensation of lyrics"—truncated summaries of the stories in the songs, presented with a deadpan irony and an alertness to the mundane surrealism of many of the narratives. He traced the lyrics back to their roots in a common stock, and at the same time emphasized the actual historical events that often gave rise to them. Smith's idiosyncratic selection of American music was a bold and sensitive collage, an avant-garde transformation of a vernacular idiom.

The anthology was filled with what seemed to listeners in the fifties and still seems to us today an assortment of archaic, other-worldly sounds; voices and instruments tuned to scales and deploying textures left behind by or excluded from the commercial musical mainstream. The past inscribed on these LPs was only a quarter of a century gone, but it did seem another country. Like Guthrie's book, the anthology alerted Dylan to the existence of other American traditions—ones he could make use of in inventing and expressing himself.

Smith saw his *Anthology,* as he did his experimental artworks, as an instrument of social enlightenment, not an antiquarian retreat. When he was presented with a Grammy shortly before his death in 1996, he said, "I'm glad to say that my dream's come true. I saw America changed by music." By which he meant, said his longtime acquaintance, Allen Ginsberg, "the whole rock 'n' roll, Bob Dylan, Beatnik, post-Beatnik youth culture . . . he'd lived long enough to see the philosophy of the homeless and the Negro and the minorities and the impoverished—of which he was one, starving in the Bowery—alter the consciousness of America sufficiently to affect the politics." [32]

For Dylan, the anthology was not only a link to the lost art of the late twenties, but also, through Harry Smith's sensibility, to the bohemian avant-garde of the fifties. As Dylan said, "I came out of the wilderness and just naturally fell in with the beat scene, the bohemian, be-bop crowd, it was pretty much connected." Dylan relished the Beats' shock tactics and was intrigued by their candor about drugs and sexuality. Beat prosody entered his songwriting armory as surely as the methods of Guthrie and the discoveries of the *Anthology.* In promoting a re-newed interest in publicly performed poetry, the Beats also stimulated the coffeehouse scene in which the second folk revival gestated. This was a do-it-yourself poetry to complement a do-it-yourself music.

But in the mid-fifties, this small group of social pioneers found themselves in near total isolation. The gulf between their beliefs, cultural practices, personal habits, and those recognized by official

America seemed unbridgeable. Unlike the political activists, they glo-ried in their isolation, in their apparent irrelevance, and in the free-dom it gave them. Rejecting the Puritanism shared by the American mainstream and the old left, they plunged into subcultures: crim-inal, musical, racial, drug and sex-related. They kept their ears peeled for a new demotic—and through their encounter with bebop-era black jazz they fashioned a jargon that, by the end of the decade, would be parodied across the country. This jargon was to prove one of the major sources for Dylan's extraordinary speech—it was not long after he arrived in the Village that he began layering the hillbilly with the hipster.

Ginsberg hailed from an immigrant Jewish family immersed in Communist Party activity. He was always both a rebellious and affec-tionate son of the old left. He inherited from his reading of Whitman and his upbringing in the popular front years an interest in American national identity, but he gave it a new twist. In 1956, in San Francisco, he wrote "America," a long-lined, rhythmically seductive, joke-filled ad-dress to the native land that adopts a tone neither Whitman nor Guthrie ever essayed: "Go fuck yourself with your atom bomb." As well as prais-ing marijuana and homosexuality and satirizing cold war paranoia ("them Russians them Russians and them Chinamen"), the poem in-vokes the then largely hidden history of the American left: Tom Mooney, Scottsboro, Sacco and Vanzetti, the Wobblies, America's "one million Trotskyites."

> It occurs to me that I am America
> I am talking to myself again

Through sheer bardic energy, Ginsberg sought to transform his isola-tion into its opposite. Though the poem ends on a note of cheerful re-solve ("America, I'm putting my queer shoulder to the wheel"), it places Ginsberg, at the outset of his career, in an embattled but somehow sym-biotic relationship with "America:"

> Your machinery is too much for me
> It made me want to be a saint [33]

The Beats are also a reminder that the spirit of the pre–World War I *Masses* still flourished in hidden corners of America, preeminently in Greenwich Village, which had long been home to a variety of leftist traditions, many of them fiercely anti-Stalinist. The World War II years had been the heyday for the CP-linked popular front artists, but they were dog days for pacifists, anarchists, and Trotskyists. However, the crisis of Stalinism in the fifties created a vacuum on the left that other tendencies began to fill. Anarcho-pacifists and cultural critics—Paul Goodman, Kenneth Rexroth, Dave Dellinger—began to get a hearing among a select few. The new American peace movement of the late fifties was dominated by neither the Communist Party nor the liberal Democrats; its revolt against the cold war was infused with the "plague on both your houses" spirit of the Beat poets and organizations like the *Catholic Worker,* edited by that survivor of the first Village generation, Dorothy Day, and the radical pacifists of the Fellowship of Reconciliation. Activists from this tradition were also responsible for founding Pacifica Radio, whose New York City arm, WBAI, began broadcasting in 1960, providing an in-house forum for the latest avatar of the Village tradition.

After nearly a decade in Europe, Alan Lomax returned to the United States in 1958. The man who had done so much to create the first folk revival was now on hand for the flowering of the second. "The modern American folk-song revival began back in the thirties as a cultural movement, with overtones of social reform," he wrote in *Sing Out!* "In the last ten years, our gigantic entertainment industry, even though it is as yet only mildly interested in folk music, has turned this cultural movement into a small boom." [34]

In the late fifties, the Kingston Trio and the New Christy Minstrels had enjoyed commercial success with easy-listening arrangements of old folk tunes. They were followed by a posse of imitators, but, at the same time, a less commercial side of folk music was also flourishing. *Sing Out!,* under Irwin Silber's editorship, no longer looking to Moscow but still defiantly of the left, reached a circulation of 15,000. Izzy Young, an anarchist from the Bronx, had opened his Folklore Center on Macdougal Street in 1957, and in 1961 it was the subject of an impromptu Dylan verse:

> I came down to New York town,
> Got out and started walking around,
> I's up around 62nd Street,
> All of a sudden comes a cop on his beat;
> Said my hair was too long,
> Said my boots were too dirty,
> Said my hat was un-American,
> Said he'd throw me in jail.
>
> On MacDougal Street I saw a cubby hole,
> I went in to get out of the cold . . .

At the Folklore Center, "They got real records and real books, / Anybody can walk in and look."

> When you come down here you're on common ground—
> Common people ground—
> Common guitar people ground—
> WE NEED EVERY INCH OF IT![35]

For the fresh-faced Dylan, the subway ride from uptown to downtown was a voyage from alienation and rejection to acceptance and community. The folk revival offered something unavailable in commercial youth culture as he'd known it:

> The thing about rock 'n' roll is that for me anyway it wasn't enough. Tutti Frutti and Blue Suede Shoes were great catchphrases and driving pulse rhythms and you could get high on the energy but they weren't serious or didn't reflect life in a realistic way. I knew that when I got into folk music, it was more of a serious type of thing. The songs are filled with more despair, more sadness, more triumph, more faith in the supernatural, much deeper feelings . . . life is full of complexities and rock 'n' roll didn't reflect that.[36]

When Dylan arrived in the Village, the folk scene was still a ghetto whose appeal was limited to a few. It was already, however, a counterculture in miniature—a self-defined minority with a uniform dress and a common frame of reference. But unlike the mass counterculture of the late sixties that it helped to breed, the folk revival was characterized by earnestness and restraint. It was self-consciously opposed to the glitzy superficiality and addled consumerism it associated with America's mass youth culture. In its place it offered something untainted by packaging, by commerce, something that was part of a greater and more enduring whole, something with a mission. The spectacle of white middle-class kids setting themselves apart from and in opposition to the society that had granted them privileges their parents hardly dreamed of puzzled and irritated many commentators (then as now). But what was clear from the beginning was that the critique of commercialism, the rejection of the manufactured pabulum of corporate America, wasn't merely ideological. Young people came to the folk revival looking for a personal experience of a type they felt was denied to them elsewhere. They came looking for the authentic.

And the princess and the prince discuss
What's real and what is not . . .
                    —"GATES OF EDEN"

What the Marxist critic Theodor Adorno called "the jargon of authenticity" had been present in the first folk revival, but it was elevated to a higher and wider status during the second. It was applied to musical performance, artistic purpose, personal style; it coursed through the shared understanding of history, tradition, politics, the "folk" and the "people," and it levied existential demands: honesty was the touchtone. In manner and dress, unadorned plainness was preferred. Anything standardized or mass manufactured was despised (except, of course, acoustic guitars, folk magazines, and sheet music). When it came to musical subject matter, teenage melodrama was discarded in favor of venerable sagas of work and physical hardship and early death; these songs crystallized the struggles of past generations; they were seen as rooted in real experience, tinged with hard-earned wisdom. Not surprisingly, for white, middle-class folksingers who had grown up in the fifties, and were singing the songs of the thirties and forties, the demand for authenticity was, from the beginning, a paradoxical one.

The word derives from the Greek *autos* ("self") plus *hentos* ("to make"). In common use it means something original, genuine, not a copy or simulation, something that is what it professes to be. But ever since the rise of industrial production, the spread of market relations and the congregation of humanity in vast anonymous cities, the authentic has carried additional connotations that make it both less precise and more potent. The world was no longer experienced as "self-made" but as an aggregate of products and conditions produced by remote forces. There was an emotional absence, difficult to define, but perceived and felt wherever the new form of social organization spread. The sense that there was something artificial in the culture bred by the new society was reflected in the commonplace nineteenth-century dichotomy between organic and mechanical, rooted and cosmopolitan. The idea of the authentic emerged both in opposition to and out of the heart of a laissez-faire society. In the conditions of mid–twentieth-century America, its appeal was powerfully reenforced.

Ever since it began to be named, collected and catalogued in the late eighteenth and early nineteenth century, folk music (and folk dances and customs) had been seen as organic and rooted and therefore somehow an antidote to alienation—something counterposed, at various times and by various critics, to modernity, modishness, mass culture, or elite decadence. The folk music revival of the late fifties and early sixties shared with previous folk revivals a discontent with the civilization of industrialization, and a search for a balm to that discontent in the products of "the folk." Folk music promised a healing of the breach between production and consumption, performer and audience. It promised community and continuity.

Adorno argued that the jargon of authenticity was an illusory, self-indulgent, and futile attempt to evade the dissatisfactions of capitalist society. "While the jargon overflows with the pretense of deep human emotion, it is just as standardized as the world that it officially negates ... the perpetual charge against reification, a charge which the jargon itself represents, is itself reified." In a passage that could easily be applied to the folk revival (and much more), he warns: "The stereotypes of the jargon ... seem to guarantee that one is not doing what in fact one is doing—bleating with the crowd ... those stereotypes ... guarantee that one has achieved it all oneself, as an unmistakably free person."[37] Or as Dylan put it, "There's no success like failure, and failure's no success at all."

The folk revival notion of what constituted authentic folk music was itself an artificial construct, strongly influenced by the work of Lomax, Smith, and others. Two great folk artists, John Lee Hooker and Muddy Waters, had been exploring the expressive capacity of the electric guitar for years, but they unplugged for the folk boom and reinvented themselves, briefly, as acoustic troubadours. Dylan arrived on the scene wearing his Woody Guthrie mask—a mask of authenticity. As early as 1960, the Village's bohemian heritage was being packaged for tourists; Dylan himself made a few dollars posing as a "beatnik" for souvenir photographs.

Visiting Guthrie, he met Ramblin' Jack Elliott, just returned from five years in Europe. Dylan already knew and admired his recordings. Elliott had a vast repertoire of cowboy songs and had made himself the major living interpreter of Guthrie's works, though he showed little interest in the politics that fired his hero. But Elliott didn't just sing the songs, he lived them. In his vocal delivery and his demeanor both on and off stage, he seemed the authentic embodiment of hard traveling individualism. But Ramblin' Jack, it turned out, much to Dylan's amazed amusement, had been born Elliott Adnopoz, the Brooklyn-reared son of a Jewish doctor. Did this make him a phony? Dylan never thought so. In fact, Rambin Jack's example helped liberate him. From his teenage years, Jack had hit the road and immersed himself in the world he'd learned about from the songs. He surrendered himself to the tradition and made the tradition his own. He might be an invention, but he offered a frisson of reality often missing on the folk scene.

Dylan was alert to the perils of authenticity—and wove some of his best songs out of its conundrums. Today, "authenticity therapy" is offered on the web; ready-faded, "stone-washed" jeans are a commonplace; and everything from cars to pasta sauces are flogged to us invoking the authentic. For the critic Jean Baudrillard, this invocation of the authentic is inevitably the signal that we are in the realm of the fake-authentic. But postmodern self-invention—the permutation of off-the-peg identities, without regard to the demands of authenticity— has bred its own dissatisfactions. The desire to reclaim the self from an inhuman social reality, to find meaning in something bigger, other, truer, older, is more powerful than ever—because more than ever the world is experienced as anything but self-made. These are longings that corporate branding cannot satisfy.

For some in the folk revival, authenticity consisted in truth-to-history. Arrangements and instrumentation were dutifully researched and the results shared with audiences. Dylan belonged to a different school. He was never the kind of folksinger who sought to disappear from the song and present it as an artifact. His approach, from the beginning, was with the blues singers for whom adding yourself to the tradition was what the tradition was all about.

Dylan's understanding of that tradition was enhanced by the release in 1961 of *King of the Delta Blues Singers,* a collection of recordings made by Robert Johnson in the mid-thirties. While he was preparing his From Spirituals to Swing concert John Hammond had stumbled across Johnson's discs in the Columbia storeroom and was startled by their power. He hoped to bring Johnson north to join his Carnegie Hall company, but the young bluesman had vanished from sight. Hammond shared his latest enthusiasm with Alan Lomax, who went hunting for Johnson on his next Mississippi field trip, only to learn from his mother that the prodigy had died in mysterious circumstances.[38] For two decades Johnson's work lay in the vaults until Hammond persuaded

Columbia to issue the 1961 compilation, which was to influence young musicians on both sides of the Atlantic.

The album appears amid other in-group totems on the cover of *Bringing It All Back Home*. In Johnson's high-pitched, keening voice, metallic multi-voiced guitar, and mysterious lyrics there was an anguished complexity that struck the listeners of Dylan's generation as distinctly modern. This was a man about whom next to nothing was known, yet who was there in full on the record, in every nuance, in every drawl, in every bent guitar note. For Dylan and his friends, Johnson became an icon of the kind of authenticity they were seeking, an authenticity in which the individual and the music formed a seamless whole.

Soon after being introduced to the Columbia reissue, Dylan added Johnson's "Ramblin on My Mind" and "Kindhearted Woman" to his set. He told Izzy Young he was writing a song called "The Death of Robert Johnson." [39] He later inserted lyrics from Johnson's "Stones in My Passway" into "Corrina, Corrina" ("I got a bird that whistles . . ."). In many ways, Johnson embodied Dylan's emerging aesthetic. In the free-verse liner notes he wrote for a Joan Baez album, he ruminated on why it was that he had been so resistant to "Joanie's" voice and its pure, sweet tone:

The only beauty's ugly, man
The crackin' shakin' breakin' sounds're
The only beauty I understand

———————————

In those early days in the Village Dylan was befriended by Dave Van Ronk, only five years his senior but with a wealth of experience Dylan could only envy. Growing up in an Irish working-class environment in Brooklyn, he sought refuge from a regimented Catholic education in music—jazz and especially trad jazz, New Orleans style, the purist's choice. From there he moved on to the blues, fashioned a growling singing voice and plumbed the mysteries of the acoustic guitar. He was happily passing his time in the merchant marine when Odetta convinced him he could make a living as a folksinger. Van Ronk became one of the first white, city-based musicians of his era to try to emulate the expressive vocal and finger-picking styles of the old records. He felt no shame in being a white man singing the blues, since he held himself to the same high standards as the original blues masters.

Unlike some of Dylan's Village cohorts, Van Ronk never begrudged the younger man his later success. He remembered him as an enthralling performer, even before he wrote any of his own songs, with "a gung-ho, unrelenting quality, a take-no-prisoners approach that was really very effective." Dylan learned from Van Ronk's repertoire and technique and soaked up what he needed from Van Ronk's knowledge of poetry and history. Somewhere along the way Van Ronk had become a socialist with a decidedly anti-Stalinist bent (in the mid-sixties he was a member of the Trotskyist Workers League).[40] In 1959, he had collaborated with an anarchist printer named Dick Ellington to produce *The Bosses' Songbook—Songs to Stifle the Flames of Discontent*, which included the "Ballad of a Party Folk Singer":[41]

> Their material is corny, but their motives are the purest
> And their spirits will never be broke
> And they go right on with their noble crusade
> Of teaching folk songs to the folk

Van Ronk was skeptical about the politics of the folk revival, not least its romance with America. "There is this social patriotism running though all of them, but really less in Dylan. It makes me sick, because I'm an internationalist myself. I don't think the American people are any special repository of goodness and duty, nor are they a special repository of evil." Van Ronk's little anti-Stalinist songbook included a revision of Woody Guthrie's anthem surprisingly close in sprit to the two excised verses of the original 1940 composition:

> This land is their land, it is not our land
> From their rich apartments to their Cadillac carland
> From their Wall Street office to their Hollywood Starland
> This land is not for you and me.

The "America" of the popular front had resurfaced in the folk revival of the late fifties and early sixties. But superimposed over its legacy was the ubiquitous cold war liberal narrative of social progress, of the rational superiority and inexorable spread of "American values." What was assumed by this narrative was assumed by the young people entering the folk revival. It was their starting point. This liberal faith in "American ideals" had a more directly formative impact on these young people's consciousness than the heritage of the thirties and forties, which they had to seek out (to the disaffected minority, it was the seeking out that made it attractive). For them the search for an alternative America was less politically programmatic than it was for Seeger or Lomax, and owed much to the rising discontents of the new consumer society. Smothered beneath the vapidly smiling billboards and the cornucopia of household goods and televisions sets there must be, they believed—prompted simultaneously by faith in and disaffection with their native land—another America, a truer and more admirable America. Talking to Izzy Young in October 1961, the still unknown Dylan claimed, "I can offer songs that tell something of this America. No foreign songs. The songs of the land that aren't offered over TV or radio and very few records. . . ."[42]

What Van Ronk identified as "the social patriotism" of the folk revival could be heard in its routine appeals to American values and traditions, its dogged attempts to construct an idealized American "people" free of their rulers' sins. In the broader political discourse of the era it wore many guises: the notion that America is the embodiment of an idea, universal and cleansed of ethnicity, the belief that America enjoys a special destiny among nations, the assumption that America is somehow *the* theater of the human soul, in which all human traits and capacities stand naked. It was a package that weighed heavily on the activists and the folksingers, including Dylan, as they began their journey through the sixties.

Asked to explain the rise of the folk revival, Van Ronk said "it was all part and parcel of the big left turn middle-class college students were making. . . . So we all owe it to Rosa Parks."[43] More precisely, they owed it all to the student sit-in movement launched by four young African Americans at a Woolworth's lunch counter in Greensboro, North Carolina, in February 1960. Within weeks the movement had spread to other cities, notably Nashville, and at a conference held in Raleigh in April, the new activists formed the Student Nonviolent Coordinating Committee.

SNCC was committed to smashing Jim Crow through nonviolent direct action. In its early years it was saturated in an ethic of personal moral witness and defined its mission in quasi-religious terms. It was also, from the outset, more militant than the other civil rights groups and more immersed in the grass roots. "We did go out and live and suffer with the everyday people," John Lewis recalled.[44] The black students brought together by SNCC were new and unexpected agents of social transformation. In the beginning, they had no institutional base and no support or recognition from the media. But their initiatives transformed people's understanding of what was necessary and what was possible. They tore the veil from American society and revealed the power of mass action. Everything that happened subsequently in America in the sixties emanates from their movement. Dylan, the folk revival, and the youth culture in general were all transformed by its emergence, and their evolution was profoundly tied to its subsequent fate.

For all the efforts of Lomax, Hammond, and the Almanac Singers, music was rarely more than an occasional accompaniment to the social movements of the thirties and forties. But in the southern United States in the early sixties, song came into its own. It was no longer an intermission in the serious politics; it was a motivator, an explainer, and as much a binding force as ideology or program. Above all, it was a weapon in the ceaseless battle against white terror that had to be waged town by town throughout the South. "The fear down here is tremendous," SNCC field secretary Phyllis Martin explained. "I didn't know whether I'd be shot at or stoned or what. But when the singing started I forgot all that."[45]

Song took on a special importance in the civil rights movement because of the African American musical tradition—already well-adapted to collective expressions of suffering and celebration—as well as the conscious efforts of political activists, black and white, to place music at the service of the movement. The insurgents adopted left-wing standards—"The Hammer Song," "We Shall Not Be Moved," "Which Side Are You On?"—as well as fitting familiar R&B and pop tunes with new topical lyrics. Ray Charles's "I'm Movin' On" became "Jim Crow's Movin' On;" Little Willie John's "Leave My Kitten Alone" became "Leave Segregation Alone." But most of all, they plundered the gospel tradition.[46]

"We Shall Overcome" was derived from Charles Tindley's gospel song "I'll Overcome Some Day" (1900), whose melody has the same nineteenth-century spiritual base as "No More Auction Block" (a critical song for Dylan), and harks back to the work songs of the southern plantations. Pete Seeger tells the story of the song's evolution:

> In 1946, several hundred employees of the American Tobacco Company in Charleston, South Carolina were on strike. They sang on the picket line to keep up their spirits. Lucille Simmons started singing the song on the picket line and changed one important word from *I* to *we*. Zilphia Horton learned it when a group of strikers visited the Highland Folk School, the Labor Education Center in Tennessee. She taught it to me and we published it as "We Shall Overcome" in our songletter, *People's Songs Bulletin,* in 1952. I taught it to Guy Carawan. . . . Guy introduced the song to the founding convention of SNCC in North Carolina [in 1960]. It swept the country.[47]

The Highlander Folk Center, founded by radical Christians in the thirties, functioned as a training ground, retreat, and political workshop for the labor and civil rights movements. It was one of the few places in the South where blacks and whites were encouraged to meet and organize together. As a result, it was under constant attack. Billboards went up around the South displaying a picture of Martin Luther King at Highlander with the caption *Communist Training School.* The House Un-American Activities Committee held a series of hearings into Highlander's alleged role in subverting the American way.[48]

Patient, undaunted, and far-seeing, Highlander launched an early outreach project teaching literacy skills to blacks who wanted to pass the voter registration tests. One of its first schools was organized in the Sea Islands off the coast of Charleston. (The islands were home to many of the tobacco workers who had adapted "I'll Overcome"). In 1956, at a class on John's Island, Guy Carawan, a white folksinger and activist, sang an old spiritual already favored in the labor movement: "Keep Your Hand on the Plow, Hold On." A local woman, Alice Wine, told him that she knew a different chorus—"Keep Your Eyes on the Prize." In the coming years, the song was reworked by many hands, and emerged as one of the major anthems of the movement.[49]

The gospel original—a typically idiosyncratic version of which Dylan recorded on his first album—aims to exhort and uplift. It offers redemption from current tribulations in a future that can be attained through spiritual striving.

> I'm going to heaven and I hain't a-going to stop,
> There hain't going to be no stumbling-block.

As in other freedom songs, there's a great deal carried over from the original: above all, the sense of determination. And some of the Biblical imagery proved remarkably apposite: "Keep Your Eyes on the Prize" retains the line:

> Paul and Silas, bound in jail, had no money for to go their bail

But the new version transforms the very nature of the struggle described in "Gospel Plow."

> The only thing we did wrong,
> Stayed in the wilderness a day too long.

> But the one thing we did right,
> Was the day we started to fight.

This lyric transition from spiritual to secular, individual to collective, passivity to activism was, in part, the work of particular individuals engaged in concrete social struggles. It was a transition involving personal and political interaction between the Sea Islands, Highlander, and the sit-ins and freedom rides.

The new anthems from the front lines of the civil rights struggle in the South quickly received a hearing in New York. The Congress of Racial Equality (CORE) and SNCC published volumes of them. In late 1960, Folkways released a *Nashville Sit-In* album compiled by Guy Carawan and the Highlander people, featuring the refashioned "We Shall Overcome," and followed it up with *1961: We Shall Overcome: Songs of the Freedom Rides and Sit-Ins.* Folkways may have been a small, specialist label, but even so, never before had the music of resistance been recorded and disseminated so instantaneously. Both of these records would have been known to Dylan, who in any case had heard the songs at hootenannies and benefits.

During the winter of 1961–62, the city of Albany, in southwest Georgia, witnessed one of the bitterest and most costly battles of the early civil rights years. Wave after wave of protest action resulted in nearly a thousand blacks jailed, but no tangible victories. However, in this struggle, large numbers of older blacks joined the students, and singing acquired a new centrality. "The harmonies and intensities of naked voices became a trademark of the Albany movement," wrote historian Taylor Branch. Among the songs that sustained the Albany community in its trials were "Oh Freedom," "This Little Light of Mine," and the defiant "Ain't Gonna Let Nobody Turn Me Round." All were featured on an LP, *Freedom in the Air—Albany, Georgia,* produced by Alan Lomax and Guy Carawan for Vanguard in 1962.

Out of the Albany campaign emerged the SNCC Freedom Singers— among them, the nineteen-year-old Bernice Johnson, who was studying music at the local state college. As a result of her role in the local protests, Johnson was expelled from college and fired from her job. She plunged full-time into the movement and married SNCC organizer Cordell Reagon, also a member of the Freedom Singers. (As Bernice Johnson Reagon she later founded the female a cappella group Sweet Honey in the Rock.) Looking back on the Albany experience, she recalled the stylistic changes the freedom songs underwent as they were taken up by a genuine mass movement:

A lot of the older people in the Albany movement were entrenched in older black cultural tradition and not as much into the black culture you'll find in the colleges—rhythm and blues and arranged spirituals. A lot of the sit-in songs were out of the rhythm and blues idiom or the arranged spiritual idiom. Those songs, as they went through Albany, Georgia, got brought back to the root level of black choral traditional music.[50]

From Albany, the Freedom Singers carried the message far and wide. They sang in halls and churches and streets and jails. They also sang on northern college campuses, where they became, in Julian Bond's words, SNCC's "public face." They used the songs to explain the movement to an audience bred, for the most part, in relative comfort and at a safe distance from the cruelties of Jim Crow. They provided, in Johnson Reagon's words, "a singing newspaper," simultaneously raising funds and consciousness. Dylan met them during their visits to New York in 1962. Johnson Reagon sang at the Carnegie Hall hootenanny at which Dylan premiered "A Hard Rain's A-Gonna Fall."

The freedom songs, more even than the example of Guthrie, inspired Dylan to adapt traditional material to new ends, specifically the ends of political intervention. It was the great participatory drama of the civil rights movement that infused Dylan, and others, with the desire, confidence, and capacity to make the old traditions anew, as Alan Lomax had demanded. It also stirred deeper longings. "Singing voiced the basic position of the movement, of taking action on your life," said Johnson Reagon. That mingling of the movement, the songs and the lure of self-fulfilment unleashed the creative energies of the folk revival and its major artist.

In their attempts to exercise their basic rights in a peaceful and dignified manner, the black youth of the South were met by violent reaction, often supported by state agencies. Vincent Harding wrote of the inner cost of this experience: "Every time they smashed away some obstacle to black freedom, and equality, another larger, newly perceived hindrance loomed before them, challenging the last ounce of their strength and their spirit." This dynamic of aspiration and frustration, hope and anger informs Dylan's music throughout the protest period, and haunts it for years after.

The Congress of Racial Equality had been founded in 1942 by a small group of Gandhian socialists, among them A.J. Muste and Bayard Rustin. In 1947, the group launched the Journey of Reconciliation, an early attempt to desegregate interstate public transport by nonviolent direct action. Nearly extinguished in the fifties, CORE chapters in the northern cities reemerged in the wake of the sit-ins in the South. In late 1961 the organization relaunched the Journey of Reconciliation as the Freedom Rides, which met with well-publicized violence as they made their way south. Along with SNCC (based mainly in the South), CORE was the organization for people who wanted to do something at the grass roots, who wanted to participate directly in social change. Unburdened by Stalinism and cold war liberalism, self-consciously interracial, it drew in increasing numbers of young activists, both black and white.

One of them was Suze Rotolo, Dylan's girlfriend, who booked the unknown singer into a CORE benefit gig to be held in February 1962. Dylan decided to write something for the occasion. The result was "The Death of Emmett Till," his first protest song. Dropping by the Folklore Center, he boasted to Izzy Young that it was "the best thing I've ever written" (not saying much at the time). Two weeks later, he sang it on WBAI, to an enthusiastic response from program host Cynthia Gooding. Dylan never released the song and soon dismissed it as "bullshit."[51] It is certainly heavy-handed and sappy (its final verse is an excruciating example of the social patriotism Van Ronk decried). But the choice of subject was an interesting one. In 1956, at the age of fourteen, the Chicago-based Till had been brutally murdered by racists while on a visit to Mississippi. Dylan was born in the same year as Till, as was Muhammad Ali, who has always cited the Till murder as a critical moment in the formation of his own racial consciousness. It was also pivotal in the life of Medgar Evers, the NAACP field secretary in Mississippi who investigated the case and watched in helpless horror as the perpetrators walked free.

From the beginning, Dylan had little interest in dreams of interracial harmony or paeans to patiently born suffering. What spurs his writing is racist violence, the brutality and madness of the white backlash. In 1961, Dylan regularly performed a version of Lord Buckley's satirical rant, "Black Cross," about an intelligent black man murdered by idiot whites. He followed "Emmett Till" with "The Ballad of Donald White," the life story of a black man speaking from death row. "They killed him because he couldn't find no room in life," Dylan explained. "They killed him and when they did I lost some of my room in my life. When are some people gonna wake up and see that sometimes people aren't really their enemies, but their victims?" [52]

In the two years following "Emmett Till," some 200 original compositions poured from Dylan's pen, including the protest songs that made his name. He dealt with race, war, class, and social change itself. He wrote about poverty, violence, outcasts, prisoners, friendship, and love. Because Dylan so decisively and rapidly repudiated his protest songs, critics and biographers have been tempted to dismiss them as simplistic and derivative, somehow not the "real Dylan." But these songs are not only an immense achievement in their own right, they are the foundation of Dylan's subsequent evolution. And they are as personal—as deeply felt, as much an expression of the artist's personality—as anything else he wrote. That's one reason they still carry a powerful charge.

There was nothing new in setting topical lyrics to familiar or traditional tunes. Black soldiers in the Civil War did it with "John Brown's Body." In the 1880s, miners rewrote "The Vacant Chair" (about the Lincoln assassination) as "The Miners' Lifeguard;" the IWW turned "Just Before the Battle Mother" (a Civil War ballad) into "I'm Too Old to Be a Scab." Joe Hill, the master of the art—he remade "In the Sweet Bye and Bye" as "The Preacher and the Slave"—explained his thinking:

A song is learned by heart and repeated over and over, and if a person can put a few common sense facts into a song and dress them up in a cloak of humor, he will succeed in reaching a great number of workers who are too unintelligent or too indifferent to read.[53]

An echo of that patronizing populism can be heard in the Almanac Singers' advice to "sing the truth as simply as you can and repeat it as many times as it has to be repeated." Dylan's approach was different. He wasn't out to educate or agitate, but to participate and to express himself. As he explained in the Newport Folk Festival program of 1963:

> I can't sing "John Johanna"* cause it's his story an' his people's story—
> I gotta sing "With God on My Side" cause it's my story an' my people's story—

Dylan arrived as a political actor with knowledge and ideas gleaned largely from records. The songs led him to the politics and the politics unlocked his songwriting gifts. The struggles over equality and peace unfolding around him provided an objective correlative for the feelings coursing through him. In his study of the Basement Tapes, *Invisible Republic,* Greil Marcus criticizes the protest songs on the grounds that there are "no individuals in them," only social types. Not so: they are filled with the nascent individuality of Dylan himself. Remember that he was composing his bittersweet, love-hate songs—"Don't Think Twice," "Boots of Spanish Leather," "One Too Many Mornings"—at the same time and in much the same artistic vein as his "finger pointin' " songs: moodily aggrieved and tenderly utopian at the same time.

Later, Dylan liked to claim that he was only "jumping into the scene to be heard" and irritated Joan Baez by telling her he wrote "Masters of War" for the money. Biographers who take this claim seriously underestimate Dylan's impish perversity—and misjudge the context. In the years during which Dylan wrote his protest songs, the overwhelming majority of white American youth subscribed to opinions that ranged only within the narrow band between deeply conservative and cautiously liberal. The politics he embraced in these songs were fashionable only among a small minority. That minority, however, was linked to a movement on the rise. This movement gave Dylan a stance from which to view a confusing world, a musical outlet for his inchoate emotions,

---

* A song from Harry Smith's *Anthology.*

and an appreciative audience. In these plainspoken democratic songs, Dylan was writing for and taking his place within a vanguard. There were easier ways to get attention or make a buck.

These topical songs have proved surprisingly durable. That the songs served in the first instance as instruments of self-expression for a particular young individual makes them no less authentic as expressions of a collective experience. On the contrary, Dylan's songs live inside the historical moment in a way that more programmatic efforts do not. As a result, they live beyond that moment. They rise out of their era and speak to ours, not least because of Dylan's hard-edged, increasingly radical political perspective.

As a teenager in Hibbing, Bob Dylan had been struck by the surreally inhuman logic of the fallout shelter boom—and in this he was not alone. In the late fifties, a small but significant section of American youth was getting worried about the bomb. In 1959, a Student Peace Union was formed, based on a rejection of both superpower blocs. Within a year it had chapters on one hundred campuses and boasted 3,000 national members. In the spring of 1960, to the surprise of the media and veterans of the left alike, 1,000 New Yorkers—mostly college students—publicly defied the city's annual civil defense drill, which they found both farcical and horrifying. Their anxieties were not assuaged when the new president, elected on a pledge to close a fictitious "missile gap" with the Soviets, boosted military spending and in April 1961 authorized the CIA-organized invasion of Cuba. In early 1962, a student march against nuclear testing drew 5,000 to Washington—the biggest protest march in the capital since the thirties, and a harbinger of much that was to come.[54]

Around the same time, shortly after he completed "Emmett Till," Dylan told Izzy Young that he wanted to write "something about fall out and bomb-testing." But he "didn't want it to be a slogan song. Too many of the protest songs are bad music. . . . The bomb songs, especially, are usually awkward and with bad music." On February 22, Young wrote in his notebook: "Bob Dylan just rolled in and wants to sing a new song about fallout shelters [called] 'Let Me Die in My Footsteps.' . . ." *

The song is a marvelously determined, fresh-faced refusal to take part in the fraud of civil defense and the larger insanity of the nuclear weapons race. More than that, it uses a visceral reaction to a perverse social policy to make an argument that is both wider in political scope and more intimately personal. It sounds themes that reappear in Dylan's work over many years and in many guises. The bomb shelters are symptoms of a life-fearing mentality: "some people thinkin' that the end is close by / 'Stead of learnin' to live they are learning to die." The nuclear threat was part of the strategy through which we are ruled: "There's always been people that have to cause fear / They've been talking of the war now for many long years." And it was also the ultimate expression of a profoundly wrong turn in human development:

> If I had rubies and riches and crowns
> I'd buy the whole world and change things around
> I'd throw all the guns and the tanks in the sea
> For they are mistakes of a past history.

Dylan insists that we cannot leave our world to the experts and stakes a claim for the presumption of youth in a society whose elders are steering it to war:

> I don't know if I'm smart but I think I can see
> When someone is pullin' the wool over me

And in the spirit of Ginsberg, he counterposes the miracle of life to the institutions of death:

> Let me drink from the waters where the mountain streams flood
> Let the smell of wildflowers flow free through my blood

---

* Although he played "Let Me Die in My Footsteps" frequently over the coming months it was left off *Freewheelin'* and only released in 1991 on the *Bootleg Series*. About the same time, Dylan wrote a poem in Young's notebook, "Go Away You Bomb" ("I hate you cause you make my life seem like nothin' at all").

In the song's conclusion Dylan again invokes the "social patriotism" that irritated Van Ronk. The antidote to the fallout shelters can be found in: "Nevada, New Mexico, Arizona, Idaho / Let every state in this union seep in your souls." This was a straightjacket Dylan was soon to burst out of.

In February 1962, Pete Seeger took Dylan to meet Sis Cunningham and Gordon Friesen, who were in the midst of launching their new "topical song magazine," *Broadside*. Cunningham and Friesen were products of the labor battles of the thirties, had been involved with the Almanac Singers, and had preserved their political commitments through the isolation and calumny of the McCarthy years. Dylan played them a new composition, "Talkin' John Birch Paranoid Blues," a satire on anti-Communist paranoia—which duly appeared in print in the new magazine's first issue. Some have seen this episode as an example of the ever-cunning Dylan ingratiating himself with potential patrons. The boy was on the make in the Village and he wanted the veteran leftists' support. Whatever truth there may be in that speculation, what is certain is that at this time defying and deriding anticommunism—not only a right-wing shibboleth but also one of the foundation stones of the liberal support for the cold war—would have been regarded by most as a serious career risk. And all Sis and Gordon had to offer was publication in a new, noncommercial, small circulation magazine. For the next year, Dylan attended the monthly *Broadside* songwriters' meetings and contributed twenty-nine original "topical" songs to the magazine, which also published new work by Phil Ochs, Tom Paxton, Buffy Sainte-Marie, Len Chandler, and Peter La Farge (whom Dylan considered the most skillful of the pack).[55]

"Talkin' John Birch Paranoid Blues" sizzles with comic disbelief at the delusional antics of the red-hunters. Dylan had lessons in the stifling absurdities of McCarthyism close to hand, in the fate of Woody Guthrie's associates. Seeger himself had been indicted in 1956 for contempt of Congress—in refusing to answer questions, he cited the First and not the Fifth Amendment—and in 1961 had been sentenced to ten years' imprisonment; he was technically out on appeal when he took

Dylan to meet the *Broadside* founders. His case was finally dismissed by the courts later that year. Nonetheless, Seeger was blacklisted by *Hootenanny*, ABC's attempt to cash in on the folk revival. As a result, Baez, Dylan, and others refused to appear on the program. In 1963, when Dylan turned up at a CBS studio to rehearse for his first national network TV appearance—on *The Ed Sullivan Show*—he played the John Birch satire. He was asked to play something else. He refused. His appearance was canceled.[56]

At the time, both the peace and civil rights movements were wracked by debates about relations with Communists or people alleged to be Communists. Martin Luther King was cajoled into dissociating himself from some of his closest advisers because of their alleged links with the Communist Party, past or present. The Student Peace Union was under internal and external pressure (the latter in the form of media-hungry Congressional committees) to repudiate not only "communism," but also any individual with ties to any form of organized Marxism. But the radical youth who formed the cadre of SNCC, and others who would soon form the cadre of Students for a Democratic Society (SDS), were increasingly convinced that McCarthyism was a far greater danger to freedom than any Communist conspiracy. To them, the search for reds under the bed had become ludicrous—and Dylan gave expression to that nascent contempt in his talking blues. Already, in 1960, students had disrupted a House Un-American Activities Committee hearing in San Francisco. Later in the decade, Jerry Rubin, Abbie Hoffman, and others debunked the proceedings through parody and pantomime. In place of the deliberately sober and solemn approach of the leftists who had faced the inquisition in the forties and fifties, Dylan and his contemporaries dismissed the entire witch-hunting enterprise with caustic mockery. In so doing, they shook off a crippling political inhibition, and embarked on a journey toward a more all-embracing critique of their country and its role in the world.

Dylan wrote "Blowin' in the Wind" somewhere in the Village—backstage at Gerde's or in a café opposite the Gaslight—at the beginning of April 1962. He introduced an early performance with the caveat: "This here ain't a protest song or anything like that, cause I don't write protest songs. . . . I'm just writing it as something to be said, for somebody, by somebody."[57] Though it was to be more than a year before recordings of the song were released, it spread rapidly through the folk set. In May, Dylan sang it on WBAI accompanied by Pete Seeger and Sis Cunningham. Weeks later, the lyrics were plastered across the cover of the sixth issue of *Broadside*. By word of mouth, it soon acquired the status of underground sing-along standard.

"Blowin' in the Wind" slipped easily into the folk revival repertoire: its musical formula and lyrical style were already familiar. The melody, as Seeger was the first to spot and as Dylan has acknowledged, is in part a reworking of the tune of "No More Auction Block (Many Thousands Gone)"—a song first sung by escaped slaves in Canada before the Civil War. Paul Robeson performed and recorded it; Odetta picked it up from him and Dylan picked it up from her. When he sang "Auction Block" in the Village in 1962, he gave it a fierce, haunted quality not found in the stately lamentations of Robeson or Odetta.

In retrospect, "Blowin' in the Wind" seems timeless, abstract, naive. But in context its glancing references to the great social challenges of the day—racism and war—carried a powerful topical punch. Listeners had no doubt what Dylan was referring to when he asked when the "cannon balls" would be "forever banned" or how long it would be before "some people are allowed to be free." The song is delicately poised between hope and impatience. It is filled with a sense that a long-awaited transformation is both imminent and frustratingly out of reach. The ambiguous refrain—"the answer, my friend, is blowin' in the wind"—gropes for the unnameable. In this it touches a mood explored in Dylan's work through the rest of the decade. The "answer" is here, and not here; it exists, a force felt all around us, but remains elusive.

When Peter, Paul and Mary's smooth and earnest cover version was released in June 1963, it sold 300,000 copies in two weeks, making it the fastest selling single in Warner Brothers' history. This unexpected intrusion of social consciousness into the pop charts* took pundits by surprise, and the media ruminated over the significance of the latest youth phenomenon and its unkempt troubadour hero. But there was no mystery to the song's success. In the weeks before the Peter, Paul and Mary single was released, U.S. television screens had been filled with images from Birmingham, Alabama, where thousands of marching black children had been attacked by police with dogs and fire hoses. "How many times can a man turn his head / and pretend that he just doesn't see?" The same insistent demand that now, not tomorrow, is the time to tackle injustice, fills the open letter Martin Luther King wrote from his Birmingham jail cell.

Peter, Paul and Mary were only the first of many to cover "Blowin' in the Wind." One of the artists who tried his hand with the song was Sam Cooke, the gospel star turned crossover teen idol. Cooke covered the song as part of his ceaseless efforts to fashion a mass, multiracial audience; ironically, for him, Dylan's brave new song was a commercial opportunity—it was already familiar to a section of the white audience he wanted to reach.[58] But he was also drawn to the song because of his growing political engagement, and lamented to friends that it had to be a white boy who first dared talk about these realities on the jukeboxes. The success of "Blowin' in the Wind" helped inspire Cooke's own composition, the magnificent "A Change Is Gonna Come," the first masterpiece of socially aware soul, written in late 1964. Even in 1966, when the sixteen-year-old Stevie Wonder decided to record "Blowin' in the Wind," Motown bosses worried that their prodigy would be tainted by political controversy. Wonder's zestful rendition topped the R&B charts, and in the years to come the politics of race and war would become ever more explicit in black popular music.

Dylan himself never saw the song as a rallying cry but as a challenge—to the establishment and the movement, to the apathetic and the active. In the notes he wrote for *Broadside* in 1962, he declared:

* The other enduring hit of that summer was Lesley Gore's "It's My Party" (". . . and I'll cry if I want to").

Too many of these hip people are telling me where the answer is, but oh, I don't believe that. I still say it's in the wind and just like a restless piece of paper, it's got to come down some time. . . . But the only trouble is that no one picks up the answer when it comes down so not too many people get to see and know it . . . and then it flies away again. . . . I still say that some of the biggest criminals are those who turn their heads away when they see wrong and know it's wrong. I'm only 21 years old and I know that there's been too many wars. . . . You people over 21 should know better . . . cause after all, you're older and smarter.

Soon after "Blowin' in the Wind" made its way around the coffee-houses, Dave Van Ronk told the song's author it was "incredibly dumb." Dylan may have agreed, because within a year he dropped the tune from live performances—except for mandatory sing-alongs at folk festivals and the March on Washington. In 1971, when Dylan—after a long hiatus in his public support for good causes—appeared at the Concert for Bangladesh organized by George Harrison, the former Beatle suggested he sing "Blowin' in the Wind." An irritated Dylan asked Harrison whether he still performed "I Wanna Hold Your Hand." But the primitive Beatles classic did not carry the political resonance of the primitive Dylan classic, and Harrison was right to see its appositeness to a concert whose central purpose was a moral appeal to the comfortable and affluent to assist the poor and disaster-stricken—not tomorrow, but today. This was con-firmed by the audience response, when Dylan, yielding to Harrison, but seizing the moment, belted out the familiar number from the stage.[59]

In June of 1962, the UAW-owned FDR Camp at Port Huron, north of Detroit, hosted the annual convention of Students for a Democratic So-ciety. The then little-known SDS was the student wing of the League for Industrial Democracy (LID), a venerable social democratic think tank long committed to a stringent anticommunism. After five days of meet-ings, the fifty-nine delegates—ostensibly representing SDS's 2,000 stu-dent contacts—adopted the Port Huron Statement, which was to become the most widely circulated and influential manifesto of the new (white, American) left, though it was created under the auspices of the old. Spurred by the protests against the bomb, the exponential growth of the civil rights movement, and many of the same discontents that drew young people to the folk revival, its authors consciously sought to map out a vision of American social change that would ring true for a new student generation.[60]

The statement eschewed the vocabulary of the old left. The words *capitalism, imperialism, class,* and *revolution* were nowhere to be found. Its specific proposals for reform were modest. It envisioned working in a renewed Democratic Party. But it was saturated with intimations that deeper and more radical change would be needed. "America rests in national stalemate," the students declared. "America is without community, impulse, without the inner momentum necessary. . . . Americans are in withdrawal from public life, from any collective effort at directing their own affairs."

The critique of American society in the Port Huron Statement was as much cultural as political. Speaking as young people to young people, the authors portrayed themselves as a generation shadowed by the bomb. They lamented "the decline of utopia and hope" but saw signs that "students are breaking the crust of apathy." Unlike the old left, they stressed individual freedom and creativity, which they argued were being stifled by the conformist, bureaucratic order of postwar America. "The goal of man and society should be human independence . . . finding a meaning in life that is personally authentic . . ." Politics itself would have to be redefined. Its function would be "bringing people out of isolation and into community." Tactics, strategy, and ideology were tied together under the ringing rubric of "participatory democracy."

The moment that created "Blowin' in the Wind" also created the Port Huron Statement, which shares the song's mixture of idealism and subdued impatience, as well as its longing for a bigger answer to the growing questions posed by the events of the day—the civil rights movement, the nuclear threat, and the bland complacency of the cultural mainstream. "We have no formulas, no closed theories . . ." the statement cautioned. Skeptical of both the liberal and Communist traditions, severed from organized labor by the cold war, and emboldened by their own experience of material comfort, they paraded their innocent openness. Year zero had been declared on the American left. It was a historical moment that was to shape Dylan's trajectory in the coming years as well as the evolution of many others, not least SDS itself.

As a result of events at Port Huron, the young SDS leaders were upbraided by their elder LID sponsors. It was an article of faith for them that members of Communist and "totalitarian" groups had no place in the democratic left. Yet at the outset of the Port Huron meeting the student delegates had voted to grant observer status to a member of a Communist Party youth organization. The LID veterans were also worried that the statement was too evenhanded in its denunciation of U.S. and Soviet foreign policies. Worse yet, it openly opposed what it called "an unreasoning anti-Communism." The SDS people couldn't see what the problem was. A generation gap had opened.

In July 1962, Dylan prefaced the *Freewheelin'* recording of "Bob Dylan's Blues" by saying: "Unlike most of the songs nowadays that are being written uptown in Tin Pan Alley—that's where most of the folk songs come from nowadays—this wasn't written up there, this was written somewhere down in the USA." It's a reworking of Guthrie's Rainbow Room jibe, a claim of authenticity, and a restatement of the Lomax credo that true folk music reflected American reality. But the reality that Dylan writes about in this off-the-cuff number includes the TV figures of the Lone Ranger and Tonto, sports cars ("I don't have no sports car / And I don't even care to have one"), and a final admonition by Dylan to an imagined acolyte (at this stage he had none):

You want to be like me
Pull out your six-shooter
And rob every bank you can see
Tell the judge I said it was all right

Dylan played and wrote songs about outlaws of all kinds, and frequently imagined himself as one. But already in "Bob Dylan's Blues" he displaces outlawry into a satirical realm. This slim one-and-a-half joke song may be based on a venerable blues, but it hints at a different world, one in which the authentic is contradictory and American reality frustratingly elusive.

——————————————

It's often claimed that Dylan wrote "A Hard Rain's A-Gonna Fall" in response to the Cuban missile crisis. Dylan himself seems to believe it. "I was in Bleecker Street in New York," he recalled some years later. "People sat around wondering if it was the end and so did I. . . . it was a song of desperation. What could we do? Could we control men on the verge of wiping us out? The words came fast, very fast. It was a song of terror. Line after line, trying to capture the feeling of nothingness." [61] Nonetheless, the fact remains that Dylan premiered "Hard Rain" at a Carnegie Hall hootenanny organized by Pete Seeger on September 22, 1962, some weeks before the U2 spotted the Soviet missiles on Cuban soil. It was only on October 22 that Kennedy announced his naval blockade and the crisis erupted in the headlines.

None of which makes "Hard Rain" any less relevant to the missile crisis. The audience at Carnegie Hall seemed impressed by the new song, and Seeger himself quickly incorporated it into his repertoire. For these people, and for Dylan, the real possibility of nuclear extinction had been in the air for some time. Dylan was able to write "Hard Rain" "before the event" not because he was a prophetic mystic, but because he was a political artist in a political milieu with an astute sense of the prevailing anxieties. The urgency and despair out of which Dylan says he wrote the song were undeniably real.

"A Hard Rain's A-Gonna Fall" is the first of Dylan's songs to be comprised of a series of disconnected, enigmatic images (an indulgence in obscurity to which he would not return for two years). The song borrows its quizzical refrain from "Lord Randal," a Child* ballad ("Oh, where have you been, Lord Randal, my son?") and is driven by an insis-

* Francis Child, a Harvard professor, published his five-volume *English and Scottish Popular Ballads* between 1882 and 1898. It became the founding canon of folk song.

tent if rough-edged rhythm that anticipates his later turn to rock 'n' roll. The singer's vision in this song is panoptic: evoking global destruction ("seven sad forests" and "a dozen dead oceans") as well as more metaphorical disasters ("ten thousand talkers whose tongues were all broken," "a newborn babe with wild wolves all around it"). He hears not only "the roar of a wave that could drown the whole world" but also "the song of a poet who died in the gutter." Finally, he ventures out into a postapocalypse landscape that is also the reality of the here and now:

> Where the executioner's face is always well hidden,
> Where hunger is ugly, where souls are forgotten,
> Where black is the color, where none is the number

And he vows, with more confidence than in "Let Me Die in My Footsteps," written only seven months earlier, to "tell it and think it and speak it and breathe it."

At Carnegie Hall, Dylan introduced his audience to another new song, "Ballad of Hollis Brown," the tale of a man driven to murder and suicide by poverty. (The melody is derived from the traditional "Pretty Polly.") The language was as pared down as that of "Hard Rain" was luxuriant, but like "Hard Rain" it beats with a stark, bleak terror. This song has been disparaged as "hysterical" but that's what it needs to be; it's the hysteria of poverty and powerlessness. Dylan's presentation of the self-destruction of the oppressed makes the blood run cold. "Hollis Brown" touches the tragic monumentality of the folk ballads it's based on. Unlike them, it was written not for people who knew poverty all too well but for people who scarcely acknowledged it existed. Dylan was writing about what Michael Harrington called the "other America," about the casualties of class that crossed racial boundaries.

Weeks after writing "Hard Rain" and "Hollis Brown," Dylan returned to the theme of racial violence with "Oxford Town," his response to that autumn's events at the University of Mississippi. When James Meredith sought enrollment as Ole Miss's first black student, whites across the South reacted in horror. In a bravura display of reactionary defiance, Governor Ross Barnett blocked Meredith's path. The Kennedy administration was forced to intervene. Federal agents escorted Meredith to his dormitory. In the most violent student disturbances of the decade, several thousand white college boys (pumped up by the regional media and the governor himself, and assisted by highway patrolmen and local police) besieged the campus, attacked the federal marshals guarding Meredith, slashed tires, hurled Molotov cocktails, bricks and lead pipes, and fired shotguns. "Two men died 'neath the Mississippi moon," Dylan sings, accurately—and another 28 were shot and 160 wounded. In the end, the Kennedy administration deployed 23,000 troops—three times the population of Oxford—to subdue the white resistance to Meredith.[62] Dylan's song is plainspoken and moving, if one-dimensional. He seems to have played it live only once—on his sole visit to Oxford, Mississippi, in 1991.[63]

After "Oxford Town," Dylan returned to an antimilitarist theme in "John Brown," the tale of an innocent sent "off to war to fight on a foreign shore" (the song does not appear on any of Dylan's sixties albums, but it became a staple of his live performances in the nineties, along with other antiwar material). The young soldier's proud mother dispatches him with the advice: "Do what the captain says, lots of medals you will get." She brags to the neighbors "about her son with his uniform and gun, / And these things you called a good old-fashioned war." And Dylan hammers home the ghastly refrain: "Oh! Good old-fashioned war!"

The same year Dylan wrote "John Brown," the Kingston Trio were enjoying success with Pete Seeger's "Where Have All the Flowers Gone," which included an antiwar verse considered daring in its time:

> Where have all the soldiers gone
> Gone to graveyards ev'ry one
> When will they ever learn?

Dylan's song is less wistful and more graphic in its account of the costs of war. When the soldier returns from overseas and is met at the station by his mother, she is shocked at his condition:

> Oh his face was all shot up and his hand was all blown off
> And he wore a metal brace around his waist.

He whispered kind of slow, in a voice she did not know,
While she couldn't even recognize his face!

Though the disabled soldier's "mouth can hardly move," he manages
to address his mother in all his bitterness:

"Don't you remember, Ma, when I went off to war
You thought it was the best thing I could do?"

Then he tells her something of the reality of war. He tells her how in the
midst of battle he asked himself, "God, what am I doing here?"

But the thing that scared me most was when my enemy came close
And I saw that his face looked just like mine.

And a terrified, indignant Dylan wails in refrain: "Oh! Lord! Just like
mine!" Finally, Brown recalls how "through the thunder rolling and
stink" it came to him that he "was just a puppet in a play." In "John
Brown" Dylan told the story of Ron Kovic—disabled Vietnam veteran,
antiwar crusader and author of *Born on the Fourth of July*—some seven
years before Kovic lived through the nightmare and drew the lesson of
the song from his own experience. The writing in "John Brown" is
sometimes cumbersome, the naturalism is crude, and the hysteria less
disciplined than in "Hollis Brown," but in its repugnance at jingoism,
glancing references to class, filial rage, and anguished opening to an internationalist vision, the song shows Dylan working to synthesise
something new, a contemporary folk music that was emotionally raw
and politically uncompromising. In "John Brown" social patriotism has
begun to go sour. Not long after writing the song, Dylan would make
his first trip abroad. Albert Grossman had somehow persuaded the
BBC to cast Dylan in a small role in an original drama, and to pay his
fare across the Atlantic.

In April 1951, the Communist Party of Great Britain organized a conference in London on "the American threat to British culture." That
threat emanated, it was argued, from the drive by American big busi-

ness to foist "the American way of life"—greed, violence, and racism—on the British people, not least through the popularity of Hollywood films and "commercial dance music." The party condemned a number of films—*Kiss of Death, The Set-Up, White Heat, Brute Force,* all now considered noir classics—for promoting sadism. The BBC was attacked for preferring American over British songwriters. American popular music played on "the hopes and frustrations of the people . . . brushing aside the idea of struggle." It was a music of "wish fulfillment" and "sloppy eroticism," "drugging the minds of the people," most worryingly, young people: "Our youngsters are being brought up to know no other films or songs than American. They are being encouraged to wear American clothes, speak with American accents, ape American ways." The antidote to this poison was "to popularize and re-discover our cultural heritage . . . to develop a popular, progressive culture based on our traditions." [64]

If the aim was to reach out to coming generations of working-class British youth, the party's antagonism to American popular culture was to prove a major misjudgment. Ironically, the party itself, in its turn to folk culture, helped foster a growing interest in American musical idioms. The Communist Party's early Ballads and Blues events—which an expatriate Alan Lomax helped to organize—were refreshingly eclectic, featuring both British folk and American jazz and blues artists, not least Big Bill Broonzy, who had also graced Hammond's From Spirituals to Swing gig in 1938. As Raphael Samuels recalled, the early British folk revival displayed a relaxed and innovative attitude toward heritage. It broke from the conservative pastoralism of the old Cecil Sharp* societies and preferred smoky pubs to concert halls. [65]

---

* The English folklorist Cecil Sharp (1859–1924) started the Morris dance revival and collected traditional ballads in the British countryside. Between 1916 and 1918 he visited southern Appalachia, where he found variants of old English and Scottish folk songs long forgotten in their native lands. "I should say that they [the white people of the mountains] are just exactly what the English peasant was one hundred or more years ago," he wrote. "They are happy, contented, and live simply and healthily, and I am not at all sure that any of us can introduce them to anything better than this."

It was out of this new interest in old American music—especially New Orleans jazz—that the skiffle fad emerged in the mid-fifties. Lonnie Donegan had a hit with a thumping version of Leadbelly's "Rock Island Line" and across the country teenagers emulated him—which was easy enough, because the musical elements of skiffle were rudimentary. When he arrived in London in 1955, Ramblin' Jack Elliott was startled to find these familiar tunes clothed in English accents; he concluded that English skiffle wasn't "worth shit." But Alan Lomax disagreed.

> At first it seemed very strange to me to hear these songs, which I had recorded from convicts in the prisons of the south, coming out of the mouths of young men who had suffered, comparatively speaking, so little. But I soon realized that these young people felt themselves to be in a prison—composed of class-and-caste lines, the shrinking British empire, the dull job, the lack of money—things like these. They were shouting at the prison walls, like so many Joshuas at the walls of Jericho.[66]

Lomax was prescient. Skiffle opened the door to a generation of British youth; it introduced them to the rhythmic enchantments and earthy realism of the African American tradition. It was through skiffle that Lennon met McCartney. "This American-amalgamated, British-derived Africanized music has already filled a large vacuum in the musical life of urban Britain," Lomax wrote. People were once again making their own music, and that was a phenomenon he always welcomed. Lomax urged the skifflers to continue their efforts, but warned them against indulging in "sophisticated chord progressions, like the jazz boys." Instead, he advised them to "discover the song-tradition of Great Britain . . . Probably the richest in western Europe."

During his stay in Britain, Lomax introduced Bert Lloyd (author of *The Singing Englishman,* an adventurous early Marxist essay in popular musicology) to Ewan MacColl, a working-class militant from Salford. MacColl had spent a decade as an actor and singer in left-wing theater companies but was now looking for a new approach to building a people's culture. Following Lomax's example, Lloyd and MacColl set about constructing a canon of working-class British folk music—shifting the focus from the feudal countryside to the industrial proletariat, and emphasizing a continuing tradition of protest from below. Lomax also introduced MacColl to Peggy Seeger, daughter of Charles and Ruth Crawford Seeger. The meeting inspired MacColl to write the delicately haunting "The First Time Ever I Saw Your Face," and led to a partnership that ended only with MacColl's death in 1989.*

As the American challenge to homegrown music intensified, one wing of the folk movement became more purist. "I was convinced that we had a music that was just as vigorous as anything America had produced, and we should be pursuing some kind of national identity," MacColl explained, "not just becoming an arm of American cultural imperialism." Under the influence of MacColl and the left, many Ballads and Blues clubs turned themselves into Singer's Clubs, with policy rules governing what should and should not be performed. MacColl felt that "if the singer was English, then the songs should be from the English tradition"—which sparked off debates about the regional roots of English folk, not to mention its relationship to Irish, Scottish, and Welsh music. In 1957, there were said to be 1,500 Singer's Clubs with 11,000 members.[67]

The big boost for the British folk revival came in the following year, with the formation of the Campaign for Nuclear Disarmament and the first of the Aldermaston marches. These demonstrations were many times the size of the U.S. ban-the-bomb marches of the early sixties, and their political impact was much greater (they succeeded in making unilateral nuclear disarmament, briefly, an official Labour Party policy). They provided an impetus for the nascent new left (the first of many) and a cradle of the sixties youth culture, as working-class Young Communists, university students, and footloose beatniks mingled in a common crusade and found a common interest in guitar-based music.

The British folk revival was more overtly politicized than its U.S. counterpart, and the influence of the organized left, including the

---

* In 1969, Peggy Seeger penned "I Wanna Be an Engineer," one of the earliest musical expressions of the new wave of feminism (published first in *Broadside*).

Communist Party, was significant. As in America, however, there was a conviction that folk music was the authentic voice of the oppressed and a refuge from the soullessness of commercial mass culture. "The clubs themselves seem to have served as some kind of refuge for the sociologically orphaned," wrote Samuels, "the ex-working class from whose ranks the new generation of singers were largely recruited."[68]

When Pete Seeger toured Britain in 1961, he was impressed by the buoyancy of the folk movement and in particular by the new topical songwriting promoted by MacColl and Lloyd. He heard modern ballads for modern times—though always set to traditional tunes and traditional accompaniments—and on his return urged his American colleagues to follow the British example, which led to the launching of *Broadside*.

Dylan arrived in London on May 18, 1962. He checked into the Mayfair, where the BBC had booked him a room, but felt uncomfortable in such plush surroundings ("I knew then what it is like to be a Negro," he told Robert Shelton). He set off to the folk clubs, where he felt much more at home. Here he soaked up the contending schools of folk practice and the various political perspectives that lay behind them. He met and heard many of the younger singers, including Martin Carthy, who introduced Dylan to the original British sources of the Appalachian songs he knew from the work of Lomax and Harry Smith. "His time in England was actually crucial to his development," said Carthy, "it had a colossal effect on him."[69]

Dylan reworked Carthy's arrangement of "Scarborough Fair" into two of the best of his early love songs, "Girl from the North Country" and "Boots of Spanish Leather." Jean Ritchie's version of "Nottamun Town"—an Appalachian adaptation of a song from an English mummers' play—was refashioned into "Masters of War." In the coming months "Lord Franklin" would become the prematurely nostalgic "Bob Dylan's Dream." "The Road and the Miles to Dundee" would become "The Walls of Red Wing," which deals with the repressive conditions in a juvenile detention center. Most significantly, Dominic Behan's "The Patriot Game" (itself derived from an old Appalachian tune) would give birth to "With God on Our Side." Behan had written:

> Come all you young rebels and list while I sing
> For the love of one's country is a terrible thing.
> It banishes fear with the speed of a flame
> And it makes us all part of the patriot game.

In London Dylan learned that Behan had taken his cue from Samuel Johnson's definition of patriotism as "the last refuge of the scoundrel." The idea clearly made an impression on him, and runs through his work from "With God on Our Side" to "Tombstone Blues." * But in London he told a British interviewer. "I don't like singing to anybody but Americans. My songs say things. I sing them for people who know what I'm saying." He took this chip-on-the-shoulder American identity into the heart of the London folk scene, won over some and antagonized many.

The Singer's Club at the Pindar of Wakefield on Gray's Inn Road was run by MacColl and Peggy Seeger and reflected their priorities. Dylan sang "Masters of War" and "Ballad of Hollis Brown." MacColl and Seeger were not impressed. Strangely, Dylan was doing what Mac-Coll wanted young singers to do: use old tunes to comment on current political realities. But there was, from the beginning, something about Dylan that MacColl could not accept. "I have watched with fascination the meteoric rise of this American idol," MacColl told *Sing Out!* readers in 1965. "And I am still unable to see in him anything other than a youth of mediocre talent. Only a completely non-critical audience, nourished on the watery pap of pop music, could have fallen for such tenth rate drive. . . . What poetry? The cultivated illiteracy of his topical songs or the embarrassing schoolboy attempt at free verse?" [70]

Yet in the course of his visit to London (he also popped over to

---

* And beyond. In the 1983 "Sweetheart Like You," he writes:

> They say that patriotism is the last refuge
> To which a scoundrel clings
> Steal a little and they throw you in jail
> Steal a lot and they make you king

Paris), Dylan's work took a decidedly political turn. When he met up with his friend, the novelist and songwriter Richard Fariña, toward the end of his time abroad, he told him: "Man, there's things going on in this world you got to look at, right? You can't pretend they ain't happening. Man, I was in New York when that Cuba business came over the radio, and you think that don't put something in your head? Man, you can keep on singing about Railroad Bill and Lemon Trees, or you can step out, right?"[71] And when Dylan returned to New York he made a similar point to Shelton, "I need some more finger pointin' songs . . . Cause that's where my head's at right now."

The interchange between the English-speaking cultures on either side of the Atlantic was constant and complex throughout the decade. Without this mutual influence, it's impossible to imagine the evolution of either British or American popular music, or the dissident subcultures that sprouted in both countries. The impact of African American music on British youth was immeasurable, but there was also significant traffic in the opposite direction. A month after Dylan's visit, "Please, Please Me," the Beatles' first hit, entered the British charts. It was a momentous development for which the British Communist Party, to name but one, found itself unprepared.

Both "Masters of War" and "With God on Our Side" burst the boundaries of the soft-focus pacifism of previous antiwar songs. Both are concerned not merely with the imminence of war, but with its deeper causes, with the forces that promote and profit from fear and violence. Both are magnificently enraged and enduringly radical. Five years before students in large numbers were to take action against campus collusion with the Pentagon and the weapons industry, "Masters of War" unmasked the military-industrial complex:

> You fasten the triggers
> For the others to fire
> Then you set back and watch
> When the death count gets higher

Dylan points the finger of guilt at the war-makers and the war-profiteers and jabs it in their faces. The song is dry, sparse, and un-wavering in its indictment and its anger. The bare, archaic-sounding guitar chords hint at momentous tragedies past and to come, while the flat, steely voice speaks of hard lessons learned and not forgotten. Not least a lesson from Woody Guthrie: that the greatest criminals are those that "hide behind desks." Enraged by the omnipotent, unaccountable manipulators who threaten to annihilate his world, Dylan once again asserts his right to speak out:

How much do I know
To talk out of turn
You might say that I'm young
You might say I'm unlearned
But there's one thing I know
Though I'm younger than you
Even Jesus would never
Forgive what you do

Fully aware of his temerity in speaking out, he is nonetheless convinced of its urgent necessity. Paradoxically, the sense of impotence in the face of a prospective nuclear holocaust emboldened both Dylan and his generation. Confronted with such recklessness, there was no time to waste and nothing to lose. A voice had to be raised—if only to pronounce a curse. The climactic verse (which Joan Baez refused to sing) is morbidly unforgiving:

I will follow your casket
In the pale afternoon
And I'll watch while you're lowered
Down to your deathbed
And I'll stand o'er your grave
'Til I'm sure that you're dead

The vindictive note was uncharacteristic of the civil rights and peace movements of the first half of the decade—but it was characteristic

Dylan. And it strengthens the song. For this is not merely a desire to bury a group of wicked individuals, but to bury a social interest and a system that breeds war.

That Dylan was no liberal even before he made his break with the liberals is confirmed by "With God on Our Side," another composition of early 1963. Here he subjects the epic narrative of American history and national identity to an iconoclastic revision worthy of Malcolm X. Effacing himself in the first verse ("Oh my name it is nothin' / My age it means less"), he notes that he was taught that "the land that I live in / Had God on its side." He then embarks on a coruscating survey of the genocide and militarism engendered by this nationalist fundamentalism. "Oh the history books tell it / They tell it so well"—but they do not tell the truth: about the Indians, about the Spanish-American War and World War I, about the post–World War II rehabilitation of ex-Nazis. Dylan brings the story up to the minute, observing "I've learned to hate Russians / All through my whole life," and spells out what this latest incarnation of the national mission means:

> But now we got weapons
> Of the chemical dust
> If fire them we're forced to
> Then fire them we must
> One push of the button
> And a shot the world wide
> And you never ask questions
> When God's on your side.

In defining the current nuclear competition with the Soviets as the most recent episode in a history of murder and hypocrisy, Dylan spews contempt on the liberal justifications for the cold war and U.S. overseas interventions. In this song, Dylan expresses the embitterment of a generation of politically innocent young Americans who discovered with shock that the people they had been told were the good guys were actually something else entirely—the experience eloquently described by SDS president Carl Oglesby at a demonstration against the Vietnam

War in October 1965: "Others will make of it that I sound mighty anti-American. To these, I say: don't blame *me* for *that!* Blame those who mouthed my liberal values and broke my American heart." [72] In response to the growing horrors of Vietnam, more and more were to question their country's historical record. The "social patriotism" that had inspired activists in the first half of the sixties came to seem naive or worse, and the radical analysis and uncompromising contempt of songs like "With God on Our Side" more truthful, politically and emotionally.

The cold war and the bomb were always, for Dylan, as much a state of mind as a geopolitical reality. In the coming years, the ban-the-bomb movement would give way to the much larger anti–Vietnam War movement, which Dylan would shun. But the horror and absurdity of nuclear weapons competition, the insanity of a system that claimed "a world war can be won," continued to haunt his music.

In April 1963, Dylan penned yet another song about the death of a black man. "Who Killed Davey Moore?" * is a rapid response to the fatal outcome of Moore's featherweight title fight against Sugar Ramos (Moore died on March 23; Dylan premiered the song on April 12.). It is a concise but sweeping analysis of the ethical complicity of a whole society in the (avoidable) death of a single man. The cock robin refrain is used to nominate and expose the guilty. One by one, Dylan allows them to condemn themselves out of their own mouths. Anyone familiar with boxing and its history will recognize all the routine rationalizations, as the referee, the crowd, the manager, the gamblers, and the boxing writers wash their hands of the dead boxer's blood: "Boxing ain't to blame, / There's just as much danger in a football game . . . Fist fighting is here to stay, / It's just the old American way."

In the final verse he focuses on the winner of the fatal fight. Dylan tells us he "came here from Cuba's shore / Where boxing ain't allowed

---

* The song was recorded by Pete Seeger, though not by Dylan himself. His unique Town Hall performance can be heard on the *Official Bootleg Series*, 1991.

no more." This line got a big cheer when Dylan debuted the song at his milestone Town Hall concert (an indication of the explicitly leftist identity that bound Dylan and his audience at this point). But neither Dylan nor the audience had got it quite right. Revolutionary Cuba did not ban boxing; on the contrary, in the coming years Cuba would produce a rich array of world-dominating boxing talent, from Teofilo Stevenson to Felix Savon. The vehicle for this sporting efflorescence was a planned program of state intervention and funding. What Cuba had banned was "professional boxing," prizefighting. Despite the error, Dylan was wise enough to place money at the center of boxing's ethical morass. "I hit him, yes, it's true, / But that's what I am paid to do."

On April 16, 1963, Martin Luther King wrote from his jail cell in Birmingham:

> It's better to go to jail in dignity than accept segregation in humility. . . .
> There comes a time when the cup of endurance runs over, and men are
> no longer willing to be plunged into the abyss of despair.[73]

Two weeks later, on May 2, 4,000 black children marched through the city center demanding an end to Jim Crow. The subsequent police assault was broadcast worldwide. On May 10, Birmingham's white authorities were forced to accept a deal with King and the movement. The victory renewed civil rights agitation across the South. In the ten weeks that followed there were 758 demonstrations and 14,733 arrests in 186 cities.[74]

One of those cities was Jackson, the Mississippi state capital, where local NAACP field secretary Medgar Evers was leading an increasingly militant fight against segregation.* "In the racial picture, things will never be as they were," Evers warned a local television audience, as the sit-ins and arrests mounted, "History has reached a turning point, here and over the world."[75] On the evening of June 11, President Kennedy

---

* "I got a woman in Jackson, I ain't gonna say her name / she's a brown-skinned woman / but I love her just the same"—Dylan in "Outlaw Blues," January 1965.

told a nationwide TV audience that he too had come to believe that "a great change is at hand." Under pressure from the actions in the South, and their impact in the North, Kennedy announced that he would send a major civil rights bill to Congress—a great triumph for the movement. Later that night, Evers returned home from one of the endless series of meetings through which that movement was sustained. As he stepped out of his car, he was shot to death by a hidden assassin. Three and half weeks later, on July 5, the twenty-one-year-old Bob Dylan arrived in Greenwood, Mississippi, to give his support to a SNCC voter registration drive.

For decades, the black population in the Delta country around Greenwood had been terrorized by one of the most tyrannical white supremacist regimes in the South. It was considered impossible to organize these downtrodden rural workers, people who knew only powerlessness and isolation. Bob Moses, whose selfless dedication was already legendary among SNCC workers, had arrived there in the spring of 1962, determined to crack open the monolith.[76] In June of that year, he took his first batch of local volunteers to Highlander for training. Two months later, the SNCC office in Greenwood was besieged and ransacked. One of Moses's new recruits, a sharecropper (and singer) named Fannie Lou Hamer, was punished for the crime of seeking to register to vote by being kicked off the plantation where she had lived for eighteen years.

In an attempt to starve out resistance, state officials blocked the distribution of federal food supplies in two Delta counties. On the brink of famine, the sharecroppers fought back. The turnouts for SNCC's mass meetings grew, as did the numbers seeking to register. It was a show of black defiance unprecedented in the post-Reconstruction Delta. In February 1963, gunshots were fired at a SNCC worker sitting in a car on a country road. SNCC activists from around the country poured into Greenwood, including executive secretary Jim Forman, a onetime student activist from Chicago who had visited the South as a journalist and enlisted in the struggle. Throughout March 1963, amid shootings and arson attacks, Moses and Forman organized protests, marches, and meetings, and refused to scale down the voter registration challenges. Medgar Evers visited the town and was soon followed by Dick Gregory and reporters from the national press. Having been attacked by police dogs in the course of an attempt to register voters, eight SNCC workers, including Moses and Forman, found themselves convicted of disorderly conduct and sentenced to eight months in prison. They elected to serve the time rather than appeal. However, they were quickly released as a result of a compromise deal cut by the federal government (behind the SNCC workers' backs) with the Greenwood authorities.

The movement in the Delta soon sputtered to a halt. Despite promises by the White House that the perpetrators of racist violence would be brought to account, the Justice Department dropped its suit against Greenwood in late May. In early June, in nearby Winona, local cops jailed and brutally assaulted SNCC activists, including Fannie Lou Hamer. They were on their way back from a training session at Highlander—whose premises were themselves soon raided and padlocked by state authorities, then burned to the ground.*

So by the first week of July 1963, the beleaguered Greenwood movement was in need of outside support and attention, and Dylan's visit promised both. It was the actor-singer Theodore Bikel's idea that Dylan "should get a first-hand impression of the struggle in the South." He approached Albert Grossman with the proposal, and when Grossman complained about the cost, Bikel wrote out a check. He and Dylan flew to Atlanta and then on to Jackson, where they were met by two SNCC workers who drove them to Greenwood. Here they joined Pete Seeger, Len Chandler, and the Freedom Singers, who had all come down to sing at the rally scheduled for the next morning. Throughout the journey, Bikel told Shelton, Dylan was quiet, scribbling notes on stray pieces of paper, as was his habit. "His political attitudes were less strongly formed than many of ours. It seemed a personal thing with him to be going down into the deep South."[77]

---

* Highlander was reestablished, and still flourishes.

Dylan did not arrive in Greenwood unprepared. After all, this was the land where the blues began, as Alan Lomax called it. It was the land of Dylan's early masters, Bukka White, Charley Patton, Blind Lemon Jefferson, and John Lee Hooker. It was the land where Robert Johnson, Bessie Smith, and Emmett Till had all met their fates. Through the music and the history, Dylan already knew the Delta as a place of suffering and disgrace as well as tortured resilience. But this close-up experience of Jim Crow and the people who had risen to challenge it was something different. Bikel recounts Dylan's distress at his first sight of whites-only water fountains and toilets and the awe he expressed at the courage of the activists, many in the spartan SNCC uniform of work shirts and dungarees. Briefly, he shared the austerity and fear that made up their daily lives. That first night in Greenwood he slept in a church loft. The next morning he lay flat in the back of a car as he was driven the three miles out of town to the farmyard where the rally was being staged. The midday heat was intense, and the event was postponed till later in the afternoon. In the meanwhile, Dylan conversed with Forman and Moses, as well as Julian Bond and Bernice Johnson Reagon, who told Shelton that it was at Greenwood that she felt closest to Dylan. "The Greenwood people didn't know that Pete, Theo and Bob were well known. They were just happy to be getting support. But they really liked Dylan down there in the cotton country." According to Bikel, Dylan admitted to the black farmers that "he hadn't met a colored person till he was nine years old, and he apologized that he had so little to offer."

At dusk, the visiting performers clambered onto the back of a truck next to a cotton patch and performed for an audience of some 300 black people. They were watched by police in patrol cars and Klan members—and recorded for posterity by New York filmmaker Ed Emshwiller, who was on hand with a TV crew.* Dylan chose this moment to unveil his response to the Medgar Evers killing. By all accounts, the topicality of the song gripped the audience—some of whom would have seen Evers himself in recent months. Even more, the political

* A fragment is included in *Don't Look Back*.

analysis exercised a strong appeal, as Johnson Reagon has confirmed. In contrast to the moralistic and utopian rhetoric favored by the movement at this time, Dylan's song argued that racist violence was the product of political manipulation and an unjust social system.*

> . . . the Negro's name
> Is used it is plain
> For the politician's gain

Racism is neither a natural nor an inexplicable phenomenon. "The poor white man" is taught:

> That the laws are with him
> To protect his white skin
> To keep up his hate
> So he never thinks straight
> 'Bout the shape that he's in

Dylan's exposé of the white elite's divide-and-rule strategy and his insistence on the link between poverty and racism struck powerful chords among the SNCC activists, whose thinking about the nature of the challenge they faced was undergoing rapid evolution. The concert finished with Dylan joining the Freedom Singers, Seeger, Bikel, and Chandler for renditions of "Blowin' in the Wind" and "We Shall Overcome." (Later that summer, the performance was to be reprised by much the same company at both the Newport Festival finale and the Washington march.)

Dylan's encounter with the era's premier agents of social change was brief but seems to have left a deep impression. He certainly listened carefully to the Forman-penned, Lewis-delivered SNCC speech later that summer in Washington, and over the years he made many respect-

---

* As it happened, the killer of Medgar Evers, the wealthy and well-connected Byron de la Beckwith, was not "only a pawn in their game." In the mid-sixties, two all-white juries acquitted him of the crime. In February 1994, he was finally found guilty and at the age of seventy-three was sentenced to life in prison.

ful references to the people he met in Greenwood. Soon after his stay in one of America's poorest and most oppressed communities, Dylan was whisked off to a Columbia Records sales conference in Puerto Rico. He chose to entertain the assembled reps by playing "With God on Our Side" and "Only a Pawn in Their Game" (its second public outing). The southern contingent, especially, didn't like it; many walked out. That didn't seem to bother Dylan. In contrast, when he was asked to put on a tie so that he could join the Columbia execs at an expensive restaurant, he exploded.[78]

Meanwhile, the SNCC workers in Greenwood made little headway. In the six months following the federal government's deal with the white officials, only 590 blacks succeeded in registering to vote. On election day, white voters outnumbered black by 33 to 1—in a county where the black population was twice that of the white. The frustrations of Greenwood led many in SNCC to rethink their assumptions. The problem they faced was not so much redneck prejudice as reactionary institutions: from the courthouse to the White House. Forman argued that the movement should turn to "challenging the political structure of the country." Moses conceived his "white shield" strategy, and began recruiting white northern students for what was to become the Mississippi Summer project of 1964. In a way, Moses had decided that what was needed to protect the movement in Greenwood and similar places was not one, but many Bob Dylans, and not just for a fleeting celebrity visit.

Sometime during that early summer of 1963 Dylan wrote "North Country Blues." Unlike "Only a Pawn in Their Game," it's a formally conservative exercise in first-person narrative. But in matching his tale of Mississippi to one of Minnesota, Dylan brought the systemic critique of "Only a Pawn" back home. The voice in the song belongs to a woman in an iron-mining town in the Mesabi range in northern Minnesota. Her life is the story of a community married to an industry. She speaks of the dangers of mining, of accidental death, of early marriage and child-rearing, and of times when "the lunch bucket filled every season" before "The work was cut down / To a half a day's shift with no reason." Through her tale, Dylan shows us, close-up, how decisions made afar, in the name of market forces, shatter lives.

They complained in the East,
They are paying too high.
They say that you ore ain't worth digging,
That it's much cheaper down
In the South American towns
Where the miners work almost for nothing.

"North Country Blues" must be one of the earliest musical protests against what's come to be known as globalization. Dylan's portrait of a working-class community broken by unemployment, and the drink and depression that follow, has proved dismally prescient: the narrative of "North Country Blues" has been repeated across the United States and Europe; it's become the common experience of the world. (The song anticipates Bruce Springsteen's "Youngstown" by thirty years.)

The summer is gone,
The ground's turning cold,
The stores one by one they're a-foldin'.
My children will go
As soon as they grow.
Well, there ain't nothing here now to hold them.

In a way, this impersonal tale is one of Dylan's most personal: this is a song about his home turf and some of the people he grew up with. But the song is not just a montage of personal observations; it grows out of the application to those observations of a political framework. In "North Country Blues," the community is broken by an economic system—the same system that pits white against black. The system that murdered Medgar Evers.

Three weeks after the giant march on Washington, the racists replied. On a Sunday morning, the 16th Street church in Birmingham, which had served as an organizing center during the victorious spring campaign, was bombed. Four African American girls were killed. The naked brutality of the act—and its ramifications in the context of the historic victory won at Birmingham earlier in the year—elicited songs from Dylan's friends Phil Ochs and Richard Fariña ("On Birmingham Sunday the blood ran like wine, / And the choirs kept singing of Freedom"), jazz from John Coltrane, poetry from Langston Hughes, and prose from James Baldwin. And it transformed Nina Simone, a classically trained pianist with an eclectic range of musical interests. Simone had been born in the South but had moved to New York to study at Juilliard; she had already recorded jazz, blues, and Broadway tunes. As a black woman who defied musical categories, Simone had long been acquainted with the realities of power in white-dominated America. But the Birmingham bombing put an end to her patience. She wrote her first protest song, "Mississippi Goddam," and sent it off to *Broadside*. "It erupted out of me," she recalled.

> Oh but this whole country is full of lies
> You're all gonna die and die like flies
> I don't trust you any more
> You keep on saying "Go slow!"
> "Go slow!"
> Do things gradually
> "do it slow"
> But bring more tragedy
> "do it slow"

"Mississippi Goddam" was an uncompromising outcry not just against a racist atrocity, but against a nation and its liberal defenders. But Simone dedicated far more than a song to the movement. From the autumn of 1963, she was ever-present on the front lines in the South. Bernice Johnson Reagon said she "captured the warrior energy that was present in the people. The fighting people." [79]

As usual, Dylan shied away from direct comment on big events. But in the weeks following the Birmingham bombing he wrote "The Lonesome Death of Hattie Carroll," and he never wrote better.

The story came from a newspaper clipping Gordon Friesen gave to Dylan, one of many the *Broadside* co-editor offered the singer as possible sources of topical songs.[80] In February 1963, Hattie Carroll, a middle-aged black woman, had died after being struck with a cane by William Zantzinger, a young white man from a wealthy family. The incident had taken place at a charity ball, where Zantzinger was a patron and Carroll served behind the bar. In August, Zantzinger was sentenced to six months in prison for his offense. It was a report of the sentencing that sparked Dylan's song.

He set his tale to a tune adapted from the sixteenth-century Scottish ballad, "Mary Hamilton" (like Hattie Carroll, the story of a maidservant whose life is destroyed by the whims of the powerful). He recorded the new song in the studio on October 23 and premiered it live at Carnegie Hall three days later. It left the audience stunned, as it so often has in the years since then. This is one of Dylan's most immediately accessible and affecting songs, a mesmerizing piece of storytelling that takes the audience step by step through the social mechanics of a single injustice.

In *Broadside*, Phil Ochs praised the song as a model for the new generation of songwriters. "One of his most important techniques is that he always avoids the obvious," said Ochs, who complained that "so many of the songs sent to *Broadside* . . . overstate the obvious when it doesn't need to be stated at all.[81] In "The Lonesome Death of Hattie Carroll," Dylan doesn't even bother to tell us that Carroll is black and Zantzinger is white. It wasn't necessary—not in the America of 1963. The racial context was a given. Within it, Dylan focused on Carroll as a worker and mother, and Zantzinger as a scion of wealth and privilege. Critics sometimes complain that there are no individuals in Dylan's protest songs, only social forces and abstractions. But for the purposes of this song we don't need to know anything more than we are told.

The first verse states the facts of the case, newspaper style. The baldness of the narrative is relieved by the poetic detail of the "cane that he twirled on his diamond ring finger" (and its internal rhyme with "Zanzinger," as Dylan spells it) and the vocal attention he lavishes on every syllable of "Baltimore hotel society gathering." In the second verse, a portrait of Zantzinger—his inherited wealth, his social status,

his bad manners, and indifference to the consequences of his action—
ends with the information that he was out on bail within minutes. The
third verse tells us about Hattie Carroll: her age, (fifty-one), her ten
children (actually, according to the newspaper report, she had eleven),
her life of menial labor. Three lines in succession end with the word
table (the table on which she waited and at whose head she never sat),
flatly stressing the grinding reduction of a human spirit dispossessed
and exploited by others. This verse concludes with a slow-motion
re-creation of the attack itself, the movement of the cane through the
air: "doomed and determined to destroy all the gentle."

Each of these first three verses is followed by the refrain:

You who philosophize disgrace, and criticize all fears,
Take the rag away from your face, now ain't the time for your tears.

These lines aren't easily explicated, and however you look at them, the
words retain their mystery. But the thrust, I think, is clear. To "philosophize" here seems to imply to "rationalize," to dissolve "disgrace" (a
much stronger word than *injustice,* carrying overtones of both private
and public shame) into mere words. The refrain is addressed to those
who counsel patience, the supercilious liberals who offer their sympathy, their "tears," but little else. They're the same people Nina Simone
talked about in "Mississippi Goddam," the ones who say "go slow." They
are able to react, at a safe distance, to the appalling events Dylan shares
with them. But he warns them to wait, to withhold their knee-jerk response, and thus creates the dramatic and political platform for the
devastating final verse.

The last act of "The Lonesome Death of Hattie Carroll" is played out
in the courtroom. Dylan had already written pityingly of the human
costs of an inhumane judicial system in "Donald White," "Seven
Curses," and "Percy's Song." In "Hattie Carroll" he hammers away at the
august claims of the judiciary, the spectacle designed "to show that all's
equal and the courts are on the level," that "the ladder of law has no top
and no bottom." And with a flourish of plain statement, reveals them all
to be hollow, when the judge:

. . . handed out for penalty and repentance
William Zanzinger with a six month sentence

Dylan then swoops, one last time, into the refrain, reversing the second line: "Bury the rag most deep in your face, for now is the time for your tears." The song pivots on this ending: driving home the complicity of the law, the power of wealth and its hold on the state, the institutional basis of the injustices suffered by individuals. At the same time, it challenges listeners to examine their own part in a system capable of such routine cruelty and hypocrisy.

As Ochs recognized, "Hattie Carrol" had wrought the protest idiom to a new level of formal achievement—one that strengthened its political impact. The melody is a simple fragment set to three-quarter time, recycled over metronomic strumming. Using this regularity as a springboard, Dylan cleverly varies the verse structure, elongating the narrative unit and heightening the suspense. The first verse has six lines of exposition before reaching the refrain. The second has seven. The third has eleven. The climactic fourth also has eleven—and is bolstered by the introduction, for the first time in the song, of end rhyme: half-rhymes in *level/gavel, caught'em/bottom,* before the ringing full rhyme on the punch line: *repentence/sentence.* Meanwhile, Dylan's guitar stutters, pauses and hastens, accenting key moments in the narrative.

"Like "Only a Pawn in Their Game," "Masters of War," and "With God on Our Side," "Hattie Carroll" points to the systemic nature of the problems that agitated growing numbers of young people. It does so without for a moment taking its eyes off specific individuals in a specific setting. The subsequent fate of Billy Zantzinger* would seem to bear out Dylan's analysis of why and how Hattie Carroll died. In 1991, Zantzinger was convicted by a Maryland court of collecting more than $60,000 rent on rural shanties that lacked indoor plumbing or sanitary outhouses, and which in many cases he no longer even owned. The vic-

---

* Zantzinger continues to deny his culpability in Carroll's death, and has told Dylan biographers that the song libels him.

tims were almost all poor black people. Zantzinger faced a possible jail term of twenty-five to fifty years for the offenses. In the end, he was sentenced to eighteen months—on a work-release program—and fined $50,000.[82]

The world's great age begins anew,
*   The golden years return*
The earth doth like a snake renew
*   Her winter weeds outworn*
Heaven smiles, and faiths and empires gleam,
Like wrecks of a dissolving dream.
                —PERCY BYSSHE SHELLEY, *HELLAS*

The Carnegie Hall audience that applauded "Hattie Carroll" was also treated to the premiere of "The Times They Are A-Changin'." Already, in "When The Ship Comes In," unveiled at the March on Washington, Dylan had dared to envision an all-encompassing change, a historic vindication of the oppressed and their movement. In the new song, he presented that change, that vindication, as imminent and inevitable. Most importantly, he asserted that the instrument of change was to be a generation—Dylan's generation: "Your sons and your daughters are beyond your command." He seems to have been clear about what he was doing:

> This was definitely a song with a purpose. I knew exactly what I wanted to say and for whom I wanted to say it to. You know, it was influenced by the Irish and Scottish ballads. . . . Come all ye bold highway men, come all ye miners, come all ye tender-hearted maidens. I wanted to write a big song, some kind of theme song, ya know, with short concise verses that piled up on each other in a hypnotic way. . . .[83]

Later, when the song became a millstone around his neck, Dylan disparaged it as something he wrote because it was what people wanted to hear. It's true that such a neat fit between artist and audience should always rouse suspicions. It's also true that the song's triumphalism was not reflective of Dylan's fickle mood of this period, and it cannot be found in the other songs he wrote at the time (the delicately pained "One Too Many Mornings" and the lushly pantheistic "Lay Down Your Weary Tune".) Because means and ends seem so precisely joined in "The Times They Are A-Changin' " (and because the song is so familiar), it's easy to miss what an extraordinary composition it is, for all its irritating qualities.

Like "When The Ship Comes In," it uses the Biblical language of prophecy and redemption to invoke a great secular victory (the last verse derives from the Gospel of Mark, 10:31: "But many that are first shall be last; and the last first"—Jesus' pledge to the poor). However, it lacks the humorous glee and the element of self-conscious fantasy that enliven the earlier song. "The Times They Are A-Changin' " seems animated by the conviction that right will prevail over might, that the tide of social justice is ineluctable. Who needs God when you've got history on your side? However, this is no Marxist determinism. The song's lyricism derives less from its assertion of collective invincibility than from the tender confidence of its enormous—but elementary—ambitions.

In a sense there's less of Dylan here than in his other protest songs. It's rare indeed to find him subordinating himself so entirely to the larger movement. Nonetheless, the artist is there in the song's confrontational energy and sweeping vision of a final judgment. As in "When The Ship Comes In," social change is depicted as a violent storm: "You better start swimmin' / Or you'll sink like a stone" . . . "it'll soon shake your windows and rattle your walls." Dylan embraces the irresistible whirlwind, and relishes the day when it will expose all that is hollow and false. In Biblical style, he issues a prophetic warning against complacency; he reminds the powerful that ultimately they are impotent.

The song sets a lyric of paratactic rigor and simplicity to a tune that is buoyant but also vulnerable. For all its brash self-confidence, it is careful to say "please" to its elders—even as it warns them not to obstruct the movement for change. Here, senators and congressmen are treated with a reverence that was soon to be replaced in Dylan's work by savage contempt. The media are less fortunate:

> Come writers and critics
> Who prophesize with your pen
> And keep your eyes wide
> The chance won't come again
> And don't speak too soon
> For the wheel's still in spin

It was the unexpected achievements of the civil rights movement that made this statement and "The Times They Are A-Changin' " possible and even plausible. The song blends arrogance with innocence, an individualist ethical appeal ("lend a hand") with a faith in collective action, ambitious radicalism with liberal naïveté. In doing so it expresses the consciousness of its moment precisely.

Although it is void of any specific topical reference, the song was not void of political punch—its targets knew exactly who they were, as did the audience to whom the song was addressed. "The Times They Are A-Changin' " springs from and speaks to an incipient mass movement for social transformation—a movement that was still, in late 1963, a relatively small presence within white, record-buying America. At *this* moment, in *this* song, Dylan seems to believe that *this* movement can and will rise to the challenge of bringing justice to an unjust society.

Dylan was never an activist. He absorbed his politics, like much else, by osmosis. His contribution to the movement was limited to a small number of personal appearances, a few donations—and the songs. These, however, were an inestimable gift.

NOT MUCH IS REALLY SACRED

We preserve the so-called peace of our community by deeds of petty violence every day. Look at the policeman's billy and handcuffs! Look at the jail!

—HENRY DAVID THOREAU

ON DECEMBER 13, 1963, three weeks after the Kennedy assassination, Dylan arrived at the Hotel Americana in New York City to attend the Emergency Civil Liberties Committee's annual Bill of Rights dinner. The ECLC had been formed in 1951 to defend the Smith Act victims—the Communist Party leadership—when the established civil liberties groups, spooked by the cold war purge, shied away. Each year it presented its Tom Paine Award to a champion of the cause. In 1962, Bertrand Russell had been the recipient. In 1963, the prize went to Bob Dylan.

During the course of the evening Dylan drank heavily. When he got to the rostrum, he improvised a speech that managed to offend just about everyone in the house.[1] "It's took me a long time to get young and now I consider myself young and I'm proud of it," he told the 1,400 paying guests, among them veterans of countless campaigns for free speech and social justice. "It's not an old people's world." He wanted "to see faces with hair on their head . . . I look down to see the people that are governing me and making my rules—and they haven't got any hair on their head—I get very uptight about it."

So far, his audience indulged him, greeting the young man's impudence with self-conscious laughter. When he mentioned Woody Guthrie, they applauded, but Dylan reminded them: "It has sure changed in the time Woody's been here and the time I've been here. It's not that easy any more. People seem to have more fears." He went on to question, indirectly but unmistakably, whether the traditions, experience and guiding assumptions of the left had any value at all.

> I've never seen one history book that tells me how anybody feels. . . . And it don't help me one little bit to look back . . . there's no black and white, left and right to me anymore . . . I was at the March on Washington up on the platform and I looked around at all the negroes there and I didn't see any negroes that looked like none of my friends. My friends don't wear suits. My friends don't have to wear any kind of thing to prove they're respectable negroes.

In the course of the speech, Dylan declared himself in favor of free travel to Cuba, a sentiment that may have pleased most of those present but would have terrified his record executives. He also announced that he was accepting the award on behalf of SNCC and James Forman, whose perilous face-to-face confrontation with racism, he later explained, made him impatient with the comfortable detachment of middle-class do-gooders. For Dylan, the incandescent purity of SNCC's struggle in the South had exposed the emptiness not only of traditional politics, but of the entire discourse of American democracy. But in his efforts to divide the authentic from the inauthentic and to place himself on the right side of that line, he stumbled into the peroration that really got him into trouble that night:

> I'll stand up and to get uncompromisable about it, which I have to be to be honest, I just got to be, as I got to admit that the man who shot President Kennedy, Lee Oswald, I don't know exactly where, what he thought he was doing, but I got to admit that I too—I saw something of myself in him.

The young singer was vigorously booed by his elders. At that moment, to speak ill of the dead president—worse yet, to identify with his killer—was to breach the most daunting taboo in America, a taboo that neither the old left nor the liberals were prepared to violate. (Interestingly, it was the same taboo that Malcolm X had breached two weeks earlier, in the "chickens coming home to roost" crack that precipitated his final split with Elijah Muhammad.[2]) Dylan's impromptu identification with Oswald was a blunt instrument enabling him to register a sense of alienation that had gone way beyond disquiet over racism and nuclear arms. It was also in keeping with Dylan's fondness for the outlaw conceit that crops up throughout the history of popular culture and on which he was to perform increasingly complex variations in the songs he composed during the rest of the decade.

Dylan's rant wrecked the ECLC's fund-raising pitch, and left his hosts and most of the guests fuming. Within days, Corliss Lamont, the doughty civil libertarian and chairman of the ECLC, had dispatched a letter to the organization's members defending the choice of Dylan as award recipient:

> . . . it is urgent to recognize the protest of youth today and to help make it understood by the older generation. Walt Whitman and Woody Guthrie, the cultural antecedents of Bob Dylan, were not appreciated by their society until they were very old. We think that it would be better to make the effort now to comprehend what Bob Dylan is saying to and for the youth.

Under the circumstances, it was remarkably generous. Lamont enclosed the text of a lengthy verse message Dylan had sent to the ECLC, in which he reiterated his respect for the organization and tried to explain what he had meant and what he had felt at the Bill of Rights dinner:

> it is a fierce heavy feeling
> thinkin something is expected of you
> but you dont know what exactly it is . . .
> it brings forth a wierd form of guilt

He makes a point of paying his respects to the old left, but in terms that indicate the distance that separates him (and his generation) from them:

I'm speakin now of the people I've met
who were strugglin for their lives an other peoples'
lives in the thirties an forties an the fifties
an I look t their times
I reach out t their times
an, in a sense, am jealous of their times

The tone of address is humble throughout, but in the end Dylan declares, "I do not apologize for being me nor any part of me." He offered
to make up any losses the ECLC had incurred because of his behavior,
but never made good on the promise.

Soon after the ECLC debacle, Dylan dropped in on a meeting of the
SDS national council in New York City.[3] He was joined by another unexpected celebrity guest, Alger Hiss, a ghost from the old left—cheered
by the seventy activists present as a martyr of the anti-Communist
crusade they were rapidly outgrowing. For them, Hiss was an outcast
figure, like Dylan, and their welcoming him had little to do with
their feelings about the New Deal, the popular front, or the Soviet
Union. This small gathering of young, white, politically engaged,
mainly middle-class students felt that they were at the cutting edge of a
new mood among young people, a mood reflected in Dylan's music. His
appearance in their midst seemed to confirm their status as its vanguard. If Dylan showed, they knew they must be on to something.

The singer listened in silence to a debate about the organization's
plans for community organizing. The students wanted to move beyond
proclamations; they wanted to leave the shelter of academia behind.
They would go into the ghettos, live among the poor and share their
poverty. "Community organizing" would be the tool with which they
would build "an inter-racial movement of the poor." The radicals were
searching for an organic link to a downtrodden America that would
give flesh to the hazy but potent vision epitomized by the Port Huron
Statement. Their political restlessness was, in part, an expression of the
search for authenticity that had also coursed through the folk revival,
and found an icon in the consciously constructed persona of Bob

Dylan. "Students and poor people," wrote Tom Hayden, one of the architects of the new SDS strategy, "make each other feel real."[4]

Talking to the activists during a recess in proceedings, Dylan expressed an interest in working on one of the new projects. But, as Todd Gitlin recounts in his memoir of the sixties, "Dylan warned us to be careful—of him." He told them about the ECLC affair, explaining how he "went crazy" after seeing "these bald-headed, pot-bellied people sitting out there in suits." Clearly, Dylan assumed the SDSers would share his generational prejudice, and they did. "He was half warning us, half apologizing for his bad-boy behavior," recalls Gitlin, who also reports that Dylan offered to sing benefits for SDS.

Nothing came of that offer, or of Dylan's interest in the community organizing projects. Over the next year, he was to move decisively away from political activism and topical song. But even as he did so, his notoriety as a protest singer, and his identification with the movement, gained new impetus from the release, in January 1964, of his third album, *The Times They Are A-Changin'*—whose cover boasted a gritty monochrome photo of a cropped-haired, severe-looking Dylan, reenforcing his image of no-frills integrity and political commitment. However, the final song on the album—composed and recorded at the end of October 1963, some weeks after the other tracks—was a tantalizingly autobiographical song of self-justification called "Restless Farewell:"

Oh ev'ry foe that ever I faced,
The cause was there before we came.
And ev'ry cause that ever I fought,
I fought it full without regret or shame.

Note that Dylan insists that the "causes" are real and enduring and that his commitment to them had been authentic. But he then suggests that his engagement with them must be fleeting:

But the dark does die
As the curtain is drawn and somebody's eyes

Must meet the dawn.
And if I see the day
I'd only have to stay,
So I'll bid farewell in the night and be gone.

The song is often seen as Dylan's conscious valedictory to politics, but the muddled ideas, aspirations, anxieties and gripes that surface in his Bill of Rights rant, in his apologia to the ECLC, and in his brief encounter with SDS suggest a more uncertain, contradictory and anguished process. It was never the total caesura both Dylan and some his biographers have made it out to be. Clearly, Dylan was increasingly coming to see the protest singer identity as a personal burden and creative straightjacket. And he couldn't make it clearer that he felt himself unqualified for—indeed terrified by—the role both the movement and the media had cast him in. But even as he beat a retreat from politics, the political environment continued to shape his songs and his personal vision. As he railed against the movement, his music remained entangled in its fate.

In early February 1964, Dylan embarked on a long, wayward, drug-enhanced road trip from New York to California—an attempt to live at firsthand the literary high jinks of *On the Road*.[5] In Harlan County he visited striking coal miners. In North Carolina, he paid homage to the elderly Carl Sandburg, whose twenties compendium, *The American Songbook*, had been one of his earliest sources, and whose entire oeuvre was an exercise in social patriotism. In South Carolina he played a gig at the mainly black Emory University. In Atlanta he met up with Bernice Johnson Reagon and in Mississippi with Bob Moses and Tom Hayden. He made it to New Orleans for a drunken immersion in the Mardi Gras—where he jotted down some lines that were to evolve in the coming months into "Mr. Tambourine Man." He proceeded to Dallas where he haunted Dealey Plaza. In Colorado he stopped off at Ludlow, site of the 1913 massacre of strikers commemorated in the Woody Guthrie ballad, and then moved on to Denver, spiritual home of Kerouac's driver-hero Dean Moriarty. On the night Cassius Clay deposed Sonny Liston as world heavyweight champion in Miami, Dylan performed his first major West Coast gig, at the University of California at Berkeley, which was to be convulsed by the Free Speech Movement later that year. He seems to have been reviewing his sources in American history and literature, and even paying homage to that alternative America beloved of the folk revival.

In the course of this trip Dylan composed "Chimes of Freedom," often described as both his last protest song and the first of those songs comprised of "chains of flashing images" (Dylan's phrase) that make up the heart of his sixties canon. It's a transitional work, and as such suggests that the caesura between the protest era Dylan and the Dylan that followed may be less absolute and abrupt than it seemed at the time. Trapped in a thunder storm, Dylan and a companion take shelter in the doorway of a church. As the church bells ring out in the night, sight and sound collide in a single revelatory moment, a social epiphany in which a vast cast of the dispossessed and oppressed appear and are embraced.

Each verse begins with four lines adumbrating a single conceit (at some length and often with needless convolution): the fusing of thunder, lightning, and church bells. It's a self-conscious exercise in the "disarrangement of the senses" recommended by Rimbaud and the French symbolists whom Dylan was reading at the time. As Michael Gray has pointed out, Dylan borrows the phrase *cathedral evening* from a line in a poem by the American surrealist and Beat favorite Kenneth Patchen.[6] In comparison with the plainspoken rigors of the protest songs, the writing here is both more prolix and more compressed, and bristles with a new poetic ambition. The poetry is still forced (by the end of the year, Dylan could pull off this kind of hybrid imagery with startling fluidity). Nonetheless, the freeze-frame suspense of the first half of each verse is the platform for the outflow of empathy in the second half.

Dylan was fond of invoking the elements—like any would-be poet groping for a big effect. But here there's something more specific at work. These are the "chimes of freedom" and freedom at this time and in this place was a word that belonged to the civil rights movement. The phrase recalls the freedom songs and the emancipatory rhetoric of "The Hammer Song." This is the clash and flash of contemporary history, a metaphor for a social experience; it's the same storm he sang about in "When The Ship Comes In," but it no longer promises the vanquishing of authority and the vindication of a movement. Instead, within its garish son et lumière, Dylan elaborates a simple quatrain he first jotted down at the time of the JFK assassination: "strikin' for the gentle / strikin' for the kind / strikin' for the crippled ones / an strikin' for the blind."

In "Chimes of Freedom," this device is turned into an extended litany—eighteen lines in total—inspired by the bardic cataloguing of Whitman and Ginsberg, though without their brash moral self-confidence. Politically, it follows on from the systemic critique hinted at in "Hattie Carroll," "Pawn in Their Game," and "The Times They Are A-Changin'." In one sense it is the last, and perhaps most haunting, of Dylan's attempts at an all-embracing social narrative in a single song. The focus here, however, is not on condemning or transforming the system, but on the system's victims, those it persecutes and those it ignores or discards, the "underdog soldiers in the night," whom he names and celebrates. He starts with the SNCC workers he'd met in Greenwood ("the warriors whose strength is not to fight") and the "refugees on the unarmed road of flight," but ranges much further afield: "the guardians and protectors of the mind," poets and painters unappreciated in their day, single mothers ("the mistreated mateless mother"—not, in those days, a figure often discussed in public), "the mistitled prostitute" and the "misdemeanor outlaw." At the song's conclusion, his purview expands to include all "the countless confused, accused, misused, strung-out ones an' worse" and "every hung-up person in the whole wide universe."

It was Dylan's most sweeping vision of solidarity with all those marginalized by a monolithic society. But it was also an attempt to locate himself and his personal dilemmas within a wider context. The chimes of freedom toll not only for "the rebel" but also for "the rake," not to mention "the lonesome-hearted lovers with too personal a tale" and those who are "condemned to drift or else be kept from drifting." In his vulnerability and disaffection, Dylan sees himself here as one of many. But this is a fleeting vision, vouchsafed by the lightning and thunder of a historical juncture—the song does not posit any collective triumph for its heroes. On the contrary, these are "the aching ones whose wounds cannot be nursed."

Within six months, Dylan had dropped the song from his act—though he continued singing other protest classics for another six months after that. The Byrds included a truncated version on their first album. Roger McGuinn's resounding twelve string neatly illustrated the title and the band's harmonies soared through Dylan's ever-varying refrain. (Another, more forgettable rock version of the song appeared that same year on the album issued by celebrity spawn Dino, Desi and Billy.) Dylan himself returned to the song—along with so many others in his sprawling back catalogue—during the Never Ending Tour of the nineties. He performed it, poorly, at Bill Clinton's first inaugural. Nonetheless, "Chimes of Freedom" has enjoyed a more inspiring afterlife than many of Dylan's anthems. In 1988, Bruce Springsteen played it with the E Street Band to promote an Amnesty International tour commemorating the fortieth anniversary of the Declaration of Human Rights. Like the Byrds, Springsteen omitted the third and fourth of the six verses, but he brought a commitment and depth of feeling to the song's message that Dylan himself could rarely summon. (Weirdly, the awkward lines invoking lightning, thunder, and bells sound in Springsteen's mouth very much like the self-consciously imagistic efforts on his own early albums.) Springsteen gropes for and somehow finds the pulse of compassion that guides the song, and in doing so drives home not only the obviously apposite salute to "each unharmful gentle soul misplaced inside a jail" but Amnesty's core concept—the universality of human rights.

Springsteen went on to play "Chimes of Freedom" on the tour itself, where he was joined by, among other luminaries, the Senegalese mbalax master, Youssou N'Dour. This exquisite vocalist recorded his own version of the song for his album *Womat* in 1994: translating the intricate verses into Wolof and French, weaving them into a complex rhythm that manages to be both delicate and robust. In this alien setting the song unveils its true majesty, reaching across borders, musical and cultural. N'Dour belongs to the first generation of postcolonial Africans; he came of age in the seventies, and, as a socialist, has seen hopes shattered and ideals betrayed on a scale far greater than the disappointments that alienated Dylan from politics. For N'Dour, covering "Chimes of Freedom" was simultaneously a political gesture and a commercial crossover bid, which only reemphasizes Dylan's singular role and the strengths of the song as a meeting-point of diverse experiences.

Sometimes I'm thinkin'
I'm too high to fall.
Other times I'm thinkin' I'm
So low I don't know
If I can come up at all.
—"BLACK CROW BLUES," 1964

In May 1964, Dylan returned to England. *Freewheelin'* was in the UK top twenty, "The Times They Are A-Changin'" was out as a single and for the first time he found himself the object of frenzied teenage adulation. Since his first visit, sixteen months earlier, British popular music had been transformed, and that transformation was beginning to echo in the U.S.A. The Beatles, and soon after, the Rolling Stones, the Animals, the Who, and others introduced a new generation of white Americans to the pleasures of loud, rhythmic, soulful music; in doing so, they freely acknowledged the black American roots of their style, opening up new careers for the likes of Muddy Waters and Howlin' Wolf. Like John Hammond, they reminded white America that the African American contribution lay at the center of its popular art. This was a lesson Dylan already knew well. From the first, he liked the new British rock 'n' roll; it showed that the old formulas could be imaginatively reworked, and that white kids would spend unprecedented sums of money on this kind of sound—at least when it was made by white people.

It was to take him more than a year to adapt it fully to his own artistic uses. During this period, sticking with acoustic guitar and harmonica, he extended the range and complexity of his lyrics. In England he debuted "Mr. Tambourine Man" and "It Ain't Me, Babe" (the London *Times* interpreted the "no, no, no" refrain as a reply to the Beatles "yeah, yeah, yeah"). After the concerts, he visited Paris, Berlin, and Greece. During this trip, he worked on the songs that were to comprise his next album, *Another Side of Bob Dylan*, which he recorded on his return to New York in June. "There aren't any finger-pointin' songs in here," he told Nat Hentoff during a break in the sessions. "Me, I don't want to write for people anymore—you know, be a spokesman. From now on, I want to write from inside me . . . the way I like to write is for it to come out the way I walk or talk . . . the bomb is getting boring because what's wrong goes much deeper than the bomb . . . I'm not part of no movement. . . . I just can't make it with any organization . . ."[7] Far from patching up the breach with the left that had opened at the ECLC dinner, Dylan seemed intent on widening it.

At Newport that summer, his new songs—"All I Really Want to Do," "To Ramona," "Mr. Tambourine Man"—baffled many in the audience. Some critics compared him unfavorably to the new protest laureate, Phil Ochs. Irwin Silber penned a famous "open letter to Bob Dylan" published in *Sing Out!* in November.

You seem to be in a different kind of bag now, Bob—and I'm worried about it. I saw at Newport how you had somehow lost contact with people. It seemed to me that some of the paraphernalia of fame were getting in your way. You travel with an entourage now—with good buddies who are going to laugh when you need laughing and drink wine with you and insure your privacy—and never challenge you to face everyone else's reality again. . . . Your new songs seem to be all inner-directed now, inner probing, self-conscious—maybe even a little maudlin or a little cruel on occasion. And it's happening on stage, too. You seem to be relating to a handful of cronies behind the scenes now—rather than to the rest of us out front. . . .

As a socialist, Silber was concerned not only with the specific case of Bob Dylan but with the political questions it raised for the movement.

> We are all responsible for what's been happening to you—and to many other fine young artists. The American Success Machinery chews up geniuses at a rate of one a day and still hungers for more. Unable to produce real art on its own, the Establishment breaks creativity in protest against and nonconformity to the System. And then, through notoriety, fast money, and status, it makes it almost impossible for the artist to function and grow. It is a process that must be constantly guarded against and fought.[8]

Silber later acknowledged the futility of a public appeal to an artist to follow a particular aesthetic path.* But he was prescient in identifying the cost that celebrity would extract from Dylan, and the impact it was bound to have on his music. The disappointment reflected in the open letter is an index of the value placed on Dylan's contribution. After the cultural and political constrictions of the fifties his breakthrough in the protest idiom seemed a precious achievement. Silber's letter precipitated an impassioned debate on the pages of *Sing Out!,* where the venerable arguments about the social responsibility of the artist and the varying claims of the personal and the political were restated (on all sides) with a highly unacademic urgency. Interestingly, Dylan was defended by two of the more politically engaged performers of the era, Ochs and John Sinclair ("Dylan has begun to go beneath the surface . . .").[9] The explanation for his retreat from politics offered by

---

* In 1968, Silber reconsidered Dylan: "Dylan did desert—not us but an outmoded style of values which had become unequal to the task of reclaiming America. 'This land is not your land,' Dylan told us in 1965. But some of us raised on the songs of Guthrie and Seeger . . . were not ready to accept the revolutionary implications of Dylan's statements . . . Dylan is our poet—not our leader."

Dylan himself shortly after Newport 1964 is riddled with political analysis.

> All I can say is politics is not my thing at all. I'm not really part of any society, like THEIR society. Any cat that's very evidently on the outside, criticizing their society, because he is on the outside, he's not in it anyway, and he's not gonna make a dent . . . it ain't gonna work. I'm just not gonna be part of it. I'm not gonna make a dent or anything, so why be part of it by even trying to criticize it? That's a waste of time. The kids know that . . . the kids today, by the time they're twenty-one, they realize it's all bullshit. I know it's all bullshit.[10]

Illogical, arrogant, and self-indulgent, yes, but completely of its time. Indeed, as the American sixties wore on, these kinds of tangled, anguished responses to the whole question of political activity were heard ever more frequently.

Despite the victory of the Civil Rights Act, for the activists on the ground the reality seemed one of deadlock and reaction. In early 1964, the openly segregationist presidential campaign of Alabama governor George Wallace gobbled up more than 30 percent of the vote in Democratic primaries in Indiana, Wisconsin, and Maryland. The power of the race card had been revealed; the white backlash had begun (rolling into our own day). Yet at this stage only 5 percent of eligible blacks in the state of Mississippi were permitted to vote.

The Mississippi Summer Project of 1964 was Bob Moses's master plan for busting open the dungeon of the Deep South. At first, his proposal to recruit white northern students to provide a protective shield for a black voter registration drive was met with ambivalence. There were complaints that the media cared only for white people's suffering, and that this strategy would make black people yet more dependent on white goodwill. But during the spring of 1964, Moses and his SNCC colleagues toured the North and signed on a dedicated band of young whites. At training sessions, the new recruits were impressed with the challenges they would face. "Don't come to Mississippi this summer to save the Negro," Bob Moses told them. "Only come if you understand, really understand, that his freedom and yours are one." He offered no quick victories: "Maybe all we're going to do is live through this summer. In Mississippi, that will be much." [11]

On June 21, before the bulk of the white student volunteers had reached the state, three young civil rights workers, James Chaney, Andrew Goodman, and Mickey Schwerner were murdered. Chaney was a Mississippi black man and CORE activist. Schwerner was a northern white leftist, who'd been working for CORE in the South for several years. Andrew Goodman was a neophyte—one of the white youth recruited and trained by SNCC only months earlier.

The cost of Mississippi Summer was daunting. Besides the dead, there were 1,000 arrests, 80 beatings, 35 church burnings, 30 bombings, 35 shootings. The FBI agents sent into the state spent more time investigating the civil rights activists than tracking down the killers. J. Edgar Hoover attacked SNCC and the Mississippi project as red fronts. [12]

Of course, there were red (socialist, Marxist) ideas surfacing in discussions among the young Mississippi volunteers, along with many other ideas—about black nationalism, third world liberation, sex and drugs. Mississippi Summer was a laboratory, one of the points of confluence that shaped the decade. It was wracked with tensions—between black and white, locals and outsiders, leaders and would-be leaders, believers in nonviolence and advocates of self-defense—but it was undeniably creative.

Moses's target was August's Democratic Party national convention in Atlantic City, where he aimed to challenge and replace the all-white official state delegation. Despite the violence, the activists succeeded in signing up 80,000 black people to the newly founded Mississippi Freedom Democratic Party. They elected their own multiracial delegation and sent it to Atlantic City. Fannie Lou Hamer, the sharecropper now serving as vice chair of the MFDP, presented its case to the national party's credentials committee:

If the Freedom Democratic party is not seated now, I question America. Is this America, the land of the free and the home of the brave, where we have to sleep with telephones off the hooks because our lives be threatened daily because we want to live as decent human beings, in America? [13]

Lyndon Johnson was scandalized by Hamer's tone, and determined to keep the MFDP out and the official delegation in. Civil rights activists came under huge pressure from their erstwhile liberal patrons to accept a compromise—whereby they would have two nonvoting delegates seated along with the white supremacists. In defiance of the blandishments of King and the threats of the NAACP, Hubert Humphrey, and Walter Reuther, the MFDP delegates voted overwhelmingly to reject the deal; they were excluded from the convention. After all the suffering of the previous months, it was a bitter defeat. Bob Moses left Atlantic City vowing never to speak to a white man again. Nor was he the only one to suffer shell shock in the wake of Mississippi Summer. "As far as I'm concerned, that was the turning point of the civil rights movement," said John Lewis. "We had made our way to the very center of the system. We had played by the rules, done everything we were supposed to do, had played the game exactly as required, had arrived at the doorstep and found the door slammed in our face." [14]

As a student at Ohio State, Phil Ochs set out on his musical career performing in local coffeehouses as one of the Singing Socialists. [15] Then he dropped out of college and headed for Bleecker Street, arriving a year after Dylan. The *Broadside* team welcomed him and he was soon supplying the magazine with a flow of new topical songs—more than forty in eighteen months. At Newport in 1963, while Dylan dominated the main stage, Ochs made an impression at the topical song workshop with "Too Many Martyrs," his own response to the Medgar Evers killing (it also includes a reference to Emmett Till).

Too many martyrs, too many dead
Too many lies, too many empty words we've said

This was in 1963, and there were many empty words still to be spoken, and many martyrs still to be made. Already, the impatience and the anger rise up within the lament, just as they do in Dylan's early music. But Ochs was always a very different creature from Dylan. For a start, he was a much keener reader of the newspapers than Dylan, and, unlike Dylan, had a genuine intellectual curiosity about politics. His first album, *All the News That's Fit to Sing,* was released in early 1964, on the heels of Dylan's *The Times They Are A-Changin'.* There are songs about automation and unemployment, unjust imprisonments, poverty and slums, a tribute to Woody Guthrie and the Guthrie-like "Power and Glory," an appeal to reclaim America for American ideals ("her power shall rest on the strength of her freedom"). Ochs's undoubted social patriotism was, however, always inflected with an informed internationalism. The first album also includes attacks on militarism, an appeal for free travel to Cuba, a song about a Mexican peasant revolutionary, a satire on the missile crisis and "Talking Vietnam," the first musical protest against the embryonic war—composed half a year before the Gulf of Tonkin incident. He flays the cynicism of U.S. policy in supporting the corrupt south Vietnamese regime ("south east Asia's Birmingham") and propping up "Diem-ocracy—rule by one family and 15,000 American troops."

In the course of 1964, as Dylan withdrew from current events, Ochs rushed to embrace them, in song and action. He responded to the Harlem riot—the first of the decade's major inner-city rebellions—with "In the Heat of the Summer," where he mourned the violence but also saw it as an expression of political desperation: "We had to make somebody listen." Ochs traveled south to take part in Mississippi Summer, and unleashed his social patriotic disgust in "Here's To The State of Mississippi" ("Oh, here's to the land you've torn out the heart of / Mississippi find yourself another country to be part of"). In "Links On the Chain" he sang about the historical failure of the labor movement to support the struggle for black freedom. Long before it was fashionable, he sneered at the selective service system in "Draft Dodger Rag," whose jauntily cynical satire anticipates Country Joe's "I-Feel-Like-I'm-Fixin'-To-Die Rag."

These songs made Ochs the star of Newport 1964, where he became "the new Dylan"—the first of many cursed with that tag. *Broadside* declared him "the most important voice in the movement." One Newport reviewer described the contrast between the committed Ochs and the introverted Dylan as "meaning vs. innocuousness, sincerity vs. utter disregard for the tastes of the audience; idealistic principle vs. self-conscious egotism." But Ochs had no interest in this rivalry, and vigorously defended Dylan. "To cater to an audience's taste is not to respect them." Ochs remained a staunch champion of Dylan's genius and his right to pursue his artistic destiny. Dylan was less generous. In private, he needled Ochs, telling him he was "a journalist, not a songwriter," and that his music was "bullshit . . . you're just wasting your time." [16]

Ochs's songs were never as multilayered as Dylan's, and always more reliant on topical reference for their impact. As a singer and performer his range was narrow. But he wrote with wit, intelligence, and passion. He believed that songs and singers could and should make a difference.

His moment proved brief, but he made good use of it. Through the mid-sixties, Ochs sustained a musically conservative but politically radical critique of U.S. policy at home and abroad. In Santo Domingo, he denounced the invasion of the Dominican Republic (at a time when concern over this action was confined to a minute minority). He responded to the student revolt at Berkeley that autumn with the wryly impudent "I'm Going to Say it Now." Toward the end of the year, he declared his independence from the war machine in "I Ain't Marchin' Anymore," his most successful anthem. Like Dylan's "With God on Our Side," this song takes the form of a revisionist historical survey of U.S. military adventures, but is more precise in locating the political forces that motivate them:

Now the labor leader's screamin' when they close the missile plants,
United Fruit screams at the Cuban shore,
Call it "Peace" or call it "Treason"
Call it "Love" or call it "Reason"
But I ain't marchin' any more.

In January 1965, while Dylan was putting the finishing touches on *Bringing It All Back Home,* Ochs returned to their once common theme, the death of Medgar Evers, only to use it as a launching pad for an attack on onetime allies as politically charged as Dylan's was musically and poetically. "I cried when they shot Medgar Evers / Tears ran down my spine . . . But Malcolm X got what was coming / He got what he asked for this time / So love me, love me, love me, I'm a liberal." For Ochs, the liberals' desire for a comfortable life, their fear of radical change, led in the end to collusion with imperial war, racism, and domestic repression.

> I cheered when Humphrey was chosen
> My faith in the system restored
> I'm glad the commies were thrown out
> of the AFL-CIO board
> I love Puerto Ricans and Negros
> as long as they don't move next door
> So love me, love me, love me, I'm a liberal

At this time, liberal Democrat support for civil rights and for the nascent antiwar movement was regarded by many as a precious asset. Here Ochs was going out of his way to offend important allies. (Though his approach was soft-edged compared to the version Jello Biafra recorded in the nineties.) Later that year, Ochs returned to the theme—the necessary parting of the ways between liberals and radicals—in "The Ringing of Revolution." In a live recording, he introduced the new song to the audience by describing it as a movie in which "John Wayne plays Lyndon Johnson. Lyndon Johnson plays God. I play Bobby Dylan, the young Bobby Dylan." It was an uneasy joke. Ochs had been crowned as the king of protest when Dylan vacated the throne. But he was more aware than most that the movement was changing, and that the challenges to politically engaged artists were becoming more daunting.

One of the extraordinary things Dylan does in his post-protest songs is to offer a critique of politics itself as a field of human endeavor. In the midst of a wave of mass political radicalization, he interrogates the political as a category. No song on *Another Side* distressed Dylan's friends in the movement more than "My Back Pages," in which he transmutes the rude incoherence of his ECLC rant into the organized density of art. The lilting refrain—"I was so much older then / I'm younger than that now"—must be one of the most lyrical expressions of political apostasy ever penned. It is a recantation, in every sense of the word. Usually, political apostates justify themselves by invoking the inevitable supercession of youth and rebelliousness by maturity and responsibility. ("He who is not a radical when young has no heart," an old saying goes, "he who remains a radical when old has no head.") Dylan reverses the polarity. The retreat from politics is a retreat from false and stale categories and acquired, secondhand attitudes. The antidote is a proud embrace of innocence and spontaneity. The refrain encapsulates the movement from the pretense of knowing it all to the confession of knowing nothing.

In the song's opening verse, Dylan ridicules his earlier, protest-phase self. With the "crimson flames" of indignation roaring in his head, he had set out on "flaming roads / Using ideas as my maps:"

> . . . "Rip down all hate," I screamed
> Lies that life is black and white
> Spoke from my skull.

So much for the simplistic love vs. hate duality on which so much of the early civil rights and peace movement rhetoric relied (never much to Dylan's taste). But Dylan now switches from his own erstwhile naïveté to an attack on the dead culture of political activism: "memorizing politics / Of ancient history" (the sagas of the old left). He pours bile on the "self-ordained professor" who

> Too serious to fool
> Spouted out that liberty
> Is just equality in school

The critique here is that the politically engaged lack the humor and playfulness that were always important to Dylan. But the verse also suggests that their definition of liberty/freedom is too abstract—a mere slogan. There is also a reference to the movement's preoccupation with school desegregation and its limitations; there's more to freedom—the kind he'd been singing about in "Chimes of Freedom"—than integrated schools. As so often at this point in Dylan's evolution, his argument with the movement is partly that its definition of the political doesn't go far enough, isn't radical enough, partly that it is in itself a prison, a restraint, and partly that it is pompous and lame and no fun at all.

> "Equality," I spoke the word
> As if a wedding vow.
> Ah, but I was so much older then,
> I'm younger than that now.

Although in some way freedom remains, at this moment, within Dylan's lexicon, it seems equality is out. Here he can sound like a reactionary sniffily rejecting egalitarian ideologies, or Blake denouncing "mechanistic Deism," or a streetwise cynic who's wary of abstractions and the people dedicated to them. In the end, most of all, it is the inner cost of political activism that Dylan rejects; its certainties, its Manichaeism, are a betrayal of his own identity and autonomy: "I'd become my enemy / In the instant that I preach." Dylan is alarmed by the discovery of authoritarianism at the heart of the challenge to authority—and within himself. It's not only the repressive self-righteousness of the left that angers Dylan. He's groping after something more:

> Yes, my guard stood hard when abstract threats
> Too noble to neglect
> Deceived me into thinking
> I had something to protect

The impersonal demands of politics create the illusion that one has an investment in society—a theme sounded later that year in "Gates of Eden," "It's All Over Now, Baby Blue," and "It's Alright Ma (I'm Only Bleeding)." One is nothing and one owns nothing: recognizing that is the only starting point for real freedom and authenticity, the only way to escape social control, to recapture yourself. In the final lines Dylan wallows in existential confusion:

Good and bad, I define these terms
Quite clear, no doubt, somehow.

The song ends with Dylan mocking his own incoherence. It's a cry of disorientation—and an acceptance of that condition in defiance of others' expectations. Yet in this song of recantation, there is continuity. The inadequacy of liberal responses to America's growing social crises is the premise here as much as it is in "Hattie Carroll." And the assertion of youth's right to speak out—from "Let Me Die in My Footsteps" to "The Times They Are A-Changin' "—is extended and deepened. Youth must reject the categories inherited from the past and define its own terms. Indeed, youth itself has become the touchstone of authenticity. A tremendously empowering notion for the generation whom it first infected, but also, as it turned out, a cul-de-sac, and less of a revolutionary posture than it seemed at the time.

It's been suggested that "To Ramona" is really addressed to Freedom Singer Bernice Johnson Reagon, whose own entrenched political commitment did not stop her from defending Dylan's choice of a different path. While it's always a mistake to treat Dylan's lyrics as part of an autobiographical roman à clef, this song does comes into greater focus if one reads it as addressed to a youthful veteran of the civil rights movement—someone wounded in the battle, psychologically, and taking a rare respite from the front line. "I can tell you are torn / Between stayin' and returnin' / On back to the South." Dylan's declaration that "there's no use in tryin' / T' deal with the dyin' " refers to the losses endured on the civil rights front lines—losses that Dylan had been writing about for several years. The song is one of Dylan's seduction songs; like Marvell's "To His Coy Mistress," it is an elaborate argument for the woman addressed to have sex with him. The song emphasizes the physicality of the attraction—Ramona's "cracked country lips" and "magnetic movements"—but in the course of his appeal Dylan delivers an attack on the movement to which the object of his affections has dedicated herself—as if it were his rival in love. He tells her she has chained herself to an illusion:

> It's all just a dream, babe,
> A vacuum, a scheme, babe,
> That sucks you into feelin' like this.

An illusion propagated by charlatans out to exploit her:

> I can see that your head
> Has been twisted and fed
> By worthless foam from the mouth.
> You've been fooled into thinking
> That the finishin' end is at hand.

For Dylan in 1964, there was no imminent victory on hand for the civil rights movement; the promised nonviolent triumph over the forces of injustice had turned into a prolonged and bloody endurance test. He then asks the woman to evaluate herself in light of her own professed political beliefs:

> I've heard you say many times
> That you're better 'n no one
> And no one is better 'n you.
> If you really believe that,
> You know you got
> Nothing to win and nothing to lose.

As in "My Back Pages," Dylan is claiming that any sense of investment in society—even through the movement to change it—is deluded. And those "forces and friends" that say otherwise are bent on controlling and appropriating people like Ramona and Dylan himself:

> They hype you and type you,
> Making you feel
> That you must be exactly like them.

The severity of Dylan's assault on the activists and their pretensions is, however, undercut by the song's gentle country waltz melancholy. It is clear that Dylan too has nothing to offer; he admits "deep in my heart / I know there is no help I can bring." This is one romantic suit he knows from the start he will not win.

The antipolitics of "My Back Pages" and "To Ramona" is only one expression of the changing artistic personality revealed on *Another Side*. In "All I Really Want to Do" Dylan assures the object of his erotic pursuit that he does not want to "analyze, categorize" her. In "It Ain't Me, Babe" he rejects a lover because she insists on casting him in a prefabricated mold; she is unwilling to accept his weaknesses (and philandering). "Everything inside is made of stone," he declares, a tremendous line whose power lies in its self-evident untruthfulness. What "It Ain't Me, Babe" poignantly champions is human fallibility, or, rather, Dylan's fallibility. As in the antipolitical songs, his immediate personal needs dovetail with a repudiation of attempts to pigeonhole human desires or reduce individual identities. On this album, it's not only dogmatism but often intellect itself that seems the enemy. "Spanish Harlem Incident" sounds like a good title for a protest song, but in fact it's a hymn to ephemeral sensuality—charged, perhaps naively, with racial implications. As in many white fantasies, the black woman is "too hot for taming." Dylan is self-conscious about his whiteness:

> The night is pitch black, come an' make my
> Pale face fit into place, ah, please!

The fantasy figure embodies a groping for a reality beyond the stifling categories of social norms: the singer needs to touch the woman "So I can tell if I'm really real." Dylan's search for the authentic always carried complex racial implications, as it did (and does) for many white people. In 1964, he told Robert Shelton:

> It's not that I'm pessimistic about Negroes' rights, but the word Negro sounds foolish coming from my mouth. What's a Negro? I don't know

what a Negro is. What's a Negro—a black person? How black? What's a Negro? A person living in a two room shack with 12 kids? A lot of white people live in a two room shack with 12 kids. Does this make them Negro? What's a Negro—someone with African blood? A lot of white people have African blood. What's a Negro? An Ethiopian kind of thing? That's not Negro—that's ancient religious pajama-riding freaks. I've got nothing against Negro rights. I never did. Anybody who is taught to get his kicks off a superiority feeling—man, that's a drag.[17]

Shelton did Dylan a favor by keeping these comments to himself—they would have alienated a lot more people than his ECLC rant. They display Dylan's uneasiness with categories in general, and might be seen as an early attempt at deconstructing racial identity. But they are also an example of the masked racial unease that snaked through sections of the counterculture, as hip white youth took to using words like *spade* and even *nigger* in an attempt to bolster their street cred. This posture was, in part, a reaction against the cloying sentimentality of early civil rights rhetoric, but it was also a fearful attitudinal maneuver, a defensive ploy by members of a generation forced to confront the grievances of a people with whom most had little direct contact, and whose challenge inspired, provoked, and threatened them.

Of course, many on the left saw Dylan's turn from politics as little more than opportunism. They were reeling from an abrupt and painful repudiation. After all, Dylan hadn't put that much time or energy into trying to change things before he decided it wasn't worth the effort. And this recantation hadn't been forced upon him by any inquisition. So was it "just for a handful of silver he left us? / Just for a ribbon to stick in his coat?," as Browning asked of Wordsworth. Was it, as suspected by some on the left, Albert Grossman's appetite for the big time? Or Dylan's narcissistic vanity?

Clearly, the ambitious artist that was stirring inside Dylan feared being stereotyped as a protest singer and servant of good causes. And he would have been aware—if only through Woody Guthrie's experiences—of the left's bad habit of grabbing on to creative artists and try-ing to program their output. In that light, Dylan's repudiation of the movement appears as an act of wilful self-liberation, a necessary step in his artistic evolution. But if that's all it had been, if it represented noth-ing more than a private maneuver, it wouldn't have produced so much in the way of lasting music; it wouldn't have touched and continued to touch others.

The moralism of the American left in these years—embodied in both the civil rights and peace movements—was indeed wearing. The stern challenge to bear witness against injustice, whose echoes fill "Blowin' in the Wind," seemed to leave little room for private indul-gence. Dylan's response should be seen as part of a political battle to clear space for the personal, a battle fought as much within as against the left.* Like other young people, Dylan had been alerted by a dramat-ically shifting social environment to the greater richness of his own inner life, and, like others, he wanted the freedom to explore that mys-terious and enticing landscape.

Dylan's political disillusionment resonates with historical parallels. His spiritual kin can be found among artists and intellectuals from other generations scorched by the flames of social revolt, from Wordsworth and Coleridge to Koestler and *The God That Failed*. You can hear something of "My Back Pages" in Yeats's "Meditation in Time of Civil War:"

> We had fed the heart on fantasies
> The heart's grown brutal from the fare
> More substance in our enmities than in our loves

---

* About the same time Dylan was writing "My Back Pages" and "To Ramona," a group of SNCC women activists issued a historic challenge to sexist practices within SNCC it-self—and came up against a barrage of male mockery. Many of the criticisms made by the SNCC women echo Dylan's grievances against the movement: it did not practice what it preached, it exploited its adherents, its leaders were trapped within their own egos. Like Dylan, but with different purposes and to different effect, the SNCC women were redrawing the boundaries between the personal and the political. The moment that produced Dylan's apostasy also contained the seeds of the women's movement that was to stride boldly forward at the very end of the decade.

In Dylan's case, the trajectory that yields this perspective is extraordinarily telescoped. He makes a huge amount out of what was, by historic standards, a brief, largely secondhand experience. The point, however, is not the depth or detail of his personal political commitment, but its grip on his imagination; the emotional violence of Dylan's reaction against the movement was a measure of the importance it once held for him.

Dylan's turn away from politics was to become a recurring motif of the era, as wave after wave of young people engaged in and were scorched by political activity. Strange as it may sound when speaking of such a politically polarized era, this shift from the public to the personal was to prove a defining moment in the American sixties. In reaction to the sheer velocity of events, the agonizing ebb and flow of struggle, an anti-authoritarian anti-politics emerged. It's remarkable that the sense of futility should be so widely felt and expressed in what is viewed, in retrospect, as an era of inexorable progress. Of course, at the time there seemed nothing inexorable about it. In light of the obstacles thrown in their way, the forces of change seemed puny and inadequate. Dylan's songs trace a familiar movement from messianic expectation to cynical defeatism. However, as in many of his love songs, the sense of futility seems to set in even as the note of conquest is sounded.

In retrospect, Dylan's premature political disillusionment reflected not only the stresses of revolt and reaction, but also the relentless packaging of experience and identity in a consumer society. For Dylan and many others, one level of consciousness seemed to be quickly superseded by another; if you stayed at one level too long you risked being as obsolescent—and as inauthentic—as last year's fashions. Thus, Dylan helped make activism cool, and he helped make it uncool.

The songs of Dylan's apostasy belong especially to those who have remained politically engaged. They'll resonate with any activist who's ever been fed up to the back teeth with "the corpse evangelists," or feared that he or she was becoming one of them; with anyone exhausted by the posturing, dogmatism, and millennial self-confidence to which the left is prone; with anyone who has felt used and abused in the struggle; anyone who has wondered about his or her own motives and the motives of his or her comrades; anyone reeling from the disappointment of a strike or a campaign or a grand strategy (the failure of the revolution to arrive or the realization that the would-be leaders of the revolution are no better than the rest); anyone who has ever yearned for some release from the demanding effort to match action to belief. In many years of political activism, I've more than once binged on the Dylan of this period, and relished his emotive attack on a movement that so rarely lives up to its claims.

Political engagement requires a degree of certainty—about public realities and the impact of public actions—and there are times when sustaining that degree of certainty is difficult in the extreme. Yet, as Dylan himself had pointed out in his earlier songs, our rulers thrive on our uncertainties ("the words that are used for to get the ship confused . . ."); we have to work constantly to reestablish our own right to speak and act. (That's why many are drawn to political sects; people need reenforcement to go against the grain.) And while it's an error to make a religion of struggle and sacrifice, it's an illusion to think the world can be improved without them. Sadly, Dylan's apostasy did prove a forerunner of much that was to come—a flood tide of post-sixties political recantations and personal reinventions.

Within a year of writing "Chimes of Freedom," Dylan no longer wanted any part of the storms of social change. In the dryly mournful "Farewell Angelina" (recorded during the *Bringing It All Back Home* sessions of January 1965 but left off the album), he openly declares his desire to escape from a society in crisis:

> The machine guns are roaring
> The puppets heave rocks
> The fiends nail time bombs
> To the hands of the clocks
> Call me any name you like
> I will never deny it
> Farewell Angelina
> The sky is erupting
> I must go where it's quiet.

The political drama being played out around Dylan is the necessary and compelling context for the endless dreams of escape that fill the songs that followed his protest period. Throughout the sixties, Dylan is writing both within the historical tide and against it.

Throughout Mississippi Summer, the activists found solace in music. "Beyond the freedom songs," John Lewis recalled, "we had the music on the radio to see us through the summer. All those hours driving all those miles in all those cars went a little bit easier with the rhythms coming out of those dashboard radios. Popular music always had its place right beside the protest songs. . . ." The activists were stirred by Martha and the Vandellas' "Dancing in the Street," Mary Wells's "My Guy," but perhaps most of all by the Impressions' "Keep on Pushing." [18]

By 1964, the Impressions had enjoyed a string of hits in both R&B and pop charts, and had established themselves as the leading exponents of Chicago soul, a polished blend of gospel harmonies, brass, strings, and rhythm guitar, both wistful and danceable. Their creative pulse was supplied by singer-guitarist-composer-arranger Curtis Mayfield, who was a year younger than Dylan. Raised by a single mother in Chicago's Cabrini Green projects, Mayfield knew poverty and the ghetto firsthand. Through the church, he imbibed the living gospel tradition, and from his mother an early acquaintance with poetry, notably the verse that Paul Laurence Dunbar—the son of a fugitive slave—had published in the early twentieth century. [19]

From the age of fifteen, Mayfield worked as a full-time musician. With the Impressions in the early sixties, he forged a sound that was as smooth and gentle as Dylan's was harsh and challenging. In contrast to the dominant male R&B tradition, Mayfield's love songs—like Sam Cooke's and Smokey Robinson's—were tinged with vulnerability and self-doubt. ("Gypsy Woman," the Impressions' hit of 1961, may have been in Dylan's mind when he wrote "Spanish Harlem Incident.") Mayfield was a musical craftsman of both delicacy and power. He brought the succinct wit of Broadway and Tin Pan Alley to the swirling emotions of the black church.

In the first half of the sixties, most R&B and soul performers steered clear of direct involvement or public association with the civil rights movement. That task was left to the folkies, the jazz vanguard, and the Hollywood celebrities. For the emerging black soul stars, authenticity came cheap; their struggle was for survival; they were avowedly and unashamedly commercial artists. For many, a hit record was the difference between penury and a modest degree of comfort. There were already so many barriers between themselves and the wider marketplace that the notion of erecting even more exercised little appeal. Politics was considered the kiss of death—far more risky for blacks than for whites. But the unfolding drama of the civil rights movement transformed both the soul stars and the environment in which they worked. Mayfield had listened to the freedom songs and he knew that Dylan and the folkies had achieved commercial success with politically tinged material. He may also have remembered one of Dunbar's *Lyrics of Lowly Life:*

Keep a-pluggin' away
When you've rising storms to quell
When opposing waters swell
It will never fail to tell
Keep a-pluggin' away

Mayfield asked himself: "Why does it always have to be a love song?" "Keep on Pushing," recorded in Chicago in March 1964, became the first of the "message" songs he was to continue to write until his death in 1999. At first glance, its lyrics seem even barer of explicit topical reference than "Blowin' in the Wind." In summoning fortitude in the face of tribulation, it recalls countless African American spirituals. But it makes no mention of God or heaven and in its context—the summer of 1964—its politics were plain.

Now look a yonder
What's that I see

A great big stone wall
Stands there ahead of me
But I've got my pride
And I'll move on aside
And keep on pushin'

The activists found themselves humming this song because it gave them something they could not do without. What sustained the movement was precisely the sensation that it was *in movement*—that this was a collective advancing toward a destination. Mayfield calls on his listeners not to be daunted by the challenges facing them, while also acknowledging how hard their task is, how much patience has already been spent. "Keep on Pushing" established Mayfield as one of the era's great comforters and consolers, an artist of hope, a banisher of despair, but by no means an escapist. Amiri Baraka, who had recently decamped from the Village to Harlem, and turned from Beat bohemian to black nationalist, observed that, for black people, "Keep on Pushing" "provided a core of legitimate social feeling, though mainly metaphorical and allegorical." [20]

In October 1964, the Impressions returned to the studio to record Mayfield's second social anthem, the sublime "People Get Ready." Dylan admired the song, and recorded it in a Basement Tapes session in 1967 and again for a film soundtrack in 1989.

People get ready, there's a train a comin'
You don't need no baggage, you just get on board
All you need is faith to hear the diesels hummin'
You don't need no ticket, you just thank the lord

The train carrying passengers to deliverance is a gospel music archetype. It appears, most famously, in "This Train (Is Bound for Glory)"—which gave Woody Guthrie the title of his book, and which had been recorded by numerous black gospel choirs, as well as Sister Rosetta Tharpe and Big Bill Broonzy. Dylan sang it in his early folk sets, and it was to be a popular item in the Wailers early repertoire. Though the lyrics vary, they all insist that on "this train" there's room only for the righteous. "This train don't carry no gamblers / No two-bit whores or midnight ramblers."

In Mayfield's song, the train is still "the train to Jordan" but it is also the movement—like the ship in Dylan's "When The Ship Comes In." And its company is as all-embracing as Dylan's in "Chimes of Freedom." This train is "picking up passengers from coast-to-coast." Though Mayfield jettisons the moralistic demands of the old gospel song, his vision of salvation is not quite all-inclusive. "There ain't no room for the hopeless sinner / who would hurt all mankind just to save his own; / have pity on those whose chances grow thinner / there is no hiding place against the kingdom's throne."

You can find train imagery in Dylan's work of all periods, and the gospel train itself makes a dramatic reappearance in the Christian songs of 1979–80. In his mid-sixties songs, however, trains are symbols of loneliness and transience, disappearing into enigmatic distances. In "I'll Keep It with Mine," he moans: "The conductor he's weary, / He's still stuck on the line . . ." and of course, as the song title says, "It Takes a Train to Cry." In 1999, Bruce Springsteen revisited "This Train" in "Land of Hope and Dreams," and in the spirit of both Guthrie and Mayfield he welcomes on board just about all those who'd been kept off in the gospel original (sinners, drinkers, whores). But the train here is merely a means of escape; it's not going anywhere. It's the train of rock 'n' roll, of the musical camaraderie that in Springsteen's vision fills the void left by the decline of mass movements.

"People Get Ready" was born in and speaks to a different experience. Like the gospel standards, the freedom songs, and the folk anthems, it engages in a collective address and promises a collective deliverance from a social agony. It was to be three years before *power to the people* became a common catchphrase; Mayfield's language anticipates that development, but note how much more intimately he uses the populist rhetoric. He talks directly to "people," not indirectly about "the people." The delicate vocals tremble with the sacrifices of generations, balanced by a steady determination to remain generous of spirit. The guitar solos (which influenced Robbie Robertson) are poignantly muted. This isn't a facile optimism, but a resilience that fully know the travails of the past and those to come.

Like Dylan's, Mayfield's work is a bridge between the early and late sixties, between innocence and sophistication. "Keep on Pushing" and "People Get Ready," along with Sam Cooke's posthumously released "A Change Is Gonna Come," inaugurated a period during which increasingly hard-hitting social commentary emerged as a staple of black popular music. At this point, Mayfield was already something of a one-man industry. In addition to his work with the Impressions, he was writing and arranging for a variety of other Chicago soul artists. From 1965, he concentrated increasingly on developing his own sound and securing greater artistic and financial independence. That turn in his career is unimaginable without the stimulus of the civil rights movement.

The artistic ambition and desire for personal autonomy that fueled Dylan's rejection of politics fueled Mayfield's embrace of them. The historical moment that severed Dylan from the movement brought Mayfield closer to it. As Dylan renounced the duties of political protest, Mayfield shouldered them. He did so with humility and determination, and while remaining within a commercial framework and a popular musical idiom. "Our purpose is to educate as well as entertain," he said cheerfully in 1965. "Painless preaching is as good a term as any for what we do." [21]

Dylan began writing "Mr. Tambourine Man" in New Orleans in February 1964, premiered it in London in May, but decided to leave it off *Another Side*, recorded in August. The song was his most ambitious and original to date, and it's revealing that Dylan—who usually preferred to dash off a tune and record it without further ado—nursed and refined the song for more than eight months before deciding to release one of the many versions recorded in January 1965 at the *Bringing It All Back Home* studio sessions.

Dylan has explained that the title is a reference to Bruce Langhorne, the black guitarist who provided studio backing for many a folksinger.

Langhorne liked to sport an outlandishly large Turkish tambourine, and this image was the starting point (but little more) for Dylan's sensuously fantastic journey on the "magic swirlin' ship." [22] Fittingly, Langhorne himself provides the chiming guitar accompaniment on the album version of the song—his calm embellishment of Dylan's flowing lyrics helping to emphasize the touching evanescence of the vision conjured up by the song.

In "Mr. Tambourine Man" Dylan stretched himself as he had never done before, entered new artistic territory and created a landscape distinctively his own. Yet the song is also atypical of the master in its unbroken gentle yearning, its lack of bitterness, its unashamed, unironic pursuit of transcendence. The song evokes the dawn ("the jingle-jangle morning") that comes at the end of the long day's journey into night, when "evenin's empire has returned into sand"—and the feeling of joy in a momentary suspension of the quotidian. It captures the delicious sway of surrendering one's individual will and one's awareness of grubby realities:

> I'm ready to go anywhere, I'm ready for to fade
> Into my own parade, cast your dancing spell my way,
> I promise to go under it.

This surrender leads the singer to an anonymous but somehow limitless landscape where "but for the sky there are no fences facin' "— a place where he is alone, at peace, and free to explore an infinite inner labyrinth:

> Then take me disappearin' through the smoke rings of my mind,
> Down the foggy ruins of time, far past the frozen leaves,
> The haunted, frightened trees, out to the windy beach,
> Far from the twisted reach of crazy sorrow.

Here "all memory and fate" have been driven away; both past and future have been pushed aside in favor of a lingering immersion in a fleeting present: "let me forget about today until tomorrow." "Mr. Tambourine Man" is the cry of an urban man seeking joy and revelation in splendid isolation from the crowd. But how naive and narcissistic is the picture postcard self-portrait with which it concludes:

> Yes, to dance beneath the diamond sky with one hand waving free,
> Silhouetted by the sea, circled by the circus sands

Here Dylan is imagining himself, as so many young people have, as the last man, the only man, and nature's child. A paean to escapism, "Mr. Tambourine Man" ushered in a period in which escape and its problematic nature became a thematic preoccupation. The collision of resistance from below with a long consumer boom unleashed longings for the infinite among classes of people who previously would not have been able or willing to pursue them. It was an appetite that could never be fully satisfied, either politically or personally.

Publicity is not merely an assembly of competing messages: it is a language in itself which is always being used to make the same general proposal . . . it proposes to each of us that we transform ourselves, or our lives, by buying something more . . . Publicity, situated in a future continually deferred, excludes the present and so eliminates all becoming, all development. Experience is impossible within it.

—JOHN BERGER[23]

In November 1964, Dylan added "It's Alright Ma (I'm Only Bleeding)" to his repertoire—longer, more obscure, more complex than any of his previous work. The novelty of the imagery, delivery, and form of the song blinded many at the time to the plain fact that "It's Alright Ma" is as much a protest song as anything else Dylan has written: a vision of a corrupt and dehumanized society and the fate of the sensitive, autonomous individual within it.

"That's All Right Mama," written by Mississippi blues man Arthur Big Boy Crudup, had been Elvis Presley's first hit record in 1955. (Dylan recorded his own version in 1962, but never released it). Its final

verse has a Dylan-like mingling of sexual arrogance and social resentment:

> I'm leaving town, baby
> I'm leaving town for sure
> Well, then you won't be bothered with
> Me hanging 'round your door
> Well, that's all right, that's all right,
> That's all right now mama, anyway you do.

In Dylan's song, the refrain carries much of the same sense of fragile defiance, but the experience out of which it arises, and the language in
which it's described, occupies territory unhinted at in Presley's teenage
erotica. The song opens with "darkness at the break of noon" (Milton by
way of Koestler), a total eclipse, and an instant conclusion ("there is no
sense in trying"). The guitar picking is restrained but determined, its
ominous impetus driving the song forward, as relentless as the flow of
imagery and the hammering rhymes.*

The second verse barrels through threats, bluffs, scorn, "suicide remarks," "the fool's gold mouthpieces," and "the hollow horn" that plays
"wasted words" toward the aphorism that sums up so much of Dylan's
sixties art: *he not busy being born is busy dying.* Here, as throughout the
song, Dylan is reworking and deepening the life/death polarity he first
deployed in "Let Me Die in My Footsteps."

"It's Alright Ma" is a sweeping condemnation of a society in which
the holiness of life is denied, a shameful society where "Goodness hides
behind its gates." A society of hypocrisy about sex and love and labor
and power, a society governed by "human gods" who "Make everything
from toy guns that spark / To flesh-colored Christs that glow in the
dark" and for whom the beautiful, the creative is "Nothing more than
something / They invest in." At the heart of this society is what Marx
(certainly not Dylan) called the commodity fetish—and its ideological
handmaiden in mass society, the advertising industry.

---

* In later years, Dylan tried to bring out the melodrama of "It's Alright Ma" with a heavy-
metal arrangements—the results were usually overblown.

> Advertising signs that con
> You into thinking you're the one
> That can do what's never been done
> That can win what's never been won

In a society dominated by commodities, all public discourse has grown corrupt. The power of money has rendered all social communication inauthentic:

> . . . money doesn't talk, it swears
> Obscenity, who really cares
> Propaganda, all is phony

As for the movement that claims to challenge this society, it merely enacts its rituals and feeds its power. Protest is "just one more person crying." Those who "say don't hate nothing at all / Except hatred" are part of the game, as are the sad characters "on principles baptized / To strict party platform ties / Social clubs in drag disguise." The outspoken dissenter expresses nothing but his own powerlessness ("Outsiders they can freely criticize / Tell nothing except who to idolize").

> While one who sings with his tongue on fire
> Gargles in the rat race choir
> Bent out of shape from society's pliers
> Cares not to come up any higher
> But rather get you down in the hole
> That he's in.

Is that an oblique self-portrait? A PR hustler, a TV demagogue, a movement firebrand? The point is that those who comment on society are themselves the product of that society. Inauthenticity and life denial permeate our every gesture. There is no escape from the corruption and emptiness of the public sphere—except in the autonomous individual consciousness.

"It's Alright Ma" is filled with a Gramscian conviction that the most insidious means of domination are those that secure the "spontaneous consent" of the dominated. It's a song about the "the mind-forged manacles" that Blake heard clanging as he walked the streets of London in 1792. But Dylan is without either Gramsci's or Blake's abiding belief in collective human agency and capacity. His critique of the repressive, omni-invasive character of mass culture is here as harrowing and all-inclusive—and nearly as pessimistic—as Adorno's. Nonetheless, the monstrous totality of social domination is by no means the whole of this song. Dylan defiantly asserts his autonomy and survival as an individual. It isn't an easy struggle.

> You lose yourself, you reappear
> You suddenly find you got nothing to fear
> Alone you stand with nobody near . . .

The liberating lesson is that "it is not he or she or them or it / That you belong to." The only way to escape from social control is to disinvest in society and in society's judgment.

> But I mean no harm nor put fault
> On anyone that lives in a vault
> But it's alright, Ma, if I can't please him.

Human freedom remains a reality in this song, though it is menaced on all sides. In the final verse, the confrontation between self and society is entirely antagonistic—and unresolved.

> My eyes collide head-on with stuffed graveyards
> False gods, I scuff
> At pettiness which plays so rough
> Walk upside-down inside handcuffs
> Kick my legs to crash it off
> Say okay, I have had enough
> What else can you show me?

Dylan is defiant to the end. The song concludes with a proud but despairing declaration of his own subversiveness:

> And if my thought-dreams could be seen
> They'd probably put my head in a guillotine
> But it's alright, Ma, it's life, and life only.

⌊Consciousness is the battleground on which Dylan now plants his standard. His music of the next two years would be a sustained assault in that battle. Politics had been injected into the theater of consciousness and consciousness had become the theater of liberation. ⌋It seemed the most daunting challenge the radicals had yet posed themselves. But part of its appeal was that it was, in fact, easier ground to fight on. In Dylan's case, the perception of the scale and depth of society's dishonesty issued in (or justified) a repudiation of all forms of political engagement. Nonetheless, the rage of "It's Alright Ma" against a commodified universe—and determination, somehow, to preserve a human autonomy within it—seems as apposite today as ever.

By early 1964, SNCC had been organizing for two years in the town of Selma in central Alabama. White resistance to attempts at black voter registration took on ever more violent forms, culminating in the police killing of a local youth during a demonstration in February. On March 7, 1,000 nonviolent demonstrators gathered to march the fifty-four miles to the state capital, Montgomery, to demand an end to the assault on their rights. As they crossed the Pettus Bridge spanning the Alabama River they were attacked by local police and state troopers; John Lewis was beaten unconscious and hospitalized, along with eighty others. Television cameras broadcast the images of white law enforcement officials clubbing, kicking, and tear-gassing nonresisting blacks.

In the greatest outpouring of national support the southern civil rights movement was ever to enjoy, protests and pickets spread across the country. Calls for voting rights legislation echoed in Congress and editorial columns.[24]

King and other leaders entered the fray. On March 10, a crowd of 3,000, led by King, gathered to make another attempt to cross the Pettus Bridge; once again the marchers were met by troopers and police. They were not aware that in a last-minute deal with the federal government, King had agreed to lead an orderly retreat. Confrontation was avoided, but as they followed their leaders back to base, SNCC activists sang the movement favorite, "Ain't Gonna Let No One Turn Me Round," with bitter irony.

The events in Selma forced Lyndon Johnson's hand. He appeared on television on March 15 to announce a new voting rights bill—and concluded his speech with the words, "we *shall* overcome." King and Lewis, watching the speech in a Selma hotel, were moved. Jim Forman was not. He dismissed the phrase as a "tinkling empty symbol" and later said, "Johnson spoiled a good song that day." [25] In his *Biograph* interview of 1985, Dylan seems to recall this controversy. Talking about the cooptation of rock 'n' roll, he says:

> It's like Lyndon Johnson saying we shall overcome to a nationwide audience, ridiculous . . . there's an old saying, "if you want to defeat your enemy, sing his song" and that's pretty much still true. [26]

After the president's announcement, a federal court granted a permit for a Selma to Montgomery march and federal marshals were assigned to protect it. Supporters, black and white, poured in from around the country. Len Chandler was among them, and his chant was adopted by the marchers: "Pick 'em up and lay 'em down, all the way to Selma town." Just outside their destination, they were treated to an outdoor concert featuring, among others, Nina Simone, Odetta, Peter, Paul and Mary, Joan Baez, Tony Bennett, and Leonard Bernstein. (In Philadelphia, the Impressions joined artists from Motown in a Freedom Show to raise money for the march—the first major coming out of the soul stars for the movement.) Fifty thousand joined the next day's triumphal march into Montgomery. Wallace kept out of sight. Hours later, Viola Liuzzo, a white supporter from the North, was shot dead while driving back to Selma.

The Selma actions were the last united initiative of the civil rights movement. The backstage tensions of the March on Washington were now visible to all. Among the young activists, there was an increasing impatience with nonviolence and the integrationist mantras of the early sixties. There was widespread distrust of the older leaders, including King, and criticism of their media status. Where King seemed to want to rouse the conscience of the country, SNCC wanted to rouse and organize poor blacks. One by one, it seemed, their allies had let them down.

To many in SNCC, the forward march of the civil rights movement had been halted, not only on the streets of southern towns, but at a deeper level. Formal, legal equality, it emerged, was not the same as real freedom. One week after the Voting Rights Act of 1965 was signed into law, a violent uprising swept through the Watts district of Los Angeles. After six days, it was suppressed by the national guard; thirty-four people were killed and thousands were arrested. There were other outbreaks in Cleveland, Chicago, and New York City.

The battles of the first half of the decade had expanded the aspirations and deepened the frustrations of young black people. There was a greater confidence in the resources of the black community and a greater cynicism toward the intentions of the white. As SNCC and CORE turned toward black nationalism, and the words of Malcolm X (assassinated earlier in the year) reverberated through black America, white supporters of the movement were forced to reexamine themselves and their role. If the black activists were going to lead and mobilize the black community independently of whites, what did that leave the whites to do? Some black activists suggested they should look to organizing their own community, as the black activists were doing. But what was their community? Where were its boundaries? What language did it speak?

In March 1965, Allen Ginsberg was in Prague—having been deported from Cuba—watching a rock 'n' roll band. The music and the musicians filled him with political hope and erotic longings: "Because the body moves again, the / body dances again, the body / sings again." [27] After visits to the Soviet Union and Poland, he returned to Prague in the first week of May. The government had permitted the revival of a "folk custom"—actually a nineteenth-century invention—in which the students of Prague elect a king of May. In itself, this was somewhat contro-versial: May Day was the international workers' day, not a feudal hang-over. In keeping with the folkloric and festive occasion, the students dressed in turn-of-the-century attire, bowler hats and all. But as far as the authorities were concerned, the quaint ritual turned into a danger-ously subversive saturnalia when an independent-minded crowd of 100,000 jubilantly elected Ginsberg to the ancient honor. The visiting poet paraded—drunkenly, joyously—through the streets, declaiming his gospel of liberation. The episode was one of the first public sight-ings of the spirit that infused the Prague Spring of 1968, and it's signifi-cant that both rock 'n' roll and American Beat poetry fed into that brief flowering.

On May 7, Ginsberg was deported to Britain. On the plane to Lon-don he wrote "Kral Majales," in which he unashamedly blends political critique with self-celebration. "Communist and Capitalist assholes tan-gle and the just man is arrested or robbed or had his head cut off. . . . I am the King of May, which is the power of sexual youth . . . And tho' I am the King of May, the Marxists have beat me upon the street . . . and deported me from our Kingdom by airplane." In a self-mocking but prophetic touch, he added: "and I am the King of May, tho' paranoid, for the Kingdom of May is too beautiful to last for more than a month." [28]

In London, Ginsberg joined Dylan's entourage. The singer was in England for his third visit, the one chronicled in D.A. Pennebaker's mesmerizing documentary, *Don't Look Back*. Ginsberg can be seen in the background during the innovative opening sequence, in which Dylan, standing in an alley adjacent to the Savoy Hotel, holds up a series of large cards inscribed with tag lines from "Subterranean Homesick Blues" while the song plays on the soundtrack.

Dylan was still performing solo, with acoustic guitar, and still singing many of his protest classics. He had already recorded and re-leased the rock 'n' roll tracks on *Bringing It All Back Home*, though these were as yet little known in Britain. Once again, he was in transi-tion. Pennebaker's film shows Dylan slyly interrogating fans, friends, hangers-on, would-be interviewers, and his own growing celebrity. One of its running jokes is Dylan's nonresponse to questions about the rise of Donovan, the singer-songwriter who was being hailed as a homegrown English Dylan. The two finally meet at a party in Dylan's hotel suite, where Donovan gives an impromptu performance of his winsome hit single, "Catch the Wind," whose debt to Dylan's early work is painfully obvious. Dylan replies by playing a charging, confident, steely "It's All Over Now, Baby Blue," a song he'd written earlier in the year.

"Baby Blue" (the soubriquet is taken from a Gene Vincent song) opens with an urgent injunction: "you must leave now, take what you need . . ." The song's subject is departure, moving on, restlessness raised to a principle. In an impermanent world, it advises us to travel light, to be prepared to jettison friends, lovers, mentors, influences, even one's own identity.

> Leave your stepping stones behind something calls for you
> Forget the dead you've left they will not follow you

In "Baby Blue," the outside world is in a state of metamorphosis: "the sky too is folding over you" . . . "the carpet too is moving under you." In each verse there's a figure offering a gnomic warning: the orphan with his gun, the "empty-hand painter," the lover "who's just walked out your door," the vagabond "who's standing in the clothes that you once wore." All carry the same mysterious message: if you don't move on, you will become an alien to yourself.

What is it that's "all over now"? Whatever you believe has sustained you—the movement, folk music, your lovers, home, reputation, bank balance. In "Baby Blue," Dylan seems to whisper a prophetic reminder of the transience of social status, the flimsiness of the nooks and niches we cling to. Freedom here isn't a social aspiration or static utopian condition. It's a reality that must be seized, the bedrock of our lives that we hide from ourselves.

At the end of the film, Dylan, basking in his Albert Hall triumph, sits in the back of a limo with manager Albert Grossman and sidekick Bob

Neuwirth. Grossman quietly informs Dylan that a British newspaper has dubbed him an "anarchist." Dylan is surprised but somehow pleased ("Give the anarchist a cigarette," he barks). Grossman explains that they've picked this label "because you don't offer any solutions." Dylan wonders why they haven't called him a Communist: "In England Communists aren't . . ." he begins, and Neuwirth finishes the thought: "In England it's cool to be a Communist." Dylan rejoins: "I don't think it's cool to be an anarchist though."

Dylan and his entourage seem to be dimly aware that Britain's political culture was not the same as America's. In particular, Dylan knew that Britain had been spared the experience of McCarthyism—the cold war purge that created the great historical caesura that dogged the American left. But he also sensed and took satisfaction in the fact that in Britain too he had somehow transgressed a well-guarded cultural frontier.

After Dylan's departure, Ginsberg remained in London, reveling in the pop music and avant-garde art scene. In June he played a leading role in the International Poetry Incarnation at Albert Hall, an event that helped define—and boost the profile of—the emerging British counterculture.[29] To the organizer's surprise, 7,000 people responded to some last-minute publicity. And they didn't look or act like the people who usually attended poetry recitals. They listened to scores of poets that day, among them Christopher Logue, Lawrence Ferlinghetti, Gregory Corso, Adrian Mitchell, and Michael Horovitz.* The *Times Literary Supplement* conceded that the organizers had "made literary history by a combination of flair, courage and seized opportunities." Their aim, however, was not merely to promote new talent, but to "affirm a purely

---

* At the last minute the Russian Andrei Voznesensky and the Cuban Pablo Fernandez, under pressure from their governments, withdrew from the event, as did the Chilean Communist Pablo Neruda, who was said to be concerned that Ginsberg might take off his clothes.

poetic space," to awaken the sleeping Albion, to gather the dissident tribes.[30] "It wasn't the beginning of anything," Adrian Mitchell explained in 1966, "it was public proof that something had been accelerating for years." It was time for poetry "to bust down all the walls of its museum/tomb and learn to survive in the corrosive real world." One of the stimuli for this development was Dylan's work, which had already blurred the boundaries between poetry, popular music, and politics.

At the Albert Hall, Mitchell was the best received of the British poets. His poem, "To Whom It May Concern", with its stinging refrain, "Tell me lies about Vietnam," * "was rewarded with the biggest ovation of the evening," according to Edward Lucie-Smith's jaundiced report in *Encounter*. Mitchell also recited "You Get Used to It," a poem whose starting point was an image from Selma. ("If you've spent all your life in hell or Alabama / You get used to it.") The young people at the Albert Hall had been following events in the United States, they had been stirred by the civil rights movement and outraged by the war on Vietnam. Mitchell used those distant experiences to challenge a British audience in a language that was both popular and politically charged.

Ginsberg was the presiding sprit here, as in Prague. "Arch-celebrant, with flowing beard mantic hair radiant eyes hand-pointing drunken bear arms," Michael Horovitz called him, "navigating our course in the persona of a too-long exiled biblical prophet."[31] The visiting American recited a new poem, "Who Be Kind To," in which he poured forth the tender impressions of his recent travels. "The Liverpool Minstrels of Cavernsink / raise up their joyful voices and guitars / in electric Africa hurrah . . . Twist & / Shout, and / Gates of Eden are named / in Albion again." The long years of isolation were coming to an end. Ginsberg had found an audience among a new generation. This generation, on both sides of the Atlantic, had been prepared for his poetry and his message by the work of Bob Dylan. "Tonight let's all make love in London," he cried, ". . . the new kind of man has come to his bliss."[32]

---

* In 2003, Mitchell altered the line to "Tell me lies about Iraq."

LITTLE BOY LOST

A pardlike Spirit beautiful and swift—
A love in desolation mask'd—a Power
Girt round with weakness—it can scarce uplift
The weight of the superincumbent hour

—SHELLEY, "ADONAIS"

BETWEEN LATE 1964 and his motorcycle accident in the summer of 1966, Dylan created a body of work that remains unique in popular music. Drawing on folk, blues, country, R&B, rock 'n' roll, gospel, British beat, symbolist, modernist and Beat poetry, surrealism and Dada, advertising jargon and social commentary, Fellini and *Mad* magazine, he forged a coherent and original artistic voice and vision. I've been listening to these records since shortly after they came out, and nearly forty years on, I still find them fresh and full of surprises. Their beauty retains the power to shock and console.

The creative firestorm was brief but intense. Even in the midst of it, Dylan's art was in flux. During these twenty months there's a movement away from the public domain interrogated in *Bringing It All Back Home* and *Highway 61 Revisited* toward the more intimate universe explored in *Blonde on Blonde*. There's also a growing verbal and structural complexity, an ever more fluent and open syntax, an increasing integration of words and music and indeed of all the source elements. Throughout, there's an expanding and intensifying artistic ambition. Dylan could not stand still. He was compelled—by the interaction between social upheavals and inner demons—to explore to the limit the new genre he was creating.

The language of these songs sometimes achieves an intoxicated richness. Their eclectic vocabulary and range of reference were (and remain) exceptional in what was considered a medium for the unsophisticated. Dylan purges his style of the archaism and stilted poetic diction inherited from the folk tradition. The language is highly idiosyncratic, but entirely up-to-date. The songs are sprinkled with arresting images, epithets, verbal paradoxes. The flow of association yokes together the most heterogeneous ideas (as a skeptical Dr. Johnson said of the seventeenth-century Metaphysical poets): "Her fog, her amphetamine and her pearls," "The motorcycle black Madonna / Two-wheeled gypsy queen." Without strain, he juxtaposes rarefied imagery with the casually demotic: "you used to ride on a chrome horse with your diplomat / Who carried on his shoulder a Siamese cat / Ain't it hard, when you discover that / He wasn't really where it's at?" This is a poetic language that blends an almost effete verbal elaboration with blues rawness, intense specificity with delirious abstraction, the vivid with the vague:

> The guilty undertaker sighs,
> The lonesome organ grinder cries,
> The silver saxophones say I should refuse you.
> The cracked bells and washed-out horns
> Blow into my face with scorn,
> But it's not that way,
> I wasn't born to lose you.
> I want you, I want you,
> I want you so bad,
> Honey, I want you.

We tend to forget what an amazing achievement it was to create a popular lyrical idiom that could encompass "tax deductible charity organizations," a "leopard-skin pill box hat," "an Egyptian ring that sparkles before she speaks," "brown rice, seaweed and a dirty hot dog." Dylan opened up an established form to a range of words, references, experiences, moods, and modes not previously associated with it.

One of the trademarks of mid-sixties Dylan is the profusion of proper nouns—historical, legendary, literary, and invented. Sometimes they name places (Mobile, Juarez, Grand Street, "Housing Project Hill," "some Australian mountain range," Highway 61, Desolation Row) but more often people: Paul Revere, Belle Star, Jack the Ripper, Jezebel, John the Baptist, Galileo, Delilah, Cecil B. DeMille, Ma Rainey, F. Scott Fitzgerald, Ezra Pound, T.S. Eliot, Casanova, Einstein, Nero, Cain and Abel, the Hunchback of Notre Dame, Ophelia, Dr. Filth, Mack the Finger, Sweet Melinda, Georgia Sam, Louise and Johanna, Queen Mary, Queen Jane, the Queen of Spain, and of course, Mr. Jones and Captain A-Rab. It's as if the historical specificity of topical song were turned on its head. The aim there was to tie the song to events in the real world; the aim here is to make an unreal world sound as if it's real and vice versa. This is the experience of history recast as phantasmagoria.

In February 1965, as Dylan entered the studio to record *Bringing It All Back Home,* the U.S. launched a campaign of systematic airial bombardment against North Vietnam. The operation, code named Rolling Thunder (it's not clear whether Dylan was aware of this when he gave the same name to his 1975 touring "revue") would go on for eight years, during which time the U.S. would drop more ordinance than was dropped in the entire course of World War II. At the same time, the buildup of U.S. combat forces began in earnest. By July 1965 there were 100,000 U.S. troops in Vietnam. By the end of the year their numbers doubled, and over the following year they doubled again. In November 1965, the U.S. death toll in Vietnam reached the 1,000 mark—and would multiply by a factor of forty over the next four years.

The first major national demonstration against the Vietnam War was called by SDS in April 1965.[1] Attempts to bring together a broad coalition that would include the established ban-the-bomb groups and Democratic Party dissidents as well as student radicals and the old left foundered when the moderates feared the demonstration would appear soft on communism. To everyone's surprise, 25,000 turned up—mainly white students. Phil Ochs sang "Love Me, I'm A Liberal," scolding the erstwhile allies who had tried to undermine the demonstration, and was cheered. Ochs was joined on the platform by SNCC's Bob Moses, who linked the government's policies in Mississippi to those in the Mekong Delta. SDS president Paul Potter argued that " the people of Vietnam and the people on this demonstration are united in much more than a common concern that the war be ended. In both countries there are people struggling to build a movement that has the power to change their condition. The system that frustrates these movements is the same. All our lives, our destinies, our very hopes to live, depend on our ability to overcome that system." [2]

In the wake of the march, a fresh wave of student activists joined SDS, which had now broken formally with its parent body. Unlike the SDS founders who had drawn up the Port Huron Statement, many of whom were red-diaper babies from the Northeast, the new recruits hailed mainly from the Mid- and Southwest and came from working-class backgrounds. Jokingly, they referred to their own advent as "prairie power;" under the impact of the black insurgency and the war in Vietnam, these innocent children of the postwar boom and a conformist culture had leapt from conservatism over liberalism into radicalism. They wore cowboy boots and smoked dope. They were Dylan's people. [3]

The year-zero mentality freed this new left of inhibitions that had dogged their predecessors, it gave the young people confidence, and promoted an experimental spirit. But it also left them rudderless, without historical perspective, prone to hyberbole and apocalyptics, swinging wildly from liberal to ultraleft and back again. "SDS compressed a lifetime of politics into a handful of years—or rather, it was compressed into us," Todd Gitlin wrote of this time. "We were force-fed history." [4] That telescoping of historical experience is ingrained in Dylan's songs.

As a result of the experiences in the first half of the decade, the youth vanguard's ambitions had been widened and its frustrations deepened; extended vision went hand in hand with quickened impatience. And through much of the second half of the decade, this vanguard—both black and white—was preoccupied with "naming the system" and coming up with a means to overturn it. As Dylan put it in "Alternatives to College" (a prose work of 1964):

You wondering why there is no eternity & that you make your own eternity and why there is no music & that you make your own music & why there are no alternatives & that you make you own alternatives

In year zero, radicals had to start from scratch, and Dylan was hardly alone in insisting that the quest was about much more than politics as conventionally defined. In its search for liberation, black nationalism highlighted cultural identity and historical recovery. Among small groups of white youth (including veterans of Mississippi Summer) a self-identified counterculture was taking shape, still largely hidden from public view, mingling political radicalism and personal experiment—including experiment with sex and drugs. In 1965, the "underground press" emerged when the *Berkeley Barb* and the *East Village Other* hit the streets, appealing to tiny and isolated minorities that had begun to see themselves as embryonic communities. Both papers combined political commitment with a lively and decidedly partisan interest in popular culture (Dylan was to become staple fare for them). Day by day, collective action and personal self-expression, the two defining strands of the American sixties, became more intricately intertwined, one alternately chafing and strengthening the other.

Those who seek formal perfection will always find Dylan, even at his mid-sixties best, irritating. Clive James once wrote that the best Dylan song is never as good as its best verse, and the best verse is never as good as its best line. It's true, Dylan is uneven. In almost all the songs there are phrases, or whole verses, that are clumsy or pointless. There is an occasional reliance on formulaic filler—though far less so than is usual in popular song. Dylan in these years was carried forward by an onrushing stream of inspiration; others, less fecund, would have paused to revisit and re-edit. The rough edges are, in any case, part of the Dylan package; he's the kind of artist whose genius is unimaginable without them. In the incomparable body of work he produced between late 1964 and early 1966, serendipity is very much one of his compositional principles. Prompted by a cursory acquaintance with surrealist theory, a lot of drugs, and a search for meaning in an absurd, arbitrary universe, Dylan embraces the accidental and intuitive. His work throughout this period is full of extempore discoveries made in the course of the creative process. He free associates—with a will.

No one can doubt that the Dylan of these years was in love with rhyme. It's everywhere in these songs, pouncing, bouncing, bursting, underscoring and highlighting, registering surprise, doubt, and delight. "Subterranean Homesick Blues" is propelled by a mad rush for rhyme. It's an obvious forerunner of hip-hop, but also a descendant of the "rude railings" of the (highly urbane and politically sophisticated) sixteenth-century English poet John Skelton:

> For though my rhyme be ragged
> Tattered and jagged
> Rudely rain-beaten
> Rusty and moth-eaten
> If ye take it well therewith
> It hath in it some pith

Although he was certainly unaware of it, Dylan makes frequent use of "Skeltonics"—short, irregular lines in which rhyme is the only fixed principle. In "Subterranean Homesick Blues," the end rhymes bounce and rattle like ping-pong balls. In later songs, rhyme is interwoven more subtly with other elements but it is almost always prominent: an essential part of a literary grammar as energized, as syncopated as the rock 'n' roll music in which it is embedded. End rhyme is supplemented by internal rhyme, assonance, consonance, alliteration; indeed, the breakdown of the lyrics of these songs into discrete lines on the page is somewhat arbitrary; at Dylan's best the rhymes are experienced in the song as a flow of shifting accents and emphases.

In these years Dylan plays with and varies the basic verse structures: more than at any other period in his career. He complicates the prosody; there's an amazing, accordion-like expansion and contraction of the lyric within the melody. In "Visions of Johanna," the twenty-two-syllable line:

Sayin', "Name me someone that's not a parasite and I'll go out and say a
    prayer for him"

is sung over the same number of measures as the sixteen syllables of

We sit here stranded, though we're all doin' our best to deny it *

and "The ghost of electricity howls in the bones of her face" occupies
the same place and space in its verse as "Oh, it's so hard to get on" does
in its. Nonetheless, for all his daring, Dylan remains within the repeated
verse structure, the bedrock of popular music. And without the verse
structure, without the disciplines of popular music, Dylan flounders, as
readers of *Tarantula*† will know. It's significant that although Dylan
embarked on a number of literary projects between 1963 and 1965; he
abandoned them all after hitting his stride in "Like a Rolling Stone."
He'd found the medium he needed; there was no need for the poems,
stories, and plays he was ill-equipped to write.

From his early days in the Village, part of Dylan's appeal was his skill
as a storyteller. His approach to storytelling was always, however, somewhat off-beat; he liked shaggy dog stories, inconclusive anecdotes, and
picaresque meanderings. In one sense, in the songs of the mid-sixties,
he gives up on narrative altogether: the ballad form demands a coherence and tidiness that is incompatible with what he's seeing and feeling.
He can no longer tell the story straight because any story told straight is
a false one. Reality assaults the singer as a series of disjointed epipha-
nies, discomfiting eruptions of the inexplicable and inhuman:

Well, I woke up in the morning
There's frogs inside my socks
Your mama, she's a-hidin'
Inside the icebox
Your daddy walks in wearin'

* Shortened in performance to: "We sit here stranded though we all do our best to
deny it."
† Dylan's only extended prose work (though subtitled *poems*); written in 1964–65, published in 1971.

A Napoleon Bonaparte mask
Then you ask why I don't live here
Honey, do you have to ask?

Dylan appears here as both mesmerized spectator and unwitting partisan in an ongoing freak show. (These songs helped shape the prose Hunter S. Thompson unleashed on the world a few years later.) The mood and the method are carnivalesque: "The circus is in town." Appearances are without substance; events are no longer linked by causal connections or rational hierarchies; they take the form of a procession of the gaudy, grotesque, and sentimental.

As a child, Dylan fantasized about circuses and carnivals; when he first came to New York, he told friends he had worked as a fairground barker. He relished the hallucinatory masquerade of the Mardi Gras. He found the carnivalesque turned to serious artistic purposes in the films of Fellini, where it is both wistful and disturbing, an invocation of lost innocence and an alienated recoil from modernity. In Dylan, it is more frequently the latter, though both are there. What's interesting is that Fellini and Dylan, modern, self-conscious artists, turned to folk culture for an aesthetic absent from the formal narrative techniques of their genres. (Stravinsky, Schoenberg, Lorca, and Ensor had all been there before them).

As you listen to these albums, the images, characters, tropes sail past in a strange ether. They're experienced as free-floating metaphors, signifiers uprooted from the signified. These songs often feel like allegories but they cannot be decoded as such. Who are "the neon madmen" and why are they climbing the bricks on Grand Street? As I.A. Richards observed, the truly poetic metaphor is never merely illustrative or decorative; it is "a borrowing between and intercourse of thoughts." In mid-sixties Dylan, tenor and vehicle interact; it is usually impossible to extract one from the other, but the metaphorical resonance he achieves is undeniable.

In ceremonies of the horsemen,
Even the pawn must hold a grudge.

Or:

All your seasick sailors, they are rowing home
All your reindeer armies are all going home.*

Or:

They're selling postcards of the hanging
They're painting the passports brown

Unpacking any of these lines is time-consuming, but not as daunting as some have claimed. Take *they're selling postcards of the hanging*: the phrase conjures up the cold-hearted transformation of suffering into commodified spectacle; it sets capital punishment at the heart of a venal, media-dominated society; and it also refers to Dylan himself, to the media bent on exploiting him, and to his own willingness to market his pain in his songs, to expose himself to public view. It's an instantly evocative opening to a complex song, "Desolation Row," within which the line finds its wider and richer meaning.

While these admittedly difficult songs are more intelligible than has sometimes been made out, there's no doubt that the Dylan of this period revels in obscurity:

My warehouse eyes, my Arabian drums,
Should I leave them by your gate,
Or, sad-eyed lady, should I wait?

Not to mention "Upon the beach where hound dogs bay / At ships with tattooed sails" or "jewels and binoculars hang from the head of the mule." The fact that no Dylan fan can see these lines without singing them, ritualistically, like a mantra memorized from a foreign language, treasured, understood as a whole, gnostically, indicates that obscurity can itself be a means of communication. The sense that Dylan's songs contained coded messages to be deciphered by the hip cognoscenti, the inaccessibility that so upset Irwin Silber, actually made these songs

* Dylan flubs this lyric on *Bringing It All Back Home.*

powerfully attractive. Anything too upfront, too transparent, too easily accessible, could not be trusted.

> All these people that you mention
> Yes, I know them, they're quite lame
> I had to rearrange their faces
> And give them all another name

Of course, Dylan sells the package, obscurities and all, by the sheer conviction of his singing, which in this period displays a dynamic and tonal control he was never to surpass. (In *Don't Look Back,* he boasts to the *Time* reporter that he can hold his breath three times as long as Caruso.) David Bowie called it a "voice like sand and glue." This voice encompasses wild changes in tone and mode: from magisterial put-downs to aching longings, from melancholy lamentation to hysterical glee. It swoons and carps and pouts; it is sardonic, exultant, sensual, raunchy, philosophical, and yet it always remains a seamless entity. Within a single song, it deftly interlaces the increasingly complex verses within a sonically expanded tapestry.

In these mid-sixties masterpieces, the style is inextricable from the substance. They lead us through a distinctive poetic landscape that is unmistakably the property of an individual artist—hence the sixties neologism *Dylanesque.* Paradoxically, this very private landscape powerfully reflected a shared social reality, a reality of insurgency and reaction, and was understood as such at the time, subliminally and by inference, among a growing audience.

Complaints about the decline in musical taste begin only a little later than mankind's twofold discovery, on the threshold of histori-cal time, that music represents at once the immediate manifestation of impulse and the locus of its taming. It stirs up the dance of Mae-nads and sounds from Pan's bewitching flute, but it also rings out from the Orphic lyre, around which the visions of violence range

themselves, pacified. Whenever their peace seems to be disturbed by
bacchantic agitation, there is talk of the decline of taste.
>   —THEODOR ADORNO, "ON THE FETISH CHARACTER
>   IN MUSIC AND THE REGRESSION OF LISTENING"

Dylan's electric set at the Newport Folk Festival in July 1965 was to become, in Clinton Heylin's words, "the most written about performance in the history of rock."[5] And not without cause. Dylan's clash with the constituency from which he'd emerged, including individuals who'd sponsored his early career, was high Oedipal drama, marked by over-reaction on all sides. The moment was resonant. It was the fulcrum of the American sixties, as the early unity and idealism of the civil rights movement gave way to division and pessimism, the war in Vietnam intensified, and domestic opposition began to grow. The first glimmers of the counterculture were visible and the media was discovering that rebellion could sell. These interlinked trends infused Newport that July; they lie behind both Dylan's aggressively boundary-blurring sound and the divided response to it.

The day before Dylan's performance, there had been a backstage incident that foreshadowed the clash to come. Alan Lomax had given a grudging introduction to a session by the Paul Butterfield Blues Band, whose electrified instruments he was known to disapprove of. As he came offstage, he was confronted by an enraged Albert Grossman, who was hoping to manage the Butterfield band. The two men were soon grappling in the dirt. As a result, the Festival board voted to ban Grossman from the event, but had second thoughts when it realized that kicking out Grossman might mean losing his clients, including Dylan and Peter, Paul and Mary.

The Lomax-Grossman undercard bout carried much of the same symbolic import as the headline clash—Dylan versus (a section of) the Newport audience. Lomax was regarded by many as the incarnation of the Festival's values and historic roots. His work as an archivist, musical anthropologist, and proselytizer had made the folk revival possible. His field recordings and anthologies were foundation stones of Dylan's art and sensibility. Years later, Dylan paid tribute to him as "one of those who unlocked the secrets of this kind of music"—folk music in all its varieties. But in 1965 it was Grossman, not Lomax, who was in Dylan's corner. The smugly imperturbable entrepreneur was already widely resented at Newport, where many viewed him as a moneychanger at loose in the temple precincts. This year, his boy Dylan had grown bigger than the event itself; the singer-songwriter's every move drew crowds and cameras and created logistical chaos. Even before Dylan stepped on stage, there was a sense that the fragile ethos of the Festival was under threat.

On the bootleg recording of the Newport appearance, Peter Yarrow (of Peter, Paul and Mary) can be heard introducing Dylan to an ecstatic audience: this was "the face of folk music to the large American public," the man who had brought to it "the point of view of a poet." The groan of disappointment from the crowd when they are warned that Dylan has "only a limited time" to perform gives some notion of the expectations he aroused. But on that late Sunday afternoon Dylan confronted the 15,000-strong Newport throng as an alien. The ascetic blue jeans and work shirt had been discarded in favor of pointy leather boots, eye-popping polka dots, and dark shades. He seemed to some to be reinventing himself as a Beatlefied dandy. Backed by members of the Butterfield band, augmented by Al Kooper on organ, he played three songs: "Maggie's Farm" (released earlier that year on *Bringing It All Back Home*), "Like a Rolling Stone" (just released as a single), and an early version of what was soon to become "It Takes a Lot to Laugh, It Takes a Train to Cry" (which would be included on *Highway 61*). Accounts of his performance and the audience's reaction are numerous and conflicting. The bootleg shows Dylan on the top of his form, and while the rhythm section sometimes stutters, the performance as a whole is fresh and convincing. Mike Bloomfield's guitar crackles and Dylan's singing is artful and fluid, each phrase lovingly shaped. Nonetheless, Dylan's electric music met with the vocal disapproval of a large number of people at Newport (there's no agreement on how large a number). What's more, several prominent Festival figures made it clear that they abhorred the noise that Dylan was making. Those sixteen minutes of raging rock inaugurated a period of public conflict between Dylan and part of his audience, a drama that was to be played out in the U.S. and Europe over the coming year.

"You couldn't understand a goddamn word of what they were singing," Pete Seeger complained, years later.[6] The poor mix and the unrehearsed ensemble have been blamed for the new sound's rocky reception. But there's no doubt that the sheer volume was an issue, as it was to be at the Manchester Free Trade Hall ten months later. Dylan wanted to play loud music, and for the same reasons that many in the years (decades) to come wanted to hear it: the visceral thrill. To the soberminded side of the folk revival, the hedonism was alien. The meaning resided, at least in part, in the words, and they wanted to hear them. But the volume was part of Dylan's search for a bigger sound in more ways than one: he wanted his art to be an intense experience for all concerned, a discharge of hectic energy, a musical whole that was more than a lyric set to a tune. This was a music of emotional extravagance that the staid Newport format could not accommodate.

Of course, in going electric, Dylan was also trying to follow the new British bands up the charts. The scope for a commercial breakthrough had been confirmed by the success of the Byrds' folk-rock version of "Mr. Tambourine Man," one of the hits of the summer. The market for rock-tinged music played with electric guitars, bass and drums was clearly larger than the market for solo acoustic folk. But the accusation of sellout was and remains curious. Usually, selling out implies a compromise with popular taste, a watering-down, a sinking to a lower common denominator. But Dylan's border-busting sound of 1965 was nothing if not challenging—to radio DJs as much as to folk conservatives. "Like a Rolling Stone," released four days before Newport, was twice the length of a standard single. The language and imagery were far richer, more recondite than was customary on mainstream radio. Most importantly, the temper of the new songs was deliberately provocative. Dylan didn't sugarcoat the pill. He lacquered it with astringent.

Dylan's daring should not be underestimated. Here was an artist who abandoned a recognized niche not for facile populism but for an adventurous and demanding style, and somehow managed to find a new mass audience for it. When the bebop innovators moved away from swing-era conventions, they found themselves in an avant-garde wilderness. Dylan helped create a new audience by challenging, even offending, his existing one. For all the mixed motives, the intellectual confusion, it took guts and vision to pull this off. It also took the right mix of social circumstances, not least those upheavals from below that supplied both Dylan and his audience with the self-confidence to smash through established categories.

History vindicated Dylan, and in short order. "Like a Rolling Stone," booed at Newport, became a huge hit, detonating an explosion of ambition and experiment in the pop genre. Dylan himself proceeded to create his most majestic and complex work, proving that he could reach a mass audience without compromising his vision. "It was an artistic challenge to see if great art can be done on a jukebox," Allen Ginsberg observed, "and he proved it can."

Newport '65 is a cautionary tale for the left. It's a tale of a movement for social change blinded by dogmatism and orthodoxy, unable to embrace an original and challenging contribution. It's a tale of the dangers of condescending to popular culture, of the folly of fetishizing a genre. It's a tale of how a would-be counterculture, in seeking to program the artist, unknowingly emulated the dominant culture it sought to challenge. The people's champions, aiming to conserve the people's music, ended up ossifying it—and failed to recognize the authentic popular expression they were looking for when it took an unexpected form.

To this day, Lomax, Seeger, and their allies get a rough ride from many Dylan fans, as if their offense were fresh. But their objections to the new music were not as groundless, philistine, or shortsighted as some would claim.

It's important to understand what seemed so precious to the old guard, so worth preserving, and why Dylan going electric threatened it. The Newport Festival was a nonprofit enterprise with a social mission. It provided a then rare showcase not only for hard-hitting topical songs but also for neglected black and working-class artists. It acted as a link between the southern civil rights movement and the folk community of the urban North. Lomax, Seeger, and the like had suffered under Mc-

Carthyism, when the values of the popular front seemed to have been extirpated from American life. To them, Newport represented a cracking open of a long-closed door, a precious seed; it needed to be given appropriate nurture.

Also on the bill with Dylan that evening was Fannie Lou Hamer—the eloquently blunt MFDP militant who so affronted Johnson and Humphrey. It was possible to have someone like Hamer on the Newport platform because the Festival organizers could safely assume that the audience would share a political as well as a musical ethic. Indeed, to them, the two were one. They conceived the folk audience, and specifically the Newport crowd, not merely as an aggregate of consumers, but as a participatory community. They believed, not without reason, that this was a community whose bonds—based on shared values—would dissolve if it was invaded by market forces. And they identified these forces with teen-oriented rock 'n' roll. In keeping with a long Romantic tradition of hostility to technology—the vehicle of impersonal social dominance—they regarded amplified and studio-crafted music as inauthentic. In this context, as Oscar Brand, a veteran of the first folk revival, explained, "the electric guitar represented capitalism."

Lomax had been the pioneer of folk as a living tradition. He had responded positively to skiffle. As early as 1958, he had included rock 'n' roll in a presentation of American folk music. He had long been aware that the "folklore movement can have dangerous potentialities." It could be used to promote nationalist and racist ideas; it could be "petrified by improper use in education." In the "creative process of folklore . . . there may be many versions of a song, every one of which is as 'correct' as every other." Yet Lomax found Dylan's music of 1965 decidedly incorrect.

For Lomax, it was the democratic character of the folk tradition that made it live.

One might say that every folklore item has been voted on by a broad electorate, an audience free to choose, reject or alter according to his lights. The teller of tales or the singer of songs often affects community taste by his own style of performance; he may stoutly defend his own version as the only correct one; but he is always conscious, as few cultivated artists can be, of the needs and preferences of his audience. His is *of* his audience.[7]

That intimate relationship, that accountability of artist to audience, would not be possible when artist and audience were mediated almost exclusively by commerce, large corporations, and the electronic media. Years later, Lomax remarked:

> We now have cultural machines so powerful that one singer can reach everybody in the world, and make all the other singers feel inferior because they're not like him. Once that gets started, he gets backed by so much cash and so much power that he becomes a monstrous invader from outer space, crushing the life out of all the other human possibilities. My life has been devoted to opposing that tendency.

However wrongheaded the fear of rock 'n' roll, the apprehensions about the impact of the increasingly powerful mass media on anything that might be construed as a people's culture have proved well-founded. Dylan's innovative fusion helped to identify a new record-buying constituency, and thus proved a stepping stone in the construction of today's global music industry. Dominated by a handful of giant corporations, it is both more economically centralized and more socially segregated than ever, as executives calibrate the music to chime with ever-more refined demographics. Like the militants at the March on Washington, the defenders of the folk faith at Newport feared that their movement was being coopted by the blandishments of established power. Given the history of the sixties, and its treatment in after-years, Lomax and his allies ought to be given credit for their prescient insight into how, in a society dominated by corporate media, the cultural expressions of dissent could be transmogrified into profitable, politically malleable commodities. As the decades have rolled by, participation and collectivity—the roots of all vital popular culture—have been steadily replaced by passive individual consumerism. There have been repeated efforts to claw back the music from the corporate institutions:

punk, hip-hop, acid house, outlaw/alternative country. All have found their destinies intertwined with the industry they rose to challenge. As Lomax feared, the demands of authenticity and political independence do, in the long run, clash with those of commerce. What he misidentified, in 1965, was the field of battle and the weapons to hand.

From Newport, Dylan himself went straight back into the studio, undaunted, and cut the bulk of the demoniac tracks on *Highway 61 Revisited.* The departure from the folk revival and the embrace of electric music seemed decisive. But Dylan soon came to regret the stampede he touched off. As he made repeatedly clear in interviews, his allegiance to the old songs, to the traditions, remained undimmed, and he never ceased plundering them. In recent years, he has often lamented the weakening of the folk tradition, the severing of the links with a precorporate past. As for rock 'n' roll, he says in the *Biograph* notes of 1985, "it's now a highly visible enterprise, big establishment thing. You know things go better with Coke because Aretha Franklin told you so . . . in the beginning it wasn't anything like that. You were eligible to get busted for playing it . . . It's all been neutralized, nothing threatening, nothing magical. . . . Everything is just too commercial." [8]

Dylan returned to Newport, after an absence of more than three decades, in 2002. The Festival itself was no longer what it once was. Abandoned in 1970 (because of what its official website terms "growing social unrest"), it was revived in the mid-eighties, largely stripped of political aspirations. Today it occupies a cozy niche in the music industry. The title sponsor for the 2002 event was a company selling "natural juices" (it was also backed by Borders, the bookselling giant, and ABC television). Dylan donned a wig, false beard, and silly hat for the occasion, but played his usual set and made no reference to past events.

I don't call myself a poet because I don't like the word. I'm a trapeze artist.

—BOB DYLAN, 1965

Dylan's performance at Newport has been compared to the 1913 Paris premiere of Stravinsky's *Rite of Spring*. Although the comparison is an expression of the persistent desire to fit Dylan's work into the canon of high art, it's not entirely far-fetched. In both cases, an unexpected concatenation of the modern and the primitive flummoxed audiences raised on neat musical categories. In both cases, the defenders of the mould-breakers claimed they were creating a music as violent and disturbing as the world it was made in. But where Stravinsky was a modernist intellectual toying with the primitive, Dylan was much more an anti-intellectual primitive toying with the modernist. In the proto-punk "Outlaw Blues" he'd shouted:

> Ain't gonna hang no picture,
> Ain't gonna hang no picture frame.
> Well, I might look like Robert Ford
> But I feel just like Jesse James.*

During this period, in both interviews and songs, Dylan champions the claims of popular culture against the presumptions of the elite. He named Smokey Robinson as the greatest living poet. In the sleeve notes for *Bringing It All Back Home* he refers frequently to the conflicting claims of elite and popular culture, and aligns himself with the latter:

> . . . the fact that the white house is filled with leaders that've never been t' the apollo theater amazes me . . . if someone thinks norman mailer is

---

* Dylan knew Woody Guthrie's "Jesse James:"

> Now a bastard and coward called little Robert Ford,
> He claimed he was Frank and Jesse's friend,
> Made love to Jesse's wife and he took Jesse's life,
> And he laid poor Jesse in his grave.

> The people were surprised when Jesse lost his life,
> Wondered how he ever came to fall,
> Robert Ford, it's a fact, shot Jesse in the back,
> While Jesse hung a picture on the wall.

"No wonder folks likes to hear songs about the outlaws," Guthrie commented, "they're wrong all right, but not as half as dirty and sneakin' as some of our so-called 'higher-ups'. "

more important than hank williams, that's fine . . . i would rather model
harmonica holders than discuss aztec anthropology/english literature
. . . i know there're some people terrified of the bomb, but there are other
people terrified t' be seen carrying a modern screen magazine . . ."

Dylan rejects the notion that there are appropriate discourses for
discrete categories of expression or experience. The boundaries sepa-
rating high and low culture are blurred. The solemnity of public rituals
is punctured and satirized. Expertise and specialization are seen as pre-
tenses that substitute the part for the whole. Dylan's democratic (and
defensive) anti-intellectualism, his celebration of instinct, of change for
its own sake finds its nemesis in academic lifelessness.

You've been through all of
F. Scott Fitzgerald's books
You're very well read
It's well known

As Mr. Jones learns, art is no substitute for life, just as politics is no
substitute, and an art or a politics that cuts itself off from life—ugly,
ragged-edged, undefinable, unpredictable—becomes the enemy. In
contrast, popular culture offers immediacy, spontaneity, energy and,
above all, authenticity—an organic relationship with human experience. The contrast between the hollowness of elite art and the vivacity
and soulfulness of popular expression surfaces as an explicit theme in
"Desolation Row:"

And Ezra Pound and T.S. Eliot
Fighting in the captain's tower
While calypso singers laugh at them
And fishermen hold flowers

It reappears in "Visions of Johanna:"

Inside the museums, Infinity goes up on trial
Voices echo this is what salvation must be like after a while
But Mona Lisa musta had the highway blues
You can tell by the way she smiles

And in "Stuck Inside of Mobile with the Memphis Blues Again" Dylan spots "Shakespeare, he's in the alley / With his pointed shoes and his bells . . ." marvelously re-creating the bard as one of his troupe of spaced-out street jesters. In "Tombstone Blues," Dylan puts elite and popular art in bed together—expressions of refractory, authentically individual creativity—and identifies their common enemies in nationalist conformity, commercial exploitation, and academic institutionalization:

> Where Ma Raney and Beethoven once unwrapped their bed roll
> Tuba players now rehearse around the flagpole
> And the National Bank at a profit sells road maps for the soul
> To the old folks home and the college

In an interview in August 1965, Dylan spelled out his current views on the place of art in society:

> Great paintings shouldn't be in museums. Have you ever been in a museum? Museums are cemeteries. Paintings should be on the walls of restaurants, in dime stores, in gas stations, in men's rooms. Great paintings should be where people hang out. The only thing where it's happening is on radio and records, that's where people hang out . . . Music is the only thing that's in tune with what's happening. It's not in book form, it's not on the stage. All this art they've been talking about is nonexistent. It just remains on the shelf. It doesn't make anyone happier. Just think how many people would really feel great if they could see a Picasso in their daily diner. It's not the bomb that has to go, man, it's the museums.[9]

Thus, Dylan declared year zero of his cultural revolution, driven by the same tension between a democratic insurgency and the inadequacy of existing vehicles (institutional, ideological, cultural) that drove the SDS activists. Ironically, Dylan's Picasso-in-the-diner dadaism restates Picasso's own concern to rescue the life-enhancing, perception-changing power of art from conventional representation and the polite condescension of institutions.* For the early twentieth-century modernists, both revolutionary and reactionary, Western civilization was in a death grip, and the bourgeois culture spoon-fed to the masses was soulless. In this, they were heirs of the romantic critics of industrial capitalism who first began the quest for the authentic as an antidote to the dissatisfaction of the individual in an impersonal society. In Dylan, this long-standing critique entered mass culture itself. He articulated it in a popular idiom, into which he incorporated some of high modernism's box of tricks: fragmentation, allusion, ellipsis, rapid mood shifts, jagged juxtapositions, and challenging obscurity. Apart from the Beats, Dylan's reading was sporadic and undisciplined, but he was a magpie, and even a casual acquaintance with Eliot, cummings, the French symbolists, and the surrealists left traces in his work. For all the strident populism, Dylan in this period is without doubt a self-conscious, avant-garde artist.

Dylan prided himself on his knowledge of and roots in popular culture. But in reality, the breach between Dylan and the musical traditions he drew on was as qualitative as the breach that separated the modernists from their sources—the art of pre-Renaissance Europe or of "primitive" colonized cultures. Recorded music enabled Dylan to ransack the American musical heritage like Ezra Pound at loose in a library of medieval manuscripts. Within that heritage, Dylan responded to strongly individual voices. But where these individuals had defined themselves within a given musical idiom associated with a regional or racial identity, Dylan drew simultaneously on many idioms: Appalachian and British folk, Delta and urban blues, country and western, gospel, Chicago R&B, southern soul, Woody Guthrie, Brecht and Weill, first generation rock 'n' roll. His relationship with all these was one of choice and selection, guided by the driving desire to make something of

---

* When Colin Powell addressed the UN in early 2003, the tapestry replica of *Guernica* in front of which he sat was discreetly draped. It would seem that under the right circumstances Picasso's response to the advent of modern airial warfare retains its sting.

his own. Despite Dylan's multifarious sources, the one thing people didn't call him was eclectic.

Dylan did not respond to popular culture with the bleached blank stare of Warhol; the best of it moved him, spoke more directly to him than anything else, the worst of it pissed him off. The irony that infuses his treatment of this theme is not a postmodern one; it's firmly rooted in the individual's search for the authentic in an inauthentic society.

The liner notes for *Bringing It All Back Home* begin and end with a parable on the absurdity of Dylan's predicament:

> am standing there writing
> WHAAAT? on my favorite wall when who should
> pass by in a jet plane but my recording
> engineer "i'm here t' pick up you and your
> latest works of art. do you need any help
> with anything?"

After a lengthy aside, Dylan returns to the parable:

> an' so i answer my recording engineer
> "yes. well i could use some help in getting
> this wall in the plane"

The dilemma for Dylan was how to retain street cred in an industry that packaged and gutted the true product of the street. Having seen at firsthand the voracity of the trend-spotting media he worried about the fate of a popular art—graffiti, in the parable—when it's taken up by the corporate establishment.

Dylan was a college dropout with an audience of college students. He was an ambitiously avant-garde artist wary of pretentiousness and overearnestness, a self-conscious artist who aspired (like so many romantic poets before him) to un–self-consciousness. He was keen to legitimize his own art and to do that he had to challenge the legitimacy of the barriers that fenced in the elite; hence the double-edged name-dropping, giving a wink to the educated, the literary, the sophisticated, and at the same trashing their rarefied exclusivity.

Dylan's work of this period should be seen as part of a larger cultural movement. In literature, the sixties witnessed an impatience with "the well-wrought urn," a greater personal (and political) engagement, an invasion of informality—in the novels of Philip Roth or the poems of Robert Lowell and Adrienne Rich. The same movement can be seen in the films of the French New Wave—where high-art traditions were refreshed by pop culture and politics. Retrospectively, Dylan's work and his posture seem to have presaged a wave of canon-busting. By virtue of his artistic achievement and social impact, Dylan helped establish popular culture as an object worthy of academic study. Then, inevitably, the paradox of the authentic kicked in. On being informed that a museum of rock 'n' roll was to open, Dylan commented, "Nothing surprises me any more."

Hatred, to you I have entrusted my treasure
—RIMBAUD, *SAISON EN ENFER*

Among the many remarkable features of "Like a Rolling Stone" is the fact that the song with which Dylan cracked the pop charts was one of unremitting spitefulness. Having done so once, he had a stab at the same thing twice more within a few months, releasing "Positively 4th Street" in September 1965 and "Can You Please Crawl Out Your Window?" in December. Indeed, for the crime of pointing out the repetition involved in the last of the trio, Phil Ochs found himself banished from Dylan's inner circle.[10]

One of the movement's traits that Dylan carried with him into his post-protest phase was the combative self-righteousness he had claimed to spurn on *Another Side*. The exultantly vindictive note of the three singles of late 1965 was already there in "When The Ship Comes In"; "Masters of War" and "Hattie Carroll" had been unyieldingly unforgiving. But in the songs of 1965 the spleen is strictly person to person. It becomes, in a way, the real matter of the music. Dylan here unashamedly glories in the weakness or misfortune of others. This upfront indulgence in personal unpleasantness was a far cry from the demure, upbeat or sentimental attitudes favored by both folk and pop conventions. In more ways than one, it was a new kind of sound in mainstream white popular culture.

Muddy Waters, a onetime Lomax protégé, recorded his R&B classic, "Rollin' Stone," in 1951. At the time, its success was confined to the black market, but it became a cult item for young British blues fans and gave Jagger, Richards, and Jones the name for their band. The lyric is a declaration of personal independence—a macho disavowal of responsibility or permanence of affections:

> Well, my mother told my father,
> just before I was born,
> "I got a boy child's comin,
> He's gonna be, he's gonna be a rollin' stone"

Dylan's song seizes on the metaphor from a different angle. It becomes a punishment and a prison, but also a common fate, an underlying reality. From the snare-shot opening and the surge of organ and piano, "Like a Rolling Stone" is permeated by a kind of ecstasy of schadenfreude. The ensemble rises and falls on waves of bitterness. The guitar gloats. The voice taunts: "How does it feel?" In this sustained six-minute epic of vituperation, the writing is relentlessly single-minded, yet ever-surprising. The sense of millennial confrontation that riddled Dylan's protest phase here takes on a life of its own, abstracted from any but the most personal context, and unleashed as a scornful, unpitying spirit—which was also a spirit of unmistakable freshness and energy. One of Blake's "Proverbs of Hell" commands: "Drive your cart and your plough over the bones of the dead," and there's something of the same diabolic exuberance in Dylan.

"Like a Rolling Stone" is addressed to someone raised in privilege who finds herself fallen among the dispossessed:

> You've gone to the finest school all right, Miss Lonely
> But you know you only used to get juiced in it

And nobody has ever taught you how to live on the street
And now you find out you're gonna have to get used to it

In her heyday, the song's subject used and abused the people around her, and mistook their service for personal loyalty. Class resentment mingles here with the resentment of a rejected lover, and the eager triumphalism of an erstwhile outcast.

The seminal status of "Like a Rolling Stone" is about more than its impact on the rock 'n' roll format. It's about the song's intimate rage and almost amoral assertion of personal autonomy—a defiant response to a world that insisted on tearing away that autonomy at every turn. "Like a Rolling Stone" was Whitman's "barbaric yawp" broadcast on AM radio.

"Positively 4th Street" has always been seen as Dylan's fuck-you to the folk set. It was indeed written shortly after the Newport clash, and 4th Street in the Village was full of folk- and protest-era associations for Dylan. But apart from the title, the song is deliberately unspecific; there's no setting here, just the drama of the singer spurning false friendship. Compared to "Like a Rolling Stone," its language is plain and its verse form simple. The song lambastes insincerity and opportunism ("You just want to be on / The side that's winning") but also displays a perverse preoccupation with social hierarchy and power relations.

And now I know you're dissatisfied
With your position and your place
Don't you understand
It's not my problem

Sometimes, the status consciousness seems pure teen angst:

I know the reason
That you talk behind my back
I used to be among the crowd
You're in with

The least commercially successful of the three singles, "Can You Please Crawl Out Your Window?" was also, musically, the closest to the pop-rock sounds then topping the charts. With its cymbal figure, aggressive guitar licks, and catchy chorus it sounds like the British beat of the Animals or Them. Unlike the earlier singles, this was a seduction song, with Dylan trying to win the favors of the woman in question by savaging her current lover. It was jokier and gentler, but Ochs was right to see its kinship with "Like a Rolling Stone" and "Positively 4th Street."

The targets of the singer's contempt in these songs are charged with the great sin in the Dylan mid-sixties universe: substituting pretense, artifice or image for the raw unpredictability of life: "You shouldn't let other people get your kicks for you." The rival lover in "Can You Please Crawl Out Your Window?" is one of Dylan's straw men of academic lifelessness: "With his businesslike anger and his bloodhounds that kneel . . . He just needs you to talk or to hand him his chalk." Once cast down, humbled, these people will learn how unreal and unimportant were the props they used to assert their superiority over others.

Emotions in these songs are unprettified ("You'd rather see me paralyzed"); the exultant, taunting conclusions of "Like a Rolling Stone" ("You're invisible now, you got no secrets to conceal") or "Positively 4th Street" ("what a drag it is / To see you") offer no quarter to the vanquished. Marrying vindictive glee to the adrenalin kick of rock 'n' roll, Dylan here elevated the put-down to an art form. In this respect he might be seen as a forerunner of the aggressively insulting strand of hip-hop. But, in Dylan, the snarling arrogance always carried undertones of anxiety and doubt.

In "Like a Rolling Stone" and "Positively 4th Street," the wheel of fortune has turned. Dylan has risen to the top—and revels in it—and those who mocked or spurned him have plummeted. But there is nothing permanent here. In a whirligig society, eminence is precarious. That's why the most important lesson is that "when you ain't got nothin' / you got nothin' to lose." In "Like a Rolling Stone," the disinvestment in society's trappings that Dylan counseled in "My Back Pages" or "To Ramona" or "It's Alright Ma" becomes the actual fate of the person addressed by the singer—there are no more "alibis." This fate is both a comeuppance, a fitting revenge, and a potential liberation.

In all of these songs there is an element of self-portraiture and self-address. The rival lover of "Can You Please Crawl Out Your Window?" could be Dylan himself:

Preoccupied with his vengeance
Cursing the dead that can't answer him back

In "Like a Rolling Stone," "Napoleon in rags" (ridiculed for "the language that he used") is surely a Dylan cameo. The song only attains its full poignancy when one realizes it is sung, at least in part, to the singer himself: he's the one "with no direction home." Dylan's declaration that he doesn't owe anything to anybody is, of course, a defensive ploy, an attempt to insulate himself from betrayal or disappointment, or indeed the changes in fashion and fortune that seemed to be coming thick and fast in these years. "Like a Rolling Stone" is at one and the same time a self-aggrandizing construction, an exercise in bluster, and an astonishingly candid confession.

It's evident from these songs that Dylan was more hurt by criticism than he liked to let on. Out of his retreat from the movement, his break with former associates, and his thin-skinned reaction to critics, Dylan fashioned rich, robust works of art. But they are no more or less the "authentic" Dylan than the self-abnegating songs of social protest. The posture of rude resentment was as much a mask as the Woody Guthrie accent had been. Dylan poured into and through the mask—and by means of the mask—the same sense of commitment, confrontation, and danger that had made him stand out among the folksingers. The emerging teenage audience heard it and identified with it. Bruce Springsteen recalled the moment precisely:

The first time I heard Bob Dylan, I was in the car with my mother listening to WMCA, and on came that snare shot that sounded like somebody'd kicked open the door to your mind: "Like a Rolling Stone." My mother—she was no stiff with rock 'n' roll, she liked the music—sat there for a minute, then looked at me and said, "That guy can't sing." But I knew she was wrong. I sat there and I didn't say nothing but I knew that

I was listening to the toughest voice that I had ever heard. It was lean and it sounded somehow simultaneously young and adult.[11]

Whatever you say, don't say it twice
If you find your ideas in anyone else, disown them
The man who hasn't signed anything, who has left no picture
Who was not there, who said nothing:
How can they catch him?
Cover your tracks.
    —BERTOLT BRECHT, "HANDBOOK FOR CITY-DWELLERS"

You arrive in London. You're besieged by the press. The first question you're asked is: "What is your message for young people?" You are yourself a young person, incomplete, still in formation. The world around you is changing rapidly and you're not sure what to make of it all. Under the circumstances, Dylan's answer—"Keep a good head and always carry a lightbulb"—seems as fitting as any.[12]

The young Dylan sought fame as determinedly as any ambitious entertainer. But fame quickly became a burden and a terror to him. From the moment that *Newsweek* exposed the new Woody Guthrie as a Jewish college dropout from Minnesota (and not the vagabond orphan he had claimed to be), Dylan recoiled from the media. He certainly craved and sometimes enjoyed the attention. But he bridled as they dubbed him a protest singer. He winced as they hailed him as the voice of a generation. From the beginning, he refused to smile for the cameras. From the beginning, he was jealous of his autonomy and reluctant to play the media game. Like Woody Guthrie in the Rainbow Room, Dylan faced an industry that seemed bent on stealing his soul.

As one of the first youth celebrities of the television era, Dylan's predicament was unenviable. Put yourself in his place. You don't recognize the pictures of you painted in the media. You don't know who this Bob Dylan is that people keep asking you about. You want to have fun, seek out thrills, hang with friends, have adventures, be selfish, be loved, but now all this must be done in the glare of the spotlights—all the growing and doubt and experiment. All kinds of people have expectations of you. You're asked to explain and justify everything, but you can't because you're winging it, moving restlessly forward on intuition and inspiration, and as far as you're concerned it's perfectly obvious what you're doing.

Dylan wanted to be merely an individual, and for the songs to speak for themselves. He longed to slough off the burdens of representation foisted on him by the media and the movement alike. He was desperate to reclaim his personal identity from the public sphere—not least because nothing true, nothing authentic, could survive in that sphere. Ironically, his very restlessness and elusiveness, his disregard for categories, made him ever more representative of his era and his generation. And that further complicated his search for authenticity. It seemed this was a race without a finishing line.

The inadequacy of language and the difficulties of communication in a corrupt society were already themes in his earlier work, but between 1964 and 1966, they move to the center of the canvas. The ineffability of personal experience haunts "Gates of Eden:"

> At dawn my lover comes to me
> And tells me of her dreams
> With no attempts to shovel the glimpse
> Into the ditch of what each one means
> At times I think there are no words
> But these to tell what's true
> And there are no truths outside the Gates of Eden

What stood outside the gates of Eden was nothing less than the entire social order, and certainly the media. In his battle to reclaim a self from nascent celebrity culture, Dylan engaged in these years in a running joust with the press. Bombarded by obtuse, unhip, cliché questions, or often, questions that were perfectly fair but for which he simply had no answers, he was by turns flippant, taciturn, jocular, enigmatic, surly, playful. Who was his favorite folk singer? "Peter Lorre." Was he in good health? "I don't see well on Tuesdays." Was he married? "If I answered that I'd have to lie to you." At times, he turned the press conference into a form of performance art. But witty or rude, it was all an elaborate defense mechanism. A way of speaking from behind the veil of protective silence:

> I got my dark sunglasses,
> I'm carryin' for good luck my black tooth.
> Don't ask me nothin' about nothin',
> I just might tell you the truth.

It was also an act of protest, a dadaist challenge to a reductive social order. It was a protest against labels in an era in which labels proliferated, as Dylan himself explained in the *Biograph* notes:

> Like the term beatnik or hippie. These were terms made up by maga-
> zine people who are invisible who like to put a label on something to
> cheapen it. Then it can be controlled better by other people who are
> also invisible.[13]

In this light, "Ballad of a Thin Man" looks like one of the purest songs of protest ever sung. In "The Times They Are A-Changin' " Dylan had warned the older generation: "don't criticize / What you can't understand." In "Ballad of a Thin Man" the wall of incomprehension between the conscious vanguard and mainstream society has become impenetrable. Despite its reputation for tantalizing obscurity, the lyrics seem to me plain enough. The song's starting point is Dylan's take on the media, its interest in and inability to comprehend him and his music.

> You walk into the room
> With your pencil in your hand
> You see somebody naked
> And you say, "Who is that man?"
> You try so hard
> But you don't understand
> Just what you'll say
> When you get home

From here, Dylan reworks his favorite duality: the forces of lifelessness versus the enlightened few. The cryptic drama enacted around Mr. Jones subverts his identity and exposes his hollowness. He is the man who hands in his ticket to "go watch the geek" only to discover that he himself is viewed by others as "a freak." He is the man whose assumptions are derived from books, from newspapers, from academia, from anywhere but life itself. He has to use his "contacts" to get the "facts" when "someone attacks" his "imagination;" and he's one of the well-heeled liberals Dylan thought he was attacking at the ECLC dinner:

> . . . they already expect
> You to just give a check
> To tax-deductible charity organizations

No one but Dylan would or could have turned the phrase "tax deductible charity organizations" into a rock 'n' roll howl, an irresistible sing-along punch line. The song is a nihilistically impish attack on the acceptance of a spoon-fed, prepackaged, and safely homogenized reality. It sneers at those who refuse to dare, to cross boundaries, to taste the forbidden rawness of life. Only recently have critics picked up on the sprinkling of homosexual hints in the song, though they seem rather obvious. A man is offered a bone; a sword swallower clicks his high heels; says, "here's your throat back thanks for the loan"; a man who's told he is a cow and asked for his "milk"; not to mention those lumberjacks in verse four. No one should be too surprised at finding a gay subnarrative in Dylan's work of this period. He certainly knew gay men in the Village; Allen Ginsberg had made little secret of the sexual attraction he felt toward Dylan. In any case, the gay masquerade, the reference to another hidden subculture, a world obscured and protected by an exclusive code, reenforces the main drift of the song.*

There's a long-running debate about who Mr. Jones really was, but the anonymity is part of point. Mr. Jones is anyone who stands baffled, inert, a cipher, in the face of outlandish reality. The spooky

---

* For Huey Newton's interpretation, see pages 208–209.

organ riffs (elegantly elaborated by Garth Hudson when Dylan unleashed this pointed tune on critical audiences during his 1966 tour)
suggest junky Hollywood horror, a suitably mordant accompaniment
to this deliberately disjointed "ballad." The sardonic refrain—"something is happening but you don't know what it is"—seemed deeply
alien to the spirit of "The Times They Are A-Changin,' " but was not
unrelated to it. Here too a demarcation was being celebrated, part
generational, part political, part cultural. Only here new elements—
the demarcations between private and public, between what can and
cannot be named—are superimposed. The refrain epitomized the hip
excluvisity that came naturally to those young people who saw themselves as having possession of a deeper insight than those around
them. Disgusted by the old, excited by the new, frustrated by their inability to be heard and understood, elated by their discovery of others
who shared their feelings, they wanted to be part of an underground.
Dylan's music offered them a passport to it. "Ballad of a Thin Man" is
the anthem of an in-group, a self-identified minority. Dylan wrote it
out of sense of besieged isolation, but to a growing audience his
music offered mutual discovery and a sense of inclusion. To young
people, in the end, the message was clear enough.

In February 1965, SNCC activists meeting in Atlanta had been stunned
when Bob Moses, the most universally respected figure in the organization, announced that it was "time to leave." Warning that SNCC leaders
were becoming creatures of the media, he looked at Lewis, Stokely
Carmichael, Forman, and did not spare himself. "My name is no longer
Bob Moses," he finished. "I am Bob Parris now." (Parris was his middle
name.) Then he walked out of the meeting. Those remaining behind
sang "Will the Circle Be Unbroken." A year later, Moses/Parris left the
country.[14]

"Until 1964, 'the movement' had depended upon its own people to
carry information from place to place," Julius Lester observed. "Meetings were small, 'movement' publications few and people depended

upon direct contact with each other to keep informed and since there were always a fair number of people in motion, this was not difficult." But in the mid-sixties, Lester noted, "the media became more and more prominent as the carriers of 'movement' information . . . the 'movement' took advantage of the media's new interest in it and began to consciously use and eventually depend upon the media to be the agent for information rather than depend upon its own people and organs." [15] As a result, the ties of accountability that bind leaders to movements were weakened; images and catchphrases took precedence over ideas and organization.

The underground community into which Dylan's mid-sixties music offered initiation was bound together not only by an exclusive jargon but also by a privileged, near incommunicable but somehow tangible political vision.

The contempt for authority is omnipresent in these songs. Whether it's employers, cops, politicians, preachers, or generals, they are always both dangerous and preposterous. In "Desolation Row," "the blind commissioner" is "in a trance / One hand is tied to the tight-rope walker / The other is in his pants." In "Just Like Tom Thumb's Blues," "all the authorities / They just stand around and boast / How they blackmailed the sergeant-at-arms / Into leaving his post . . ." In "I Want You," "The drunken politician leaps / Upon the street where mothers weep" and in "Memphis Blues Again," "the senator came down here / Showing ev'ryone his gun, / Handing out free tickets / To the wedding of his son."

In particular, the state and its agents—DAs, judges, deputy sheriffs, even the coast guard—are portrayed as arbitrary and violent forces erupting into the life of the individual. "The riot squad they're restless / They need somewhere to go . . ." It was definitely a symptom of the times that this young man who had known primarily comfort and success should display such a predilection for persecution fantasies:

Look out kid
It's somethin' you did
God knows when
But you're doin' it again

Retrospectively, it's surprising that the Newport audience failed to recognize "Maggie's Farm" as a song of political protest.* True, there were no explicit topical references, no comfort noises for the movement. But the song is laced with antiauthoritarian venom, class and generational resentment. One of its sources is "Down on Penny's Farm," a sharecroppers' lament that Dylan would have heard on the Harry Smith *Anthology:*

You go to the fields
And you work all day,
Till way after dark, but you get no pay,
Promise you meat or a little lard,
It's hard to be a renter on Penny's farm.

Dylan had already filched the song's chorus ("It's hard times in the country, / Down on Penny's farm") for his early "Hard Times in New York Town," but what surfaces in "Maggie's Farm" is the *Anthology* tune's complaint against expropriated labor. Though Dylan knew little of the world of work, he kept a jaundiced eye fixed on it. In this song wage labor appears as a prison propped up by ideology ("she talks to all the servants about man and god and law") and the state ("the national guard stands outside her door"). Its fury is aimed not just at the employing class but at the work ethic and the subordination of the human personality to employment. Like other Dylan songs of this period, "Maggie's Farm" is an antagonistic encounter between the aspirations of the individual and a grotesquely dehumanized society.

Well, I try my best
To be just like I am,

---

* The song's political punch endures. In Britain in the early eighties, it made an apposite anthem for those resisting Margaret Thatcher's neoliberal authoritarianism and supplied the title for cartoonist Steve Bell's long-running anti-Tory lampoon.

But everybody wants you
To be just like them.
They say sing while you slave and I just get bored.
I ain't gonna work on Maggie's farm no more.

Conformity to social expectations had always been a satirical target in bohemian subcultures. But in Dylan's songs of the mid-sixties, that conformity has become more insidious, more subtly pervasive, and more lethal to the human spirit. In "Subterranean Homesick Blues," the experience of growing up is depicted as an empty ritual designed to produce compliant servants of the system:

Ah get born, keep warm
Short pants, romance, learn to dance
Get dressed, get blessed
Try to be a success
Please her, please him, buy gifts
Don't steal, don't lift
Twenty years of schoolin'
And they put you on the day shift

The proletarianization of the white-collar, college-educated workforce was a theme of sixties left theory, as was a renewed interest in Marx's critique of the human alienation inherent in wage labor. To some extent, these trends reflected a wider effort to locate an agent of change to fill the void left by what appeared to be a politically passive industrial working class. It also reflected a sixties tendency—visible in both the United States and Western Europe—to cast the relatively privileged in the role of the dispossessed. If middle-class white boys were going to sing the blues, they had to have the blues, and how were they going to get them? They didn't know the lash of factory or field, but they still felt the discontents of a society in which their own lives seemed to be prefabricated. In "Maggie's Farm," the energy with which Dylan throws himself into single combat with the bosses seems to obviate doubts about the authenticity of his posture. Indeed, it establishes its own authenticity by its ferociously direct mode of individual declamation. Dylan doesn't write about the travails of the workplace, he places himself in direct confrontation with it. The refusal in the refrain—"I ain't gonna work on Maggie's farm no more"—is much wider than the one in "Let Me Die in My Footsteps" ("I will not go down under the ground"). For Dylan, the whole system of social inducements is a con, a ruse to secure obedience and extract labor. People subscribe to it only out of a fear of life and freedom, as he'd argued in "It's Alright, Ma":

> For them that must obey authority
> That they do not respect in any degree
> Who despise their jobs, their destinies
> Speak jealously of them that are free

Dylan sees the worship of Mammon as the core sickness of his society. It filters into and devalues all human intercourse. In "It's Alright, Ma" he rants against commercialization: those "human gods" who "Make everything from toy guns that spark / To flesh-colored Christs that glow in the dark." The sin is to seek ownership, to transform the ample and unpredictable flood of life into a commodity. Outside the Gates of Eden, "Relationships of ownership / They whisper in the wings;" in the "kingdoms of Experience" (an apt reference to Blake) "paupers change possessions / Each one wishing for what the other has got." Mammon, like the state, is to be held in contempt: "They asked me for some collateral / And I pulled down my pants."

In "Masters of War," Dylan had argued succinctly that the worship of Mammon bred war. And war and violence in general remain nullifying horrors in Dylan's mid-sixties dystopia. However, they have here become both generic and immediate. Chaos and destruction are not confined to foreign fields; in "On the Road Again," they intrude into everyday life:

> Well, there's fist fights in the kitchen
> They're enough to make me cry
> The mailman comes in
> Even he's gotta take a side

Even the butler
He's got something to prove
Then you ask why I don't live here
Honey, how come you don't move?

This is capitalist society wracked by the war of all against all. It is also, specifically, American capitalist society. In Dylan's songs of the mid-sixties, social patriotism is replaced by a sour distrust of that dangerous construct called America. The alternative America of the folk revival has vanished from sight. In "Bob Dylan's 115th Dream"—a hyped-up talking blues full of slapstick surrealism—the contempt for the very idea of America and its vaunted special place in the human family is lacerating and unforgiving. On the album cut, the first take is aborted by Dylan's hysterical giggle, which effectively sets the scene for a social journey so disorienting and disturbing that laughter seems the only suitable response. The song begins with Dylan "riding on the Mayflower" under the leadership of Captain A-Rab—blending the national foundation story with a tip of the hat to Melville's epic:

"I think I'll call it America"
I said as we hit land
I took a deep breath
I fell down, I could not stand . . .

What Dylan finds in his new world is a society of paranoia, violence, and treachery. Every effort he makes to communicate with its denizens gets him into ever deeper trouble:

Well, I rapped upon a house
With the U.S. flag upon display
I said, "Could you help me out
I got some friends down the way"
The man says, "Get out of here
I'll tear you limb from limb"
I said, "You know they refused Jesus, too"
He said, "You're not Him . . ."

Even the movement that promises an alternative to the country's dog-eat-dog brutality proves useless. Dylan runs into "a building / Advertising brotherhood" only to discover that "it was just a funeral parlor." The song's finale is an unequivocal kiss-off to America:

> But the funniest thing was
> When I was leavin' the bay
> I saw three ships a-sailin'
> They were all heading my way
> I asked the captain what his name was
> And how come he didn't drive a truck
> He said his name was Columbus
> I just said, "Good luck."

You can hear the breakdown of social patriotism once again in the raucous and macabre "Tombstone Blues," an assault on jingoism and militarism that reaches beyond "With God on Our Side;" it's not so much a public critique as a public reproduction of a private vision of a society corrupted at its core by hypocrisy and warfare. In the first verse, we learn that "The city fathers they're trying to endorse / The reincarnation of Paul Revere's horse"—our rulers forever reinventing the founding patriotic myth, which is also a legend of war. Dylan assures us that the town "has no need to be nervous." But clearly, that's not the case, for it's "Jack the Ripper who sits / At the head of the chamber of commerce." The chorus is as raw as anything in seventies punk:

> Mama's in the fact'ry
> She ain't got no shoes
> Daddy's in the alley
> He's lookin' for some food
> I'm in the kitchen
> With the tombstone blues *

---

* In the published lyrics, it's "a fuse" that Daddy's looking for. But on the record, he seems to be searching for more organic sustenance.

The existence of class exploitation and poverty is bluntly asserted, with no frills. Here Dylan is the disaffected offspring of working-class parents, gazing in disbelief and impotent rage at the social elite that rule over them. The unchanging desperation of the parents' daily lives is a counterpoint to the cruel antics of the rich and powerful. Verses three and four are probably the closest Dylan comes in this period to a statement about the horrors of Vietnam. Verse three begins with the loyal John the Baptist torturing a thief, then asking "his hero" (his god), the commander-in-chief (at this time President Lyndon Johnson), "Is there a hole for me to get sick in?"

> The Commander-in-Chief answers him while chasing a fly
> Saying, "Death to all those who would whimper and cry"
> And dropping a bar bell he points to the sky
> Saying, "The sun's not yellow it's chicken"

Verse four opens on a scene of biblical slaughter, where the king of the Philistines "saves" his soldiers by putting "jawbones on their tombstones" and flattering their graves. He "puts the pied pipers in prison and fattens the slaves / Then sends them out to the jungle." *Desert* might have been more in keeping with the Biblical setting, but in 1965, it was the *jungle* that American soldiers were being sent to. In that jungle, Dylan's warriors turn barbarous: "Gypsy Davey with a blowtorch he burns out their camps." And it's all "To win friends and influence his uncle." Who might or might not be Uncle Sam.

Underlying the songs of the mid-sixties is a conviction that public life as a whole is a savage, obscene charade. In this context, expressions of national pride or purpose are nothing but the self-serving lies of a debauched elite.

The story of Abraham's near-sacrifice of Isaac is told in Genesis, chapter 22. For no reason other than to test his servant's loyalty, God orders Abraham to murder his only son. And for no reason other than to demonstrate his loyalty, Abraham agrees and sets out on the grim task. At the final moment, as the father is about to slaughter the son, an angel intervenes to offer a sacrificial ram in the son's place. Meditating on the ancient text as an example of a distinctive mode of "representing reality," the polyglot literary critic Erich Auerbach noted the abrupt, mystery-laden character of the narrative, in which much is left unexplained, and much implied. The story is pregnant with meanings, and cries out for interpretation.[16] In traditional Christian exegesis, the sacrifice of Isaac was a prototype of Christ's sacrifice on the cross. "For the lord so loved the world that he gave his only begotten son." But artists have often responded uneasily to the pat teleology of that version. Caravaggio highlighted the anguish of Isaac, depicting the sacrifice as a violent assault with sexual overtones. Rembrandt was also fascinated by the story. In a late etching of compact power he dwells on the moment of deliverance: an angel of strength and gentleness enfolds both the ravaged, bewildered father and the unseeing victim-son.

In Kierkegaard's *Fear and Trembling,* the sheer ethical and emotional impossibility of Abraham's situation gives rise to a meditation on the individual's relationship to the absolute, and a critique of the inauthentic social and spiritual existence of bourgeois Europe. For Kierkegaard, the sentimental stress on the "happy ending" deprived the story of its grandeur and significance. But in lifting the individual out of history, he ended up, in his own way, condescending to a barbarous tale from a barbarous age. An opposite tack was chosen by Wilfrid Owen in his poem, "The Parable of the Old Men and the Young." The biblical tale is retold, succinctly, but with the props of World War I at hand: the "fire and iron" and "the parapet and trenches." When the Angel arrives with "the Ram of Pride" to take Isaac's place, Abraham rejects the offer. The poem ends:

> . . . the old man would not so; but slew his son
> And half the seed of Europe, one by one.

The generational indictment would have been recognized and immediately attractive to Dylan, though there's no reason to think he ever read Owen. Dylan encountered the Abraham and Isaac story in the course of his Jewish education, where it would have been presented as one of the dramatic highlights of the Old Testament, a tale of how God demands much from His chosen people, but in the end, at His own time and bidding, redeems all. However, in the aftershock of the European Holocaust, it wasn't at all clear to many Jews of Dylan's generation that God would ever stay the executioner's hand. (Here's where Zionism entered, offering the appearance of a redemptive denouement.) In "With God on Our Side," he'd charged human agents with self-righteously appropriating the right to slaughter, but in the opening, supercharged verse of "Highway 61 Revisited," he goes back to Genesis and puts the spotlight on God Himself (or one version of Him):

> Oh God said to Abraham, "Kill me a son"
> Abe says, "Man, you must be puttin' me on"
> God say, "No." Abe say, "What?"
> God say, "You can do what you want Abe, but
> The next time you see me comin' you better run"
> Well Abe says, "Where do you want this killin' done?"
> God says, "Out on Highway 61."

This is a rewrite of Genesis 22:1–3, and nearly as economical. In the informal and contemporary diction, there's a note of satire from the first. The song kicks off with a shrill police whistle, a demented hoot signaling both a mock emergency and manic party-making. With the galloping boogie-woogie of Al Kooper's piano in the background and Mike Bloomfield's spiky guitar commentaries, Dylan fires out the words in rapid syncopated succession, each one clear and arch, and recasts the drama as part minstrel show, part jive dialogue, and part Punch and Judy.

The god who snarls, "kill me a son," is a lazy, down-home version of the cruel, vengeful, jealous God of the Old Testament, the Urizen deity whom Blake wanted to overthrow from the seat of religion and the state (and the Moloch whom Ginsberg cursed). There's nothing here to hint of the coming of an angel of deliverance—these were the days when Dylan could not abide a happy ending. The overall tone is one of disbelief—at the cruelty of the sacrifice and the wanton arbitrariness of an authority that would demand it. Crucially, bewilderment has grown so intense it has prompted a protective emotional detachment, or at least the appearance of one. Dylan's work of this period is saturated with the hip recoil from the horrors of public life, not least the incomprehensible waste of war and violence. The characteristic rhetorical question is: Just how crazy can this scene get? A cool hysteria prevails. It is the tension between that distancing recoil and the relentlessly engaged energy of rock 'n' roll (and Dylan's own highstrung, endlessly fidgeting personality) that gives the song power and depth, and makes this unorthodox take on the biblical tale so shockingly vivid.

In Dylan's version, the locale of sacrifice has shifted from the land of Moriah to Highway 61, an American Grand Trunk Road, running from the Gulf of Mexico to the Canadian border, for much of the way following the course of the Mississippi. In its northern reaches, it passes not far from Duluth; in Dylan's youth its icy, empty stretches claimed many a speeding teenage driver. Crucially, Highway 61 links the land of the North Country blues to the setting of "Only a Pawn in Their Game." It crosses the Mississippi Delta and leads to Memphis—the first stage of the great African American migration from rural to urban, a trek that gave the world the blues, R&B, rock 'n' roll, and soul. Dylan knew Highway 61 from his visit to Greenwood and from the old blues songs themselves ("I started school one Monday mornin', baby, I throwed my books away / I wrote a note to my teacher, Lord, I'm gonna try 61 today . . . Lord, if I have to die, baby, fo' you think my time have come / I want you to bury my body, out on Highway 61"). He knew it was not only a route of escape and opportunity, but a venue of sacrifice and exploitation, a place where the human spirit was bought and sold, and where the individual was isolated. It's far from Woody

Guthrie's limitless highway and closer to Robert Johnson's infernal crossroads.*

In the second verse we learn that Highway 61 is where those who have been stripped bare by "the Welfare Department" are directed—at gunpoint. In the third it's where patriotic hucksters with Runyanesque names like "Mack the Finger" and "Louie the King" try to flog "forty red white and blue shoe strings / And a thousand telephones that don't ring." And in the fourth verse, a helter-skelter parody of biblical genealogy, the mad pedantry of racial classification ("my complexion, she said, is much too white") leads to a suggestion of incest—"the second mother was with the seventh son / And they were both out on Highway 61." In the final verse, Highway 61 is the place where war becomes a commodified spectacle:

> Now the rovin' gambler he was very bored
> He was tryin' to create a next world war
> He found a promoter who nearly fell off the floor
> He said I never engaged in this kind of thing before
> But yes I think it can be very easily done
> We'll just put some bleachers out in the sun
> And have it on Highway 61.

The song links the sacrifice of Isaac to the present-day nexus of media, money, and warfare. The military-industrial complex he'd damned in "Masters of War" has become a military-industrial-entertainment complex. Highway 61 is now not only a place of pointless suffering and cruelty, it's also a locus of commercial interchange; it's

* From Robert Johnson's "Crossroads:"

> I went to the crossroads, fell down on my knees
> Asked the Lord above, have mercy now, save poor Bob if you please
>
> Standin' at the crossroads, tried to flag a ride
> Didn't nobody seem to know me, everybody pass me by
>
> Standin' at the crossroads, baby, the risin' sun goin' down
> I believe to my soul now, po' Bob is sinkin' down

the public sphere twisted by the parasitic PR industry. It's a place where the worth of human beings is relentlessly annihilated. Judging by the trappings, it's something like contemporary America. And where does Dylan himself figure in that imagined country? His father was Abe Zimmerman; if he's associated with the "Abe" in the first verse, then Dylan becomes the sacrificial victim. No doubt Dylan, the Isaac-figure, the artist whose soul was being packaged and purchased, saw himself as one of the victims of Highway 61, even as in singing about it he made as clear a protest against its death logic, the logic of Abraham's sacrifice, as he had in "Let Me Die in My Footsteps." Only now the protest was made for its own sake, with no hope of changing anything. A grim entertainment, a jocose lifeline spun from a pitiless reality.

———————————

I saw pale Kings, and Princes too
  Pale warriors, death pale they were all;
They cried, La Belle Dame sans Merci
  Thee hath in thrall
—JOHN KEATS, "LA BELLE DAME SANS MERCI"

Cameron Crowe said that Dylan in the sixties wrote "songs about the politics of love." [17] That's apt. There's a preoccupation with claim and counterclaim, with status and power, with accusation and self-justification. There is also a wide range of emotions at work in these songs—many of them decidedly unattractive, few of them generous or affectionate, all of them intensely wrought.

Initially, what Dylan brought to the love song was a greater realism and candor. "We never did much talkin' anyway . . . you just kind of wasted my precious time . . ." He rejected the one-size-fits-all romantic typology familiar from pop music; sex, love, companionship, friendship, are carefully discriminated, but also in flux. The songs castigate insincerity and demand honesty. But they are also remarkable for their staggering self-deception and evasiveness.

Many of Dylan's songs take the form of an appeal to a woman to grant the singer her favors. In this they share common ground with the songs of the troubadours and trouvères, the *ghazals* of Persian and Urdu, African American blues, and a great deal of popular music everywhere. The lover addresses, coaxes, cajoles, argues with the beloved. As a suitor, Dylan likes to cast himself as the egalitarian lover who asks for and offers nothing, the straight-shooter who says simply, here I am, here's how I feel, what happens next is up to you. In the languorous "Mama, You Been on My Mind," he is a modest and undemanding admirer:

I am not askin' you to say words like yes or no
Please understand me, I got no place for you to go

He stresses that "it don't even matter to me where you're wakin' up tomorrow." In "It Takes a Lot to Laugh, It Takes a Train to Cry", the bluesy, plaintive atmosphere, redolent with timeless mysteries (sun, moon, woman), is interrupted by a remarkable declaration:

Well, I wanna be your lover, baby,
I don't wanna be your boss.

So Dylan did indeed apply the democratic individualism he celebrated elsewhere to personal and sexual relationships. But he was not the liberated male he made himself out to be. In "If You Gotta Go" (one of the songs from the *Bringing It All Back Home* sessions left off the album), he seems to be making an argument based on the freedom and mutual honesty of the two potential lovers: "If you gotta go / it's all right / but if you gotta go, go now / or else you gotta stay all night." While he insists there's no pressure—"I want to be with you, gal / if you want to be with me"—the song lays on the pressure, verse after verse. "I certainly don't want you thinking that I ain't got any respect," he says, but observes a few lines later: "It ain't that I'm wantin' / anything you never gave before." In "Can You Please Crawl Out Your Window?," he urges the object of his suit to choose risk over security, spontaneity over calculation, i.e. Dylan over his rival. He argues forcefully that this rival is merely using her as an adjunct to his frozen ego. But in return he offers nothing but the spur of the moment. As if to reassure her (and protect himself) the chorus ends with the repeated line: "You can go back to him any time you want to."

In "Queen Jane Approximately," Dylan offers himself as the lover of last resort, the one who demands nothing and who accepts the beloved without illusions. When "you want somebody you don't have to speak to / Won't you come see me, Queen Jane?" Dylan could hardly be accused of overselling himself. But there is almost always a sense that, despite the little he offers them, the women are getting a bargain. Indeed, in the very minimalism of his offerings there is an implied honesty and authenticity that exposes and undercuts the illusions of both his lovers and his rivals. He's the real one, and if they reject him, they reject reality. In "4th Time Around," his reworking of Lennon's "Norwegian Wood," he spells out what he offers and what he expects:

And I, I never took much
I never asked for your crutch
Now don't ask for mine

In "One of Us Must Know (Sooner or Later)," he tells a former lover, "I really did try to get close to you." But much of the song explains how he really always meant to keep this lover at a distance. And all of it is about disclaiming responsibility for the failure of the relationship: "I didn't realize how young you were . . . I couldn't see where we were goin' / but you said you knew an' I took your word."

The women cannot win in Dylan's songs. In the exquisite "Love Minus Zero / No Limit" Dylan describes his ideal lover, who "speaks like silence," is "true, like ice, like fire" and, crucially, "knows too much to argue or to judge." This was the ethic of innocence embraced by the post-protest, "younger than that now" Dylan. Strikingly, many of his accusations against women echo his criticisms of the movement; in the personal as well as the political, the great enemy is the impulse to categorize or control or appropriate others. But silence itself does seem to be what the Dylan of these songs prefers from his women. The graveyard woman, soulful mama, junkyard angel who takes care of the singer in "From a Buick 6," who can be relied on to keep his bed warm in a cold, chaotic universe, is praised because:

she don't make me nervous, she don't talk too much
She walks like Bo Diddley and she don't need no crutch*

The flawless Sad Eyed Lady celebrated at such mournful length in *Blonde on Blonde* is shown, in verse after verse, besieged by exploiters, phonies, and power freaks, but speechlessly, passively impervious to their corrupting blandishments. Yet turn this glacial indifference around and it becomes one of Dylan's major complaints against women. In the ironically titled "She Belongs to Me" (the point of the song is that she doesn't), the unattainable woman is resented because she "never stumbles," "The Law can't touch her at all." The "Bankers' nieces" are disparaged for seeking "perfection, / Expecting all the gifts that wise men bring."

Dylan flails women whom he sees as desexed and uptight, as in the portrait of Ophelia in "Desolation Row":

On her twenty-second birthday
She already is an old maid
To her, death is quite romantic
She wears an iron vest
Her profession's her religion
Her sin is her lifelessness

In "Tombstone Blues," he ridicules "the hysterical bride" who thinks she's "been made:"

Now the medicine man comes and he shuffles inside
He walks with a swagger and he says to the bride
"Stop all this weeping, swallow your pride
You will not die, it's not poison"

But it's not just those women who spurn desire who come under attack, it's also those who indulge it. In "Just Like Tom Thumb's Blues," Dylan finds himself marooned south of the border: "they got some hungry

---

* Male R&B chauvinism may be the starting point for "From a Buick 6," but it's worth noting that the song reaches into less charted realms. As in many of Dylan's compositions of this period, erotic attachments become existential conundrums.

women there / and they really make a mess out of you." One verse is dedicated to the attractions and perils of Sweet Melinda, the prostitute whom the peasants call "the goddess of gloom." Dylan warns: "She steals your voice and leaves you howling at the moon" (an orgasm reference?). Stuck inside of Mobile, Dylan responds to Ruthie's invitation to visit "her honky-tonk lagoon" by warning her: "you must know about my debutante." To which she replies: "your debutante just knows what you need / but I know what you want." A memorably insinuating line as well as an unthinking expression of the familiar dualism in male perceptions of womanhood. Sexless Ophelia or "the hungry women;" frigid or predatory; elite or earthy; unattainable or attainable—and either way despised and resented.

The double-standard saturates Dylan's love songs of this period. In "I Don't Believe You," the refrain is an unappeasable complaint: "She acts like we never have met." Yet Dylan could perform this in the same set in which he sang: "When we meet again, introduced as friends, please don't let on that you knew me when." One of the things Dylan does effectively in many of his love songs is to evoke the passage of time and its ineluctable impact on relationships. Alongside that, he also seems deeply agitated about shifts in social status, who's gone up and who's coming down, who's out and who's in.

> You will start out standing
> Proud to steal her anything she sees.
> But you will wind up peeking through her keyhole
> Down upon your knees.

In "Most Likely You Go Your Way and I'll Go Mine," he depicts love as a contest, a power game. Whoever is left on top when the music stops wins:

> Then time will tell just who fell
> And who's been left behind,
> When you go your way and I go mine.

In this song, Dylan is unsparing in his repudiation of a woman whom he sees as not being up to his own standards: "you know you're not that strong . . . you know how hard you try." But when a rival lover appears in the final verse, he also holds that against her ("You say my kisses are not like his"). This is one of a number of songs in which Dylan situates himself inside a ménage à trois. In "Visions of Johanna" he watches "Louise and her lover / so entwined." In "Can You Please Crawl Out Your Window?," "Temporary Like Achilles," and "Leopard-Skin Pill-Box Hat" ("I saw him makin' love to you / you forgot to close the garage door"), he's the third wheel, the one left on the outside, clamoring to be let in. In "She's Your Lover Now," a bitter dissection of a failed romance (cut at the *Blonde on Blonde* sessions but left off the album), he declares with an air of betrayed innocence:

> You know I was straight with you.
> You know I never tried to change you in any way

The song is remarkable for the sustained petty rage it directs at both the woman and her new lover, and the utter failure of this rage to bring even temporary relief to the singer. It's a heady and affecting mix of desire, regret, jealousy, and disgust.

"I Want You" has the simplest and most conventional of all love-song titles, but it's packed with enigmatic imagery and haunted by ambivalent emotions. The slinking, intricate first verse evokes a fluid, ghostly, treacherously ephemeral environment in which desire itself seems the only thing that's fixed and real, though not its objects. In fact, the object of Dylan's obsession in this song scarcely exists; there's no flattery, no effort to seduce her. The point of the song is that desire cannot be explained or justified. Despite rejection, competition, friends' counsel, and his own better judgment, Dylan *wants* her, and that is pain and pleasure rolled into one. In the final verse the singer is driven to assault a rival, then collapses into a stammering wreck. But in the meantime Dylan vents his anger at women in general in a harsh, stunningly cynical bridge:

> Now all my fathers, they've gone down
> True love they've been without it.
> But all their daughters put me down
> 'Cause I don't think about it.

Without doubt, misogyny and sexism are rampant in Dylan's music. In the songs of the mid-sixties, he does see women as an alien species, fascinating, necessary, but not to be trusted. The locus classicus of that prejudice has always been seen as "Just Like a Woman." However, any song that begins with the magically drowsy "nobody feels any pain" and climaxes with the howl "what's worse / Is this pain in here" must be more than the sum of its tired patriarchal put-downs. The discovery of the vulnerability of the woman/girl he desires but cannot fully possess touches and angers the singer; he revels in her weakness, seizes on it for the leverage it may give him, but finds that even then she remains elusive. The steady, circular rhythm over which the singer murmurs (the melody is subtly extended and the lyric delicately teased out) gives way to a dramatic bridge of rising frustration, and the singer's emotional collapse, segueing back to the verse with the bathetic "I just can't fit." It's a plea of utter helplessness. The vulnerability of the woman is in the end the vulnerability of the (male) singer. There's a little boy lost inside that little girl.

Dylan's appearance in these years has often been described as androgynous. (It's one reason why this image remains attractive when so much sixties machismo has palled.) Apart from "Ballad of a Thin Man," and a handful of references to queens, drag shows, and the like ("The beauty parlor is filled with sailors," "The waitress he was handsome / He wore a powder blue cape," the fifteen jugglers are "all dressed as men"), there is a broader element of sexual ambiguity, of uncertainty about personal identity, in these songs. There is also a camp theatricality in much of Dylan's delivery and self-dramatization, not least in "Just Like a Woman."

This song spawned more cover versions than any other track on *Blonde on Blonde,* including several by women—Judy Collins, Nina Simone, Roberta Flack, Stevie Nicks. My favorite is an obscure one: a jazzy, cabaret-haunted remake by Barbara Gosza, an American performer working in Europe. With the aid of a few strategically placed amendments to the lyrics, notably the substitution of *I* for *she* in the final chorus—Gosza remakes the male dirge as a torch-song celebration of lesbian love.[18] But she couldn't have done that so successfully if there wasn't, in the original itself, a powerful element of erotic ambivalence.

Dylan built "Leopard-Skin Pill-Box Hat" on Lightnin' Hopkins's "Automobile Blues," and the song shares Hopkins's sly humor. It's a neatly coded tale of erotic pursuit and jealousy, of fashion accessory turned sexual fetish ("Honey, can I jump on it sometime?"). There's a tone of comic detachment throughout, nowhere more effective than in the verse where he unexpectedly finds his doctor with the woman he desires (and to whom the song is addressed):

> You know, I don't mind him cheatin' on me
> But I sure wish he'd take that off his head
> Your brand new leopard-skin pill-box hat

Once again, Dylan finds himself a reluctant troilist. It's as if the games people play in private have proved as mind-bendingly bizarre as the public realities from which Dylan had turned away, and can only be faced with something like that mixture of sangfroid and barely disguised panic that fills "Highway 61 Revisited." Although "Leopard-Skin Pill-Box Hat" has an element of woman-baiting, its satire is broader than that. After all, the woman may be ridiculed for her attachment to a piece of frivolous millinery, but the singer himself appears positively obsessed with it.

In these songs, we see again and again the ridiculous spectacle to which people reduce themselves in pursuit of their erotic-romantic desires (which turn out more often than not to be as inauthentic as their political illusions). Sometimes, as in "Leopard-Skin Pill-Box Hat," and in the marvelous "Absolutely Sweet Marie," the despair is lightened with self-mockery. Self-pity, however, remains the prevailing mode, an unabashed, delirious self-pity that somehow leaps beyond moralism and becomes a strangely exquisite pleasure-pain in its own right. There's a simultaneous sense of huge power and total helplessness and, throughout, an undertone of vulnerability, fear, and loneliness. The songs are redeemed by the sheer authenticity of the confusion: emotions given a powerful and concise artistic expression long before they have been assimilated or understood by the person feeling them. This undigested immediacy stands in contrast to the more conscious, long-range analysis of relationships that fills *Blood on the Tracks*. The contradictions, the double standards, are all expressions of a boy-man lost in a world of temptations and frustrations, torn between the thirst for autonomy and the siren song of complete surrender. ("Yes, I guess I could live without you / if I just did not feel so all alone"). It's the richness of interlayered emotions that makes these songs live. An inverted Bessie Smith, frail and bleached out, "helpless like a rich man's child," Dylan blends lust and contempt, longing and fear. Not a healthy cocktail, perhaps, but nonetheless a potent artistic brew.

It's often said that sexual liberation in the sixties merely liberated men to exploit women. Personal freedom and frankness became masks for self-serving irresponsibility. And you can see that syndrome blazed in neon in the Dylan of the mid-sixties. But what you will also find there is a poetry of the disorientation that follows the (forever incomplete) escape from inherited sexual norms. The songs are full of Dylan's discontent with (elements of) conventional male-female relationships and with his (and others') failed attempts to construct an alternative. The political parallels are clear: in personal relationships, it was also year zero, only no one came to this launching pad without millennia of acquired expectations. You can feel Dylan scratching at the walls of his misogyny, trying to break or sneak or fake his way out of it. Then reeling back exhausted, unable to fathom or name his prison. There's a poignancy in that.

In the thirties, Theodor Adorno had declared, *"All contemporary musical life is dominated by the commodity form."* Those leftists who made democratic claims on behalf of popular music he dismissed with scorn. They missed the totality within which that music was created. "The culture industry intentionally integrates its consumers from above . . . the listener is converted, along his line of least resistance, into the acquiescent purchaser." In so doing, the industry strips listeners and artists alike of real autonomy, of the power to change the system that the music serves. "The consumption of light music contradict[s] the interests of those who consume it."

Adorno's theory was carved out in response to the defeat of revolutionary hopes and the triumph of fascism in Europe. Though he lived on to 1969, he never altered the main thrust of his critique. The real social content of popular music, he insisted, was determined not by singers and songwriters but by the manner in which it was produced and consumed. What he called "regressive listening" was, for Adorno, the hallmark of a bankrupt age. The appeal of popular music rested on "standardization" (the familiarity of genres), simplistic repetitive structures, "comfortable and fluent resolutions." In order to reproduce itself, and sustain listeners in the illusion that they ever heard anything genuinely new, popular music promoted "pseudo-individuation"—minor stylistic embellishments. In fact, "the liquidation of the individual is the real signature of the new musical situation."

To Adorno, the youth obsession with rhythmic music was symptomatic of a society where the possibilities of genuine collective action or individual autonomy had been all but blotted out. "Their primitivism is not that of the undeveloped, but that of the forcibly retarded." He mocked the "jitterbugs," whose very appellation had been "hammered into them by the entrepreneurs to make them think that they are on the inside. Their ecstasy is without content." The enthusiast for popular music was merely "the prisoner who loves his cell because he has been left nothing else to love." [19]

Thanks to recorded music and radio, the culture industry subordinated all forms of musical expression to its overriding dictates.

> It forces together the spheres of high and low art, separated for thousands of years. The seriousness of high art is destroyed by speculations about its efficacy; the seriousness of the lower perishes with the civilizational constraints imposed on the rebellious resistance inherent within it as long as social control was not yet total. [20]

Dylan would seem to invalidate Adorno. His work demonstrated the capacity of popular music to crack open the social monolith, to alter individual perceptions, to stimulate resistance. He made the familiar a vehicle for the unfamiliar.

Adorno's vision was restricted because he placed a model derived exclusively from the European art-music tradition at the center of his aesthetic universe. In doing so, he discounted not only the folk and popular musics of the West but also the "classical" musics of non-Western peoples. In a way, his demand for a disjuncture from the social mechanism was more radical and uncompromising than Dylan's. But Adorno treated popular culture as an undifferentiated mass (he would say that people like me are seduced by the veneer of differentiation). His vision of the culture industry as a force pressing remorselessly downward on atomized individuals left no room for resistance, for forces (however disparate, limited or contradictory) pressing upward.

Adorno also discounted the complex impact of the new popular access to traditional music. Through recordings, artists of Dylan's generation could select and permutate from a wider range than their forebears. In doing so, and in renovating popular music through this activity, they fulfilled the hopes Harry Smith had expressed in his *Anthology* notes. It's important to recognize that Dylan was never merely an automaton, an extension of the phonograph, absorbing and reproducing the newly available traditions. He brought to these traditions a critical perspective. That perspective was profoundly shaped by the mass movements of his era. So although the source elements and musical structures of Dylan's art may have been familiar, it was aesthetically fresh. It allowed the genuinely new—the ideas and feelings generated by a distinct historical experience—to flood into the commercial arena.

Yet the resonance of Adorno's vision has grown since his death. The culture industry—now more commercially and globally integrated—does seem something of an all-devouring protean force, insinuating its products into the daily lives of billions. It appears able to appropriate with ease even the most incendiary creations. Dylan himself seems to have come to agree with Adorno. In his usually acid comments on the music business, he's noted the homogenizing and sanitizing role of the big corporations and repeatedly complained that whenever the industry gets its hands on anything challenging, anything authentic, it neutralizes it. He saw earlier than many that the putative counterculture would be easy meat for this industry. Many of his dadaist stratagems were designed to shake his audience out of the habit of "regressive listening." Ironically, and unknowingly, Dylan smuggled into popular music much of Adorno's avowedly elitist critique. You can hear it running through songs from "It's Alright Ma" to "I Dreamed I Saw St. Augustine."

Like the British Communist Party, Adorno saw in popular music a means by which working-class youth were integrated into a system that oppressed them. But Adorno did not share the party's view that this was an expression of "cultural imperialism." For him, the problem was not that commercial music would make the new generation slaves of America but that it would make them slaves of the commodity fetish in general. His antidote to the poison of a mass culture that pacified workers was not the recovery of national or folk heritage, but a pursuit of the intransigently avant-garde, the last redoubt of musical freedom. By Adorno's own admission, however, that freedom was impotent: it could not shift the current imbalance of social forces.

Adorno seems to have prophesied the dilemma that loomed ever larger for Dylan as the sixties wore on. The new audience's "revolts against fetishism only entangle them more deeply in it. Whenever they attempt to break away from the passive status of compulsory consumers, they succumb to pseudo-activity." In what might serve as a sour epitaph on Dylan's music, Adorno proclaimed that "popular music . . . mummifies the vulgarized and decaying remnants of romantic individualism." [21]

———————————————

Everybody must get stoned. It's one of Dylan's most plainspoken lines, almost a slogan. It's unlikely it would get the airplay now that it did in late 1966. Dylan has always been coy about drug-taking, and given the prevailing wind on drugs from official America in the last three decades, that's not surprising. Still, he's the man who turned the Beatles on. The drug experience is there, in the songs, not merely in arcane references ("her fog, her amphetamine, and her pearls") but also as a kind of running subtheme.

The impact of drugs on the modern sensibility can be traced from at least the time of De Quincey, who was awed by "the apocalypse of the world inside me" induced by opium. For Baudelaire, taking hashish expressed a (self-defeating) "longing for the infinite." For Walter Benjamin, "hashish, opium or whatever else can give an introductory lesson" in what he called "profane illumination, a materialistic, anthropological inspiration." For Mezz Mezzrow, the Brooklyn Jewish jazz musician, smoking muggles and being a viper was about existing "in another plane and another sphere . . . we liked things easy and relaxed, mellow and mild, not loud or loutish." For Allen Ginsberg, the New Jersey Jewish intellectual, cannabis and hallucinogens were "stimulators of perception," instruments for "the augmentation of the senses" and "the exploration of modes of consciousness." ("I was somewhat disappointed later on," said Ginsberg, "when the counterculture developed the use of grass for party purposes rather than study purposes.") [22] For Dylan, the Minnesota Jewish folksinging college dropout, drug-taking was all these things, and more.

In the sixties recreational drug usage underwent an exponential increase, and became widespread in communities where it had hitherto been unknown. In general, the new market for drugs arose out of a desire to escape, not so much from the daily harshness of wage labor as from the uniformity and emptiness of a preplanned existence. Its spread reflected, in part, the same intersection of social insurgency with changing consumer demographics that shaped Dylan's sensibility and music.

The old left had recoiled from the druggy hipsterism of the bebop musicians, and they recoiled from the druggy hipsterism of Dylan in the mid-sixties. Ginsberg was not alone in constructing a counterargument that embraced drug-taking (of certain kinds) within a radical social vision. Indeed, the era was remarkable for the sheer weight of ideology and elevated motive foisted upon this particular form of pleasure-seeking. While the notion that drugs could or would be an instrument of social liberation now lacks force, it would be wrong to underestimate the political character that drug-taking (of certain kinds) took on at this time.

Drugs were in the forbidden zone. That was a key part of their initial attraction. To white kids, they were associated with black experience. What was on offer here was risk, release, transcendence, authenticity, harmless pleasure—all at relatively little cost, especially for those with time on their hands and money to spend. Nonetheless, it should be remembered that taking drugs, especially in those days, made you an outlaw. Smoke a joint and a wall of antagonism rose up between you and the state. That antagonism was a powerful material and psychological reality. It lies behind the persecution complex that races through "Subterranean Homesick Blues," which starts its hyperventilating progress with Johnny "in the basement / Mixing up the medicine" and Dylan "on the pavement / thinking about the government:"

Maggie comes fleet foot
Face full of black soot
Talkin' that the heat put
Plants in the bed but
The phone's tapped anyway
Maggie says that many say
They must bust in early May
Orders from the D. A.
Look out kid
Don't matter what you did
Walk on your tip toes
Don't try "No Doz"

Paranoia was a key word in the counterculture and in its construction of the drug experience. At the wrong time or place, taking drugs was a ticket to a state of unbridled apprehensiveness (see *Fear and Loathing in Las Vegas*). Social reality itself became threatening. But just because you're paranoid doesn't mean you're not being persecuted. Social reality *was* threatening. As the decade wore on, drug charges were increasingly used to harass political dissidents (among the more well-known victims were John Sinclair and John Lennon).

Incurring the potential wrath of the state reenforced a sense of social isolation among drug users but it also forged a communal bond. "I would not feel so all alone" was the consolation Dylan offered. In smoking a joint or dropping a tab of acid you became one of the underdog soldiers of the night. You became part of a community, with its own protective jargon and quicksilver references, not a few of them culled from Dylan's work. That made you feel special, privileged, one of the cognizant minority. But unlike the coded drug references of earlier subcultures, unlike the ghettoized bebop generation, the drug-related songs of the second half of the sixties—including Dylan's—reached out to ever wider layers of the population. As more people experimented with drugs, more people broke the code. But it never ceased to be a code, for all its popularity; indeed, the codedness was—as with the obscurity—part of the appeal.

Apart from "Mr. Tambourine Man" (the prototype for a thousand trippy anthems), Dylan's presentation of the drugs experience is decidedly ambivalent. The drug-taking he's writing about is less hippie than punk: it's about speed and smack and pills as much as hallucinogens and weed, about compulsion as well as escape. The drug fiends in "Desolation Row" sound miserable souls: "sexless patients" trying to blow up Dr. Filth's "leather cup," the "local loser . . . in charge of the cyanide hole." In the final verse of "Just Like Tom Thumb's Blues," there is a sense that the singer has found himself out of his depth, trapped in a murky medium that leaves him both exposed and isolated:

I started out on burgundy
But soon hit the harder stuff
Everybody said they'd stand behind me
When the game got rough
But the joke was on me
There was nobody even there to call my bluff

In "Stuck Inside of Mobile with the Memphis Blues Again," "the rainman" offers Dylan "two cures"—"Texas medicine" and "railroad gin."

An' like a fool I mixed them
An' it strangled up my mind,
An' now people just get uglier
An' I have no sense of time.

Hardly a paean to the delights of drug-taking, yet there's no moralism. The same perplexed, impotent ambivalence underpins even the deliriously unserious "Rainy Day Women #12 & 35." With its rudimentary lyrics, honky-tonk piano, trombone and tuba strutting and slurring like a drunken marching band, this track is a marvelous one-off, even in Dylan's catalogue. It's a comic charade in which the singer paints himself as a helpless victim: "they'll stone you when you're trying to be so good." "They" (friends? enemies?) appear to be inescapable and ubiquitous. Getting wrecked is here depicted as an involuntary, entirely passive experience. It's something that just sneaks up on you; an ambush by an uncontrollable and arbitrary force. The same self-mocking abdication of personal irresponsibility was celebrated jokily in the *Fabulous Furry Freak Brothers* comics. In Dylan, however, the languorous ethos takes on a more desperate edge. Getting stoned is not something you choose to do but that you're driven to do by the madness of ordinary life and your inability to master it. "They'll stone you and then say you are brave," but Dylan is not so sure. For Dylan, part of the attraction was the surrender of the will, the submission to his own weakness.

Of course, "getting stoned" carries a double meaning. The use of the active voice—the verb *to stone*—invokes the biblical punishment. It's what happens to the woman taken in adultery and the heretic alike, the turning of the community against a nominated outcast. It happens in the midst of daily life—at work, at play, every time you step on the public stage, every time you step off it—and it happens to everyone. It's as inexplicable and as insistent as the drugs ambush. In "Rainy Day Women" transcendence and persecution are inextricably mixed. As in other Dylan songs of the period, personal freedom and social fatalism appear as matched distorting mirrors.

When Dylan and his electric band played Berkeley in early December 1965, the singer handed Allen Ginsberg a fistful of free tickets, which Ginsberg distributed to poet friends like Michael McClure and Gary Snyder as well as to novelist turned LSD-dispensing Merry Prankster Ken Kesey and the Hell's Angels bikers he was courting at the time. At a party afterward, Dylan gave Ginsberg the cash to purchase a state-of-the-art, battery-operated reel-to-reel tape recorder—so that the poet could dictate his words while on the road. The tape recorder proved a vital tool in the composition of what was to become *The Fall of America*, published in 1972.[23]

That collection begins with Ginsberg "speeding through space" listening to "Radio the soul of the nation" where he hears "Bob Dylan's voice on airways, mass machine-made folksong of one soul." In "Hiway Poesy: L.A.—Albuquerque—Texas—Wichita," which he composed on tape at the end of January 1966, he also tunes into the Kinks and the Beatles, Barry McGuire's crass Dylan-simulation "Eve of Destruction" and, distressingly, Barry Sadler's pro-war hit, "The Ballad of the Green Berets."

> What patriot wrote that shit?
> Something to drive out the Indian
>   Vibrato of Buffy Sainte-Marie?
>   Doom call of McGuire?
> The heavenly echo of Dylan's despair
>   Before the silver microphone
>   in his snake suit
>   a reptile boy
>   disappearing in Time—
>   soft shoe dancing on the Moon?

Two weeks later, Ginsberg composed "Wichita Vortex Sutra," which he described as "big Shelleyan poem ending Vietnam war—wrote it on tape machine betwixt Lincoln and Wichita."[24] The poem is a restless collage of mid-American impressions: billboards, small towns, farms, factories, wastelands through which courses the mind-splitting horror of Vietnam. With the "American eagle beating its wings over Asia," on the home front "students awaken trembling in their beds / with dream of a new truth warm as meat / little girls suspecting their elders of murder / committed by some remote control machinery." For Ginsberg, the war is the ultimate expression of long-entrenched, life-denying currents in American culture:

> Carry Nation began the war on Vietnam here
> > With an angry smashing axe
> > > Attacking Wine—
> Here fifty years ago, by her violence
> Began a vortex of hatred that defoliated the Mekong Delta . . .

Against and within this dehumanized, war-deranged America, the poet raises his voice, bard-like, to bring into being a new America, purged of violence and materialism:

> I lift my voice aloud
> > Make mantra of American language now
> > > here declare the end of the War!
> > > > Ancient days' illusion!—
> And pronounce words beginning my own millennium.

And his heart is lifted as he hears Dylan's voice—the voice, he thinks, of a new America—reaching out to him through the desolate spaces:

> Oh at last again the radio opens
> > Blue Invitations!
> Angelic Dylan singing across the nation
> > "When all your children start to resent you
> > Won't you come see me, Queen Jane?"
> > His youthful voice making glad
> > > > The brown endless meadows
> > His tenderness penetrating aether
> > > Soft prayer on the airwaves . . .

"Wichita Vortex Sutra" proved to be Ginberg's major work of the sixties, and one of the most ambitious and sustained attempts to address the America of the Vietnam years in poetry. It was published in April

1966 in *The Village Voice,* and soon after appeared in the *Los Angeles Free Press,* the *Berkeley Barb,* and *Peace News* in Britain. The poetic style that had seemed esoterically experimental in the fifties had become a popular protest vehicle in the sixties. As Ginsberg's repeated invocations of him suggest, Dylan was the fulcrum of that transition. He was also, in Ginsberg's vision, the dividing line between war-making, money-mad, puritanical America and its nascent alternative, the forerunner of a "return to the original religious shamanistic prophetic priestly Bardic magic!" [25] Yet, while Ginsberg was celebrating Dylan as the elfin incarnation of a new consciousness, Dylan felt himself impotent and immured.

Whoever stubbornly insists on his mere so-being, because everything else has been cut off from him, only turns his so-being into a fetish. Cut off and fixed selfness only becomes, all the more, something external.
                    —THEODOR ADORNO, *THE JARGON OF AUTHENTICITY*

The climax of "Desolation Row" is a brutal vision of persecution in which social control is depicted as a form of torture.

> Now at midnight all the agents
> And the superhuman crew
> Come out and round up everyone
> That knows more than they do
> Then they bring them to the factory
> Where the heart-attack machine
> Is strapped across their shoulders
> And then the kerosene
> Is brought down from the castles
> By insurance men who go
> Check to see that nobody is escaping
> To Desolation Row

Here, the state, the ideologues, the forces of money conspire to distort and destroy the living human being. In the song's final lines Dylan howls:

Right now I can't read too good
Don't send me no more letters no
Not unless you mail them from
Desolation Row

"Desolation Row" is a refuge and an annihilation, the exclusive abode of authenticity, the haunt of those who have stripped themselves—or been stripped of—all social investments. Communication outside its confines is suspect at best. Dylan recorded the song days after the Newport imbroglio, along with "Just Like Tom Thumb's Blues," another study of displacement and immobility. Here Dylan finds himself stranded in some hazily illuminated, sour and stale border town limbo land. In this song, however, he seems to wallow in his predicament:

I cannot move
My fingers are all in a knot
I don't have the strength
To get up and take another shot
And my best friend, my doctor
Won't even say what it is I've got

"Just Like Tom Thumb's Blues" captures the picaresque wanderings of a tiny individual amid a world of giant forms. There's something in it of the poignancy of the gate-crasher bewildered at the welcome he has received and edgily awaiting his inevitable exposure and expulsion.* He's seduced and soon disillusioned by sex and drugs, fame and fortune—all of them only dimly apprehended as they swim in and out

* One source for the title of the song may be Rimbaud's poem "Ma Bohème"—whose second verse has been translated: "My only pair of breeches had a big hole. A dreamy Tom Thumb, shelling out rhymes on my path. My inn was at the sign of the Great Bear. My stars in the sky made gentle rustling noises."

of his ken. He learns how inconsequential he is: "Don't put on any airs when you're down on Rue Morgue Avenue." He observes the dangers surrounding him. His friend Angel "looked so fine at first" but after the local law got through with him "he left looking just like a ghost." Dylan's Tom Thumb stumbles through this fuzzy fantasy land with a kind of louche wariness.

> If you're lookin' to get silly
> You better go back to from where you came
> Because the cops don't need you
> And man they expect the same

Not a darkly threatening environment, but a treacherous one from which, in the final, bleary-eyed lines, he posits an escape to firmer ground.

> I'm going back to New York City
> I do believe I've had enough

One of the glories of this song is its creation of a viscous, opaque medium in which forward movement (if that's what it is) is felt as a drifting backward. It's a prolonged moment of suspension. There's a similar kind of drowning rock 'n' roll in "Stuck Inside of Mobile with the Memphis Blues Again," recorded six months later. Here thwarted escapism blends with a sense of impending doom. "Can this really be the end?" Dylan leans back and belts out the chorus; he seems to be (almost) enjoying the experience. The song begins with an enigma: the silence of the ragman ("I know that he don't talk") and a foregone conclusion: though the singer's prison may be a soft one ("The ladies treat me kindly"), "I know I can't escape." Communication is impossible—"the post office has been stolen / and the mailbox is locked." And forget about riding the rails because "the railroad men just drink your blood like wine." In verses four and five, we get a glimpse of what Dylan is trying to get away from: Grandpa is crazy and violent and the Senator is a reckless opportunist. But once again, Dylan's bid to escape is foiled:

An' me, I nearly got busted
An' wouldn't it be my luck
To get caught without a ticket
And be discovered beneath a truck.

Neither drugs (verse seven) nor sex (verse eight) extricate him from his limbo. In the finale, his thoughts turn again to New York and his companions from the Village—the "neon madmen" carefully assembling their latest constructions on Grand Street—and contrasts their (apparently) purposeful activity to his own stalled inertia:

An' here I sit so patiently
Waiting to find out what price
You have to pay to get out of
Going through all these things twice

The mysteriously impassable distance between Mobile, the Gulf Coast oil town, and Memphis, the great honey pot on the Mississippi, is the distance between depression and elation, isolation and community, anonymity and recognition, fatalism and freedom. The journey from one to the other is constantly obstructed, and in the end, like the circles of the ragman, returns to its starting point.*

Dylan's definitive treatment of "strandedness" is "Visions of Johanna," a song he wrote in November 1965. Unlike most of the material on *Blonde on Blonde*, he brought it to the studio as a finished composition. It has always been recognized as a major work, and it boasts one of the most intoxicating and suggestive of all Dylan openings:

Ain't it just like the night to play tricks when you're tryin' to be so quiet?
We sit here stranded, though we're all doin' our best to deny it

---

* In the nineties, the pop-flamenco guitarist Kiko Venonen released a mellifluous and danceable cover of "Memphis Blues Again," with the full lyric translated into Spanish. As a young man in fascist-governed Spain of the late sixties and early seventies, Venonen had discovered and been transformed by Dylan's music. In the mid-seventies he led an influential hippie-punk band that blended Spanish folk with American pop. Throughout his career, Venonen has remained a socialist and a critic of the music industry.

"Visions of Johanna" covers a lot of ground: sex, drugs, politics, aesthetics, philosophy. It's a song of great intimacy and epic scope. It explores a world of heightened definition and intensified indefiniteness—brilliance and murk. Dylan finds himself here most definitely "back in New York City"—a flickering, electric, ghostly cityscape. As the song builds, the internal rhymes seethe, the lyric flows and ebbs over the melody, adding to the incantatory, phantasmagoric effect. Who's Louise? Who's Johanna? If the artist needed us to know he would have left more clues. They are objects of desire and yearning, and of judgment and illusion. It is their elusiveness and unreality that's the point. "How can I explain? / Oh it's so hard to get on . . ." And he offers us a fleeting self-portrait: "Now, little boy lost, he takes himself so seriously / He brags of his misery, he likes to live dangerously."

In "Visions of Johanna" Dylan is stranded between extremes: between total freedom and abject slavery. Events have now spun not only beyond control but beyond comprehension. The sheer metamorphic intensity of reality makes it impossible to apprehend. Yet the hunger for the authentic remains unappeasable.

> The peddler now speaks to the countess who's pretending to care for him
> Sayin,' "Name me someone that's not a parasite and I'll go out and say a
>   prayer for him"

In the final verse there's an implied reckoning:

> The fiddler, he now steps to the road
> He writes ev'rything's been returned which was owed
> On the back of the fish truck that loads
> While my conscience explodes
> The harmonicas play the skeleton keys and the rain
> And these visions of Johanna are now all that remain

Exploding consciences provide the finishing touch in several Dylan compositions of this period. "Maggie's Farm" climaxes with the cry:

> I got a head full of ideas that are driving me insane

"From a Buick 6" comes to a similar screeching halt:

> Well, you know I need a steam shovel mama to keep away the dead
> I need a dump truck mama to unload my head

In the last verse of "Tombstone Blues," Dylan watches helplessly as someone else goes mad:

> Now I wish I could write you a melody so plain
> That could hold you dear lady from going insane

The individual locked inside his or her own consciousness confronts a catastrophically deceitful and exploitative social reality. The contradiction between the autonomous self and organized society seems unresolvable. That is the crisis that Dylan is trying to fight his way out of in these songs. The enemies are too fierce, too cunning, too ubiquitous—too internalized. Nonetheless, Dylan continues to insist, in his inimitably convoluted fashion, that freedom and authenticity are out there. They're real. But they come at a price:

> To live outside the law you must be honest

This great aphoristic warning sign to the movement, to the counterculture, to a generation and its successors leaps out from the strutting, swaggering, very silly "Absolutely Sweet Marie" (a saga of sexual frustration). People tend to forget the leering follow-up line, as Dylanesque in its way as the famous aphorism:

> And I know you always say that you agree

After recording *Blonde on Blonde,* Dylan embarked on a "world tour"—Australia, Sweden, Denmark, Britain, Ireland, and France—which turned into a sustained confrontation with the media and with his audience, or part of it. The antagonism of Newport became ritualized. Even, it's said, organized—by leftist folk clubs and British Communist Party members.[26]

During this tour, Dylan made some of his greatest music, and surely some of the most powerfully expressive rock 'n' roll ever. Backed by the musicians who were later to become known as The Band,* he explored his new sound to the limit. The sense of embattlement drove Dylan to ecstatic heights as a performer. The musicians, astonished by the audience aggression, followed his lead. Robertson's guitar became a second voice, answering Dylan's vocals, trading nuances, sarcasm, and euphoria.

Thanks to the *Official Bootleg* series, the legendary Manchester Free Trade Hall performance of May 17, 1966 (for years known on unofficial bootleg as the Royal Albert Hall gig), complete with the "Judas!" heckle, is now readily accessible.† Taken together, the two components of the show—a full acoustic set preceded the intermission, after which Dylan returned to plug in—display the stunning range, power, and subtlety of Dylan's art at this moment.

May 24, 1966, was Dylan's twenty-fifth birthday. That night he and his band appeared on stage at the Olympia Theatre in Paris before an enormous American flag. This seems to have distressed the audience more than the loud rock 'n' roll. There were cries of "U.S. Go Home!" (Drummer Mickey Jones says the flag was Dylan's idea.)[27] Oblivious, or rather, putting great effort into making himself appear and feel oblivious, Dylan ploughed on with his highly public exploration of an interior landscape. In London on May 27, he finished the tour at the Albert Hall. The booing and denunciation from a section of the audience were by now familiar. After ripping through "Leopard-Skin Pill-Box Hat," Dylan paused to explain:

> This is not English music you're listening to. You haven't really heard American music before. I want to say now that what you're hearing is just songs. You're not hearing anything else but words. You can take it or leave

---

* Robbie Robertson, Rick Danko, Richard Manuel, and Garth Hudson toured with Dylan; Levon Helm, the drummer, stayed at home. His place was taken by Mickey Jones.
† C.P. Lee's bracing *Like the Night: The Road to the Manchester Free Trade Hall* re-creates the context, the experience—and the joy, for those who were wise or innocent enough to relish Dylan's new music.

it. If there's something that you disagree with that's just great. I'm sick of people asking what does it all mean. It means nothing.

He proceeded to roll out "Just Like Tom Thumb's Blues." When that came to an end, someone shouted, "Play protest songs!" To which Dylan replied:

Oh come on, these are all protest songs. Aw, it's the same stuff as always. Can't you HEAR?

He followed that up with "Ballad of a Thin Man." [28] Despite the booing, there were many present who could "hear." As in the same venue a year earlier, when Ginsberg had preached to the International Poetry Festival, a new layer was being added to British youth culture. Within months, this culture would provide a home for Jimi Hendrix, a womb from which the unknown African American R&B virtuoso would emerge as psychedelic rock 'n' roll shaman, with a sound (and a hairstyle) that owed not a little to Bob Dylan.

On June 8, 1966, James Meredith, whose admission to the University of Mississippi had detonated the white riot in Oxford four years earlier, launched a one-man Memphis-to-Jackson "march against fear." Within hours, he was gunned down (though not killed) by another "bullet from the back of a bush." Activists from all wings of the movement vowed to complete his march. But as they did so, discord was constant, with the militants of SNCC and CORE—both now all-black organizations—at loggerheads with Martin Luther King and the NAACP. The marchers also faced the usual harassment from local officials and white vigilantes. On June 16, Stokely Carmichael, who had recently replaced John Lewis as SNCC national chairman, was arrested in Greenwood. On his release, he told a rally: "This is the twenty-seventh time I have been arrested. I ain't going to jail no more. We been sayin' Freedom Now for six years and we ain't got nothin'. What we gonna start sayin' now is 'Black Power!'." The slogan coursed through the country, galvanizing some and antagonizing others. [29]

Weeks later, King, making good on his pledge to bring the civil rights campaign to the cities of the North, led a march through a segregated neighborhood in Chicago. He was spat at and stoned by white mobs. "I have never seen anything so hostile and so hateful as I've seen here today," he told the press.[30] In November's elections, the white backlash took another stride forward—epitomized in Ronald Reagan's gubernatorial victory in California. The effect of the backlash was not to moderate black or student demands, but to intensify them, as their alienation from the dominant forces reached a new pitch. At the top, the movement was fracturing; at the base it was spreading into virgin territory. "By the fall of 1966," wrote Julius Lester, "the movement which had once been composed of a few political organizations was becoming a separate society, with its own newspapers, its own lifestyle, its own morality. It became like a huge river with people jumping in at every point along its banks. . . ."[31]

———————————

Dylan returned to the United States exhausted and in poor health. Albert Grossman had already booked him into a sixty-four–date U.S. tour. Publishers, film producers, reporters, and fans were all waiting, expecting something more from him. Then, in late July, driving along a back road near his manager's home in Woodstock, Dylan was thrown from his motorcycle and injured. How badly injured is a matter disputed by biographers, but what's not in doubt is that the accident gave Dylan a respite, an excuse to retreat from public life.[32] It also enhanced his mystique. For this child of Hank Williams, Robert Johnson, James Dean, and Buddy Holly, a youthful death, a death on the wing—on a motorcycle, no less—would have been all too iconic. And if anyone was headed for an early grave, it did seem to be Bob Dylan: no one could burn with such fire and not be consumed in the flames. He was indeed hurtling headlong through history, exhausted by the rapid transformations—personal, cultural, political—in the five and a half years since his arrival in Greenwich Village.

Yet Dylan did not expire on the highway, and his tortured umbilical link with the social conflicts of his age was yet to be severed.

THE WICKED MESSENGER

"To win the energies of intoxication for the revolution"—in other words, poetic politics? "We have tried that beverage. Anything, rather than that!"

—WALTER BENJAMIN, *SURREALISM*

AFTER THE MOTORCYCLE ACCIDENT, Dylan went into retreat. He would not tour again for eight years. Between the release of *Blonde on Blonde* in May 1966 and *John Wesley Harding* early in 1968, as far as the public was concerned, there was only silence. Yet during those extraordinary months, Dylan was as much a presence as an absence.

In the summer of 1967, the counterculture that had been in gestation for years in obscure corners of American society emerged into mass consciousness. In the media, it was named, celebrated, condemned, analyzed, caricatured, sensationalized. Vast numbers of mainly but by no means exclusively white middle-class youth were touched by it, in varying degrees, or somehow identified with its generational amalgam of music, drugs, sexual freedom, antiwar, antiracist and anticommercial sentiments. Dylan was one of its touchstones, and that year the pop-art profile of him by Milton Glaser appeared on dormitory walls and in suburban bedrooms. "The Times They Are A-Changin' " was three and a half years old, but it seemed much more apt now than it had in 1963, when it was a brash boast, a rallying cry for a self-righteous minority. As for "Everybody must get stoned," those lyrics didn't seem so obscure anymore. It was from this time on that the feeling spread among growing numbers of young people that wherever their head was at, Dylan had been there before.

The hunger for authenticity had taken a new turn: it was no longer to be found in tradition or immersion in a cause, but in the release of inhibitions, in self-expression and communal joy. The search for community, for a bond beyond the social mechanism, as in the folk revival and the civil rights movement, persisted, but now transposed to a less clearly defined constituency. The most political expressions of the counterculture—the Human Be-in in San Francisco, the underground press, the Diggers, the Yippies—consciously sought to wed collective action and personal liberation, social protest with hedonism. The alacrity with which oppositional styles—including a taste for Dylan—spread among white youth convinced some on the left that the millennium was at hand.

Even at the time, the hippie faux innocence was fatuous. "I'm younger than that now" without the plaintive lilt. At a Legalise Pot rally in London's Hyde Park in July, Adrian Mitchell addressed the flower-bearing teenagers: "these flowers are for love. Good."

> But is it a vague gas of love
> Which evaporates before it touches another human being
> Or is it a love that works?

He told them they needed "A love so explosive that its tremors / Will shake out of the sky / The bombers which at this minute / Are murdering Hanoi . . . A love so hot it can melt the armaments / Before they melt the entire country of Vietnam."[1] In the end, the self-conscious turn to the gentle and childlike could not withstand a reality that was anything but. For the summer of 1967 was also Vietnam summer, when 20,000 young volunteers took to the door-knockers across the U.S.A. to argue the case for an end to the war. Finally, two years on from the launch of the all-out U.S. assault, the demonstrations at home began to swell. In the spring, 100,000 rallied in New York, led by Martin Luther King; in the autumn, even more protested in Washington. But the rising tide of protest was accompanied by a rising sense of horror, a feeling of desperation. Paradoxically, the scale of the marches seemed to increase the sense of futility: so many people protesting, and still they didn't listen. The 400,000 U.S. troops in Vietnam at the beginning of the year increased to half a million by its end. Hundreds of GIs were being killed each week and many more maimed or wounded. For the Vietnamese, it was incalculably worse.

And the summer of 1967 was the summer of insurrection, violence, and death in American cities. In the black ghettoes, the aspirations and political consciousness engendered by the civil rights movement smashed up against the daily frustrations of poverty, joblessness, bad housing, rotten public services, and brutal policing. The federal government that had failed their people in the South was now dispatching them to die in Vietnam. That summer witnessed blazing disorder in fifty-eight cities, in the course of which police and national guards took forty-three black lives in Detroit and twenty-four in Newark.

Reflecting on why he had been booed by angry black youth at a meeting in Chicago, Martin Luther King explained:

> For twelve years I, and others like me, had held out radiant promises of progress. I had preached to them about my dream . . . I had urged them to have faith in America and in white society. Their hopes had soared. They were now booing because they felt we were unable to deliver on our promises. They were booing because we had urged them to have faith in people who had too often proved to be unfaithful. They were now hostile because they were watching the dream they had so readily accepted turn into a nightmare.[2]

So amid the euphoria of ecstatic rock 'n' roll and communal self-discovery, it was not at all strange for Andrew Kopkind, consistently one of the era's most sensitive reporters of the radical left, to observe: "To be white and radical in America this summer is to see horror and feel impotence." The bankruptcy of the establishment had been revealed as never before: "the old words are meaningless, the old explanations irrelevant, the old remedies useless." The only hope was that "The wretched of this American earth are together as they have never been before, in motion if not in movement."[3]

It was in 1967 that SDS completed its long, tortured repudiation of liberalism. In a speech given to the spring national council, the organization's national secretary, Greg Calvert, explained that liberals were those who "acted for others" whereas "radicals or revolutionaries" were acting for themselves, engaged in a struggle for their own freedom that was at the same time a struggle for systemic social transformation. Calvert defined SDS's tasks in language that might have described the Dylan of *Highway 61 Revisited:* "For SDS, organizing people is detaching them from American reality. When we break them out of that reality, that America, they begin to see their own lives, and America, in a new way . . . the process, really, is to allow the real person to confront the real America." [4]

Students and youth came to be seen as oppressed in their own right. To many, then as now, the comparison seemed disproportionate. But it struck a chord; it tapped into the same sense of unspecified alienation, that same lust for autonomy and authenticity that Dylan's music articulated. A top-selling SDS badge of the time promoted draft resistance with the slogan *Not with my life you don't*—parodying the title of one of that year's more lamentable Hollywood comedies.* With the first serious clashes between white antiwar demonstrators and police—in Los Angeles in June and in Oakland in October—some radicals began talking about "white riots" to complement the actions in the black ghettoes. In any case, there was an agreement that the time had come to move "from protest to resistance."

By the autumn, SDS had acquired a 30,000-strong following on some 250 campuses around the country. Its numerical strength had grown tenfold in two years—a measure of the upsurge in student radicalism, and SDS's own unique role as its vehicle and vanguard. [5] Carl Davidson described the SDS campus shock troops of 1967 as follows: "younger members, freshmen and sophomores, rapidly moving into the hippy, Bobby Dylan syndrome. Having been completely turned off by the American system of compulsory miseducation, they are staunchly anti-intellectual and rarely read anything unless it comes from the underground press syndicate." [6]

* *Not With My Wife You Don't!*

In *Playboy,* Paul Goodman anatomized the Dylanesque soul of the new student radical:

> Their solidarity based on community rather than ideology, their style of direct and frank confrontation, their democratic inclusiveness and aristocratic carelessness of status, caste or getting ahead, their selectivity of the affluent standard of living, their effort to be authentic and committed to their causes rather than merely belonging, their determination to have a say and their refusal to be processed as standard items, their extreme distrust of top-down direction, their disposition to anarchist organization and direct action, their disillusion with the system of institutions . . .[7]

For a brief moment it did seem to many that collective action and individual self-expression, the political and the cultural, could be merged to build a potent social movement. Staughton Lynd recalled: "For white radicals it was a time of politics of affirmation rather than politics of guilt." Wallace Stegner, however, was more doubtful; the young radicals, he wrote, "often seem to throb rather than think."[8]

In popular music, the experimental vein opened by mid-sixties Dylan was now being mined with gusto by others. In the spring, the Beatles released *Sergeant Pepper.* The San Francisco groups unveiled the psychedelic sound. Hendrix took Dylan's rock 'n' blues and poetry to orgiastic heights. It was the year of "White Rabbit," "Light My Fire," "A Whiter Shade of Pale," among a crop of songs marked by druggy references, obscure lyrics, and exotic sounds. In June, the first Monterey Pop Festival—self-consciously modeled on Newport—featured Hendrix's sprawling, guitar-drenched exploration of "Like a Rolling Stone." The festival was the dawn of what soon became known as "progressive rock"—rock infused with the sense of experiment, artistic seriousness, and sensory exploration that Dylan had introduced in his mid-sixties masterpieces. At Newport itself, Arlo Guthrie debuted his draft-dodger epic, "Alice's Restaurant," to an enthusiastic reception, and Country Joe and the Fish were cheered for their antiwar "I-Feel-Like-I'm-Fixin'-To-Die Rag." Both songs brimmed with political satire, and were topical in the best Newport tradition, but both were also marked by their mordant jokiness. The killing machine had become too real, too omnipresent, and gallows humor felt like the only reasonable response. Again, Dylan's work stands behind both songs.

This was also the summer of Scott McKenzie's "San Francisco (Be Sure To Wear Some Flowers In Your Hair)." No sooner had the counterculture been identified by the media than it was packaged and promoted as a product. *Time* made "the new generation" its "man of the year" and praised it for its commitment to "the western ethos—decency, tolerance, brotherhood." The fashion, film, music, and advertising industries all vied to exploit the new market. Adorno would have smiled bitterly at the ease with which political resistance was transformed into a package aesthetic experience—into a *lifestyle,* a term that enters common usage in this period. So instantaneous was the commodification of the new ethos that at the end of the summer countercultural radicals were already staging a "death of hippie" demonstration in a forlorn effort to cast off the identity fashioned for the insurgents by the media. The irony that the new mass anticonsumerism was propagated by the instruments of consumerism was clear to many at the time; perhaps less clear was that this irony had its roots in the characteristic contradictions of American sixties culture. The youth rebellion of the era was itself, in part, the product of the commercial society against which it rebelled. The insurgent response was buried deep inside the very structures that it shook: even *Leave It to Beaver* had Eddie Haskell.

Just as big business saw big profits in the nascent counterculture, sections of the left were also staking a claim, with greater historical entitlement, but in the end with considerably less success. The Yippies—a designation that both mocked and exploited facile media labels—launched themselves on the world in autumn of 1967. They were the most high profile of many left-based attempts to harness the inchoate politics of the counterculture. Tellingly, they relied almost exclusively on the media to do this. Abbie Hoffman and his comrades proved adept at exploiting television, radio, and newspapers to subvert establishment assumptions; their guerrilla marketing was cheap and cheerful and it had an impact way beyond the confines of the activist left. But it was always problematic.

The recognized leaders of radicalized American youth in the late sixties were anointed by the media; their leadership was exercised largely through symbolic gestures, images, and catchphrases. There were no mass organizations to which they were accountable, and little real dialogue between the highly visible vanguard and the volatile, rapidly swelling army of dissident students and young people. There were many slogans—some of them incisive and inspiring—but little ideology or program. "The secret of the yippie myth is that it's nonsense," wrote Jerry Rubin, proudly, in *Do It!* his 1970 bestseller, "its basic informational statement is a blank piece of paper." [9] It was, more than ever, year zero for many on the American left. The consequent political vacuum was to be filled in the years to come, alternately, by the liberal Democrats (the McCarthy and McGovern presidential campaigns) and by a bewildering variety of dogmatic ultraleftisms.

Nonetheless, thanks to the confluence of all these trends—thanks to the movement and the media—individual gestures of rebellion did take on powerful political implications, and in some cases did lead to active political engagement. In the charged circumstances of the times, choices over hair, dress, and music came to mean more than they had been in the past or would in the future. They referred to something larger than the lone teenage consumer; for many, they referred to and represented the embrace of a great social movement.

Dylan later described 1967 as "the season of hype." [10] He was singularly unimpressed by the claims being made for the counterculture, the new generation, the new rock, and the new left. These were all claims that had been lodged in his earlier work, which may have been one reason why the ever-restless one responded to the psychedelic outburst with wary cynicism. It was also one reason why, throughout this period, the mystique of Bob Dylan continued to spread and intensify. Even as he sat in silence and rural isolation, he seemed to speak to more people than ever and on a deeper level. His entire back catalogue continued to sell. In August 1967, *Bringing It All Back Home, Highway 61 Revisited,* and *Blonde on Blonde* all went gold. Columbia issued a *Greatest Hits* album to fill the void left by Dylan's retreat; within six months, it too went gold. Pennebaker's *Don't Look Back* was released, introducing the Dylan persona to far more people than had ever actually seen the man perform live. Thanks to the season of hype, Dylan's work was lapping over ever wider social circles.

During the summer of 1967, Huey Newton, Eldridge Cleaver, Bobby Seale, and colleagues met in a house in San Francisco to create a new newspaper, *The Black Panther*. As they worked through the nights honing their message, one record played repeatedly in the background, Dylan's "Ballad of a Thin Man." Seale recalled:

> This song Bobby Dylan was singing became a very big part of that whole publishing operation of the Black Panther paper. . . . This record became so related to us, even to the brothers who had held down most of the security for the set. The brothers had some big earphones . . . that would sit on your ears and had a kind of direct stereo atmosphere and when you got loaded it was something else! These brothers would get halfway high, loaded on something, and they would sit down and play this record over and over and over, especially after they began to hear Huey P. Newton interpret that record.

Moved by the song but puzzled by the lyric, Seale had asked Newton, "What the hell is a geek?" Newton explained that a geek was a circus performer who ate live chickens:

> He doesn't like eating raw meat or feathers but he does it to survive. But these people who are coming in to see him are coming in for entertainment, so they are the real freaks. And the geek knows this so during his performance, he eats the live chicken and he hands one of the members of the audience a bone, because he realizes that they are the real freaks. . . .

For Newton, the geek-freak interplay carried potent race and class overtones:

What Dylan is putting across is middle class people or upper class people who sometimes take the afternoon off and put their whole family into a limousine and they go down to the black ghettoes to watch the prostitutes and watch the decaying community. They do this for pleasure. . . . people who are disadvantaged . . . they're not interested in them coming down for entertainment. But if they'll pay them for a trick, then they'll tolerate them, or else they'll drive them out of the ghettoes. This song is hell. You've got to understand that this song is saying a hell of a lot about society.[11]

The summer of '67 was a time of hope and energy for the Panthers. In May, the hitherto obscure group of revolutionary black nationalists had seized the media spotlight when they marched onto the floor of the California State Assembly in Sacramento brandishing guns. (In fact, they had intended to sit in the gallery, but got lost en route). At the time the party could claim only seventy-odd members, all of them in two West Coast chapters. But they were brash, confident, convinced that they themselves could and would find the key to unlock the black revolt. In marrying ghetto-based community organizing, black pride, the language of anti-imperialism, and the policy of armed self-defense, they believed they had resolved the movement's mid-decade impasse. Infiltration, egomania, media addiction, and the cult of the gun had not yet turned the party's internal life into a maelstrom of feuds and personal abuse. In the wake of the Sacramento stunt, they worked to forge links with (and revitalize) the remnants of SNCC, but they weren't seeking leadership from other quarters: they were going to take the initiative and provide it themselves.

That a rock ballad written by an introverted white boy from Hibbing should mesmerize this would-be ghetto vanguard, forged out of poverty and violence, is a testament not only to Dylan's art, but also to the era that shaped it. The Panthers were a political response to many of the same tides that shaped Dylan's artistic arc: the successes and frustrations of the civil rights movement, the bankruptcy of Vietnam War liberalism, a distrust of academic or formal discourses, and a commitment to authenticity and the language of the street. They shared Dylan's rage at being patronized, as well as his contempt for middle-class liberals who let other people get their kicks for them. They had rejected "America" as a racist entity—and aligned themselves, nominally at least, with those people of color outside the United States who were resisting the U.S. government. For them, the bards of social patriotism—not to mention the prophets of peace and love—held little appeal. In contrast, Dylan's confrontational energy, his uncompromising assertion of his own autonomy, exerted an immediate emotional and intellectual appeal. Newton and his friends were determined to decipher his code, and make his song their own.

The Panthers took from Dylan's song what they needed. Newton's reading of the lyric—characteristically blending the excitement of intellectual discovery with dogmatic self-certainty—may have been singular and obsessive, but it was also apt. Dylan's carnivalesque satire was an anthem for outsiders who had declared themselves insiders, a trenchant riposte to an uncomprehending, exploitative gaze; it was not at all far-fetched to see America's race- and class-divide looming behind it. After all, it was African American culture that provided the template on which white bohemia had modeled its protective shell—that shell which Dylan inserts between himself and Mr. Jones.

The Panthers found in Dylan's art a locus for their own rage, and an analysis of white exploitation of black experience. Sadly, there was a prophetic warning in Huey Newton's interpretation of the lyric that he and his comrades failed to heed. Increasingly, they were too willing to play the geek, metaphorically chomping off live chicken heads for the benefit of the white media.

Meanwhile, the artist who had vowed "I will not go down under the ground" had burrowed into a basement in the Catskills. There, for several months in mid-1967, Dylan conducted a communal musical workshop, an experimental laboratory in which melodies, lyrics, rhythms, instrumentation, and voices could be swapped and varied and reshaped according the passing whims and moods of the participants. Crucially, there was no album-making agenda; no business pressure. This was a private affair. And in that privacy, Dylan and his colleagues—Robbie Robertson, Rick Danko, Richard Manuel, Garth Hudson, and Levon Helm (i.e. The Band)—found freedom. The freedom to plagiarize and to improvise, to say everything or nothing, to leave experiments incomplete, to indulge whims. The freedom to play. This is music liberated by its sheer inconsequentiality.

In their full glory the Basement Tapes comprise 160 recordings of more than 100 individual songs. The vast majority are covers: forgotten pop hits from the fifties, country ballads from the thirties and forties, folk revival standards, blues, rockabilly, bluegrass, songs by John Lee Hooker, Hank Snow, Johnny Cash. It's a rich and idiosyncratic selection of American people's music (the sole non-American number is Rimsky-Korsakov's "Flight of the Bumble Bee"). In among the covers are a score of Dylan originals, mingling easily in this motley company. Even The Band couldn't be sure, when Dylan brought them an unfamiliar tune, whether it was one of his own or something retrieved from his vast interior storehouse of popular song.

The Dylan originals on the Basement Tapes boast a startling profusion of memorable hooks and melodies. Song after song features swelling, emotion-choked choruses that are both instantly accessible and impenetrably mysterious. The verses, in contrast, are often wayward, half-told anecdotes, passing impressions, verbal fragments, and nonetheless seductively intriguing for that.

For five years—the first half of his twenties—Dylan had been in the van, racing ahead, sustaining a precarious balance on the crest of a wave. But at the very moment when avant-gardism was sweeping through new cultural corridors, Dylan decided to dismount. The dandified, aggressively modern surface was replaced by a self-consciously unassuming and traditional garb. The giddiness embodied, celebrated, dissected in the songs of the mid-sixties had left him exhausted. He sought safety in a retreat to the countryside that was also a retreat in time, or more precisely, a search for timelessness. The basement sessions have the air of soothing a fever—the fever of incessant innovation that Dylan had embodied so intensely for a few eventful years. Vindictiveness and righteous indignation have been replaced by a more reflective and less judgmental temper.

> And remember when you're out there
> Tryin' to heal the sick
> That you must always
> First forgive them.

In the Basement Tapes, Dylan is once again writing against the times, though also very much from within them. The songs might even be interpreted as a running critique of the ephemeral delusions of the summer of love. They are delicately balanced between absurdity and grandeur, laughter and terror, brooding fatalism and the lingering taste of freedom.

Inevitably, this private creative moment soon became public. Basement Tape tunes were quickly covered by Peter, Paul and Mary, Manfred Mann, the Byrds, and, of course, The Band themselves on *Music From Big Pink*. More significantly, unlicensed copies of the tapes circulated among ever wider circles. Within two years the Basement Tapes had become the first mass-distributed bootleg. The laid-back, downhome sound proved a trendsetter (by no means always a positive one*). What Dylan and his friends were doing in the privacy of the basement, without purpose or plan, somehow reflected the needs and mood of a broader public mesmerized and discomfited by a series of titanic social clashes.

———————————

From the moment the Basement Tapes began seeping out into the world, their musical language struck many as distinctively and self-consciously "American." Robbie Robertson and Garth Hudson both described what they were doing in Woodstock as making "American music." This thesis is at the core of Greil Marcus's study of the Basement

———

* "Turn up the Eagles, the neighbors are listening . . ."—Steely Dan.

Tapes, *Invisible Republic,* where he argues that the tapes are an invocation and exploration of "the old, weird America" whose idiosyncratic voices had been assembled in Harry Smith's *Anthology.*

While the "Americanness" of the music is something that almost everyone claims to hear, it is exceedingly difficult to define. Specific allusions are few and far between. The cast of characters and the landscape may suggest an "invisible republic," but perhaps less so than in the mid-sixties albums. Marcus locates the Basement Tapes' Americanness not so much in scattered lyric references as in the musical environment and the tone of voice—the flat, wary, masked tone that he associates with America's paradoxical historic development. While his book— easily the most thoughtful meditation on the meaning of Dylan's music—goes a long way to defining this tone, it does remain elusive.

Marcus argues that Smith's *Anthology* is unified by intimations of a "perfectly, absolutely metaphorical America—an arena of rights and obligations, freedom and restraints, crime and punishment, love and death, humor and tragedy, speech and silence . . ."[12] The American "arena" is here so widely drawn that almost any cultural product, from any nation, could qualify for inclusion. As so often in American writing about American popular culture, there is an America-shaped hole at the heart of the analysis. What the songs in Smith's *Anthology* have in common is that they were produced, initially, by and for working-class people, and mainly outside the great urban centers. Why then should Americanness be presumed to be their primary binding agent? Are these songs really any more American than Broadway or Hollywood show tunes? Only, of course, if you redefine America as essentially a rural and small-town entity. And that mythology freezes America, removes it from history, and makes it a plaything for repression and empire.

As Dylan himself was fleetingly aware, "America" is a selective construction; in the end, like other nation-states, the U.S.A. is defined more by the conflict and interaction among its constituent elements than by any lowest common denominator. The critical resort to national identity explains little and obscures the fact that many of the *Anthology* songs more closely resemble the folk art of foreign societies than Hollywood or Tin Pan Alley or rock 'n' roll. In the end, Marcus commits the same sin with which he charges Lomax and the popular front: he homogenizes a variegated tradition in pursuit of a political vision. That vision may be darker, more fatalistic than anything Lomax (or indeed Smith) would have endorsed, but it is, no less than theirs, the product of ideology and historical experience.

Nonetheless, there can be no doubt that in the basement Dylan and his colleagues were trying to reestablish a relation to a tradition from which they felt severed. The songs are saturated with memory and loss, though what is being remembered or lamented is usually unspecified and unclear. Marcus argues that:

> . . . every American harbor[s] a sense of national ending . . . a great public event locked up in the silence of the solitary. For any American it is a defining moment; no promise is so precious as in the moment one knows it can never be kept, that it belongs to the past. In 1967, in the basement of Big Pink, this event was in the air . . .[13]

The starting point in these backward-looking songs is a sense of discontinuity. Dylan turns to the past—to those things which are or seem to be permanent—out of a fear and disgust with contemporary society and its succession of passing whims. It's an escape from history into history. For Dylan it was clearly no longer year zero.

> We carried you in our arms
> On Independence Day,
> And now you'd throw us all aside
> And put us on our way.

Opening with a patriotic allusion and a parental grievance, "Tears of Rage" turned "The Times They Are A-Changin' " upside down. Here, generational alienation is presented from the parent's viewpoint:

> Now, I want you to know that while we watched
> You discover there was no one true
> Most ev'rybody really thought
> It was a childish thing to do

The naively disillusioned daughter to whom the song is apparently addressed seems not to be listening. "The Times They Are A-Changin' " is a public rallying call; "Tears of Rage" is a private howl of grief. The power of the chorus—"tears of rage, tears of grief"—lies in part in the sense that no one will hear, that no one can fathom the narrator's tragedy. "Why must I always be the thief?" he asks plaintively. Why am I always cast in this role: the criminal, the accused, the outcast? Marcus notes that Dylan sings on this track with "an ache deep in the chest, a voice thick with care." In "Tears of Rage," love has been forfeited; guilt and betrayal are mutual. "Oh what kind of love is this / which goes from bad to worse?" The song is haunted by the feeling that patriotic solidarity, national identity, intergenerational bonds have all been dissolved, both sometime in the remote past and immediately, in the here and now. There's no popular-front optimism in the America of the Basement Tapes. (Woody Guthrie is a ghost, but only one of many.) There's no faith in progress, democracy or the people. The music certainly evokes an American heritage, but it is a darker one than the sentimental banalities of either the television jingoists or the social patriots.

In the Basement Tapes, America is a hermetic enclosure. It's a construction outside of which Dylan never steps. Having abandoned year zero, Dylan now sees the same grand tragedies, the same small comforts, repeated cyclically. When, a year later, an interviewer mentioned the deaths of Kennedy and King and the war, Dylan responded: "We're talking now about things which have always happened since the beginning of time. The specific name or deed isn't any different than that which has happened previous to this. Progress hasn't contributed anything but changing face and changing situations of money and wealth."[14] This is the conservative, antimodernist Dylan who can be traced back to the folk revival. But the cyclical view is distinctly post-accident. It is also, as laid out by Dylan in the interview, glib. In the songs it has power because it's not a ready-made self-serving philosophy but an incomplete, pain-riddled vision, not a cheap answer, but a more radical posing of the question.

The Basement Tapes are filled with the sound of young men singing like old men. Young men who had prematurely acquired a ruminative sense of a lost past. Rudderless and adrift in an unstable and violent present, they longed for the enduring, for musical modes and lyric moments beyond fashion and hype. In an age of relentless neologism, the attraction of the Basement Tapes was their timeless quality. However, as Marcus notes, "there is no nostalgia in the basement recordings; they are too cold, pained, or ridiculous for that. The mechanics of time in the music are not comforting." [15] Retreat may be a palliative, but it is not a cure.

The freedom of the Basement Tapes allowed Dylan to indulge his appetite for nonsense to the full (Robertson described the sessions as "reefer run amok"). The playfulness, the casual, improvisatory approach (to music-making and to daily life) can be heard in the dry babble of "Tiny Montgomery:"

> Scratch your dad
> Do that bird
> Suck that pig
> And bring it on home

In the Basement Tapes, Dylan adopts a relaxed attitude toward the grotesque, the bizarre, the inexplicable. The encounter with the surreal inanity of the mundane is more equable, more accepting than before; the jokiness is less manic, less defensive. It's as if the artist found it a relief not to have to be serious about anything at all. He could be chirpily bucolic in "Apple Suckling Tree" and jauntily bathetic in "Please Mrs. Henry" ("I'm down on my knees, and I ain't got a dime"). He mocks his own inertia and impotence, but with a much gentler touch than in *Blonde on Blonde*. In place of that album's strangled urgency, Dylan adopts a laconic humor, a deadpan tone that speaks of resignation and self-preservation in the face of absurdity and betrayal.

Escape and escapism are among the dominant themes of the Basement Tapes, but there is always an ambivalence—about the possibility, desirability or permanence of escape. In the mournful "Goin' to Acapulco," the boys sing the chorus, "goin' to have some fun," like men facing a prison sentence. The verse offers only a wry, self-protective renunciation:

> Now, if someone offers me a joke
> I just say no thanks.
> I try to tell it like it is
> And keep away from pranks.

"You Ain't Goin' Nowhere" appears to celebrate bucolic retreat: "Oh, oh, are we gonna fly / Down in the easy chair!" But on closer inspection it proves to be a curious kind of retreat. Where the chorus hymns an escape that offers both elation and safety, the verses elaborate the paradox of a static journey. In a stark reply to his own "Baby Blue," Dylan sings:

> Pick up your money
> And pack up your tent
> You ain't goin' nowhere

Here, shelter from the storm is found in forging a connection to something deeper and more lasting.

> Strap yourself
> To the tree with roots

It's not surprising that this tune became a key track on the Byrds' influential *Sweetheart of the Rodeo,* the album that first ploughed the country-rock furrow. Still, it remains altogether more arch and discomfiting than the paeans to rural verities that were to become commonplace as the sixties turned into the seventies. In the last verse, the drawled seriocomic delivery moves dreamily from the frustrations of the world conqueror, Genghis Khan, to what sounds like a lazy person's revision of a freedom song:

> We'll climb that hill no matter how steep
> When we come up to it

The sense that there may be something ghastly lurking in the backwoods, a void at the heart of the retreat, fills "Too Much of Nothing." In the plangent chorus, there seems to be a reference to T.S. Eliot's wives

("Say hello to Valerie, say hello to Vivien"). The poet of dread-filled stasis certainly has a place in this song. The easygoing shuffle of the tune contains a subterranean foreboding:

> Now, too much of nothing
> Can make a man feel ill at ease . . .

As the singer's anxiety levels rise, so do organ and guitar in the background. The song reaches a climax of constrained panic:

> Now, it's all been done before,
> It's all been written in the book,
> But when there's too much of nothing,
> Nobody should look.

Dylan is overwhelmed by the totality of the past, the impossibility of the genuinely new. It seems that in stasis there is no peace. (It's also bad for the character: Too much of nothing "can turn a man into a liar" and "just makes a fella mean.") The same sense of unease is given comic treatment in the delightfully indecipherable "The Mighty Quinn, (Quinn The Eskimo)."

> Nobody can get no sleep,
> There's someone on ev'ryone's toes
> But when Quinn the Eskimo gets here,
> Ev'rybody's gonna wanna doze

The escape theme is turned around again in "Nothing Was Delivered," where the singer appears to be keeping someone hostage. The lyric could be addressed to anyone who has promised something and failed to deliver it (politicians, drug-dealers, advertisers, Dylan himself). Over the Fats Domino–style piano, the singer flatly, soberly explains that the time for paying debts has come.

> Now you must provide some answers
> For what you sell has not been received,
> And the sooner you come up with them,
> The sooner you can leave.

Prices have to be paid, promises redeemed, and no one is going any-where until they are. As in a number of the Basement Tapes, there is a dramatic contrast between the menacing deadpan verse and the full-throated down-home chorus.

> Nothing is better, nothing is best,
> Take care of yourself and get plenty of rest.

The longing for peace, community, and simple fellow-feeling was common ground with the summer of love. But Dylan did not share the shallow optimism of the flower children, or their embrace of an ethic of irresponsibility, or the hopes of imminent transformation that in some ways they shared with the angry radicals. He looks at human affairs here from a safe distance, but remains troubled by them. The sense of resig-nation is never complete in any of these songs. They are the songs of a man at rest, but uneasily so.

The song titled "Clothes Line Saga" on the official *Basement Tapes* album was originally labeled "Answer to Ode." In late August, the Beat-les "All You Need Is Love" was knocked off the number-one spot in the charts by a curious song by the unknown Bobbie Gentry, "Ode to Billie Joe." Gentry was born in Choctaw County, Mississippi, not far from Greenwood, and her song opens on a landscape familiar to Dylan:

> It was the third of June, another sleepy, dusty Delta day
> I was out choppin' cotton and my brother was balin' hay
> And at dinner time we stopped and we walked back to the house to eat
> And mama hollered at the back door "y'all remember to wipe your feet"

The pointless precision of the date lends the song a documentary feel. In Dylan's reply, he adopts the same technique:

> It was January the thirtieth
> And everybody was feelin' fine.
> The dogs were barking, a neighbor passed,
> Mama, of course, she said, "Hi!"

Dylan recognized in the Gentry song the use of the vocal mask that gives nothing away, that only hints at ominous truths. The surface banality stands in piquant contrast to a hidden tragedy. Indeed, the song was a hit partly because it implied that our problems, social and personal, were more troubling than we liked to admit. In Dylan, the banality itself becomes sinister; the mask becomes a trap. The uncanny normalcy paraded before us by the narrator is straight out of *Invasion of the Body Snatchers*—accurate in all details, yet utterly lifeless.

In Gentry's song, the secret sore weeping under the surface of daily routine is that "Billy Joe Mcallister jumped off the Tallahatchie bridge." The song only hints at why this happened and how the narrator was involved (an unwanted pregnancy is the usual interpretation). It's a private tragedy, a hidden disgrace. In Dylan's reply, the "secret" that troubles the placid surface of daily routine is a highly public one:

> "Have you heard the news?" he said, with a grin,
> "The Vice-President's gone mad!"
> "Where?" "Downtown." "When?" "Last night."
> "Hmm, say, that's too bad!"
> "Well, there's nothin' we can do about it," said the neighbor,
> "It's just somethin' we're gonna have to forget."
> "Yes, I guess so," said Ma,
> Then she asked me if the clothes was still wet.

The vice president in 1967 was Hubert Humphrey, the Minnesota politician whose liberal credentials had been eroded by his role in the exclusion of the MFDP at Atlantic City, and by his support for the Vietnam War. It's inconceivable that Dylan did not have him in mind. In addition, he's one of Dylan's generic authority figures, like the "blind commissioner," the "drunken politicians" and the senators who pop up in the mid-sixties songs; only now his antics elicit no disbelief. There is no struggle against futility. And that is the problem. In "Blowin' in the Wind," Dylan asked: "How can a man turn his head and pretend that he just doesn't see?" In "Clothes Line Saga," he tells a tale of those who see and hear but still turn away, their senses blighted by the continuum of normalcy. The song meanders to a close by way of a line that is the antithesis of every sentiment expressed by Dylan since he'd first picked up a guitar: "Well, I just do what I'm told." At which point, the singer returns to the family house and shuts "all the doors."

It was a bleak social vision against the fevered backdrop of the summer of '67. In this chilling tale of imperturbable American complacency, and in his intuitive sense that most Americans remained disengaged from the unfolding horrors of the age, Dylan proved more acutely aware of the real challenges facing the insurgents than many of those leading the charge. In "Clothes Line Saga", America escapes behind a closed door, and responds to the madness and betrayals of public life by shutting them out, citing impotence and cultivating amnesia.

Among the more self-conscious pieces of Americana on the tapes is "Down In the Flood," whose starting point is the blues response to the Mississippi's menacing habit of periodically breaching its banks. The harrowing flood of 1927, which displaced hundreds of thousands of African Americans, inspired three songs Dylan knew well: Bessie Smith's "Backwater Blues," Blind Lemon Jefferson's "Rising High Water Blues," and Charley Patton's "High Water Everywhere." In all of them, the singer confronts a force of nature, a community is overwhelmed. "Down in the Flood"'s invocation of a collective tragedy takes us back to Dylan's earliest work, not least his songs about the bomb. But the body of the song is preoccupied with unnamed individuals who seem to be in dispute about the desirability, practicality, and fairness of making a bid to escape the rising waters. As in many of the Basement Tapes, the mythic is offset by the anti-mythic. In the enigmatic chorus only one fact is salient: events and choices are irrevocable.

> Oh mama, ain't you gonna miss your best friend now?
> Yes, you're gonna have to find yourself
> Another best friend, somehow.

For all their jokiness and deliberate inconsequence, the Basement Tapes are permeated by a sense that loss is real, that not "everything can be replaced," "life is brief," "lost time is not found again."

"Take care of all your memories"
Said my friend, Mick
"For you cannot relive them . . ."

In the past, Dylan had spoken glibly about his own mortality, as a kind of justification for doing his own thing. The accident and the violent flux of the times seem to have shifted his mood. In the Basement Tapes, there's an echoing sorrow, a shrouded intensity, that feels like the brooding underside of all the extreme manifestations of the era.

In the soaring chorus of "This Wheel's On Fire," the out-of-control driver races toward his doom in an ecstasy of rock 'n' roll. As he detaches himself from the careening immediacy of the violent present, he reaches into the past. Each verse begins and ends with the phrase, "If your memory serves you well." But what is being summoned to memory? Only the plan to meet again, fragments of past interaction, a few bright, palpable, inexplicable details ("I was goin' to confiscate your lace / and wrap it up in a sailor's knot / and hide it in your case") flashing out from a general murkiness.

And after ev'ry plan had failed
And there was nothing more to tell,
You knew that we would meet again,
If your mem'ry served you well.

It was little more than a year since the same artist had insisted "please don't let on that you knew me when." The man who was so eager to outgrow the past, who sloughed off identities and relationships with a change in the season, and who had celebrated that freedom in song, is now prophetically intoning: "you knew that we would meet again"—and it doesn't matter whether that's in the here or the hereafter. The past surrounds us, clings to us, but we only see it and know it when it's too late.

The same frail balance between the yearning for freedom and a sense of predestined tragedy swells up inside "I Shall Be Released," the fragmentary Basement Tape destined to become a global standard. Repeated renditions have made the song robustly anthemic, but in its original incarnation it's sung by Dylan and Richard Manuel with a tremulous frailty, as if the singing were an effort to keep fear and exhaustion at bay. It's a song of simplicity and beauty that manages to be immensely evocative in its short span. Somehow its sheer sketchiness conjures up the poignancy of the desire for release and the immutable reality of confinement. It echoes with anonymous injustices committed through eons. While Dylan brings us close to the nameless, faceless narrator, at the same time he wraps this immediacy in a longer view, almost a cyclical view of freedom and incarceration that seems to take in the course of a whole lifetime. That reenforces the sense here, as elsewhere in the Basement Tapes, that the yearning for freedom is also a yearning for oblivion, for death, for immersion in the setting sun.

> I see my light come shining
> From the west unto the east.
> Any day now, any day now,
> I shall be released.

The first person narrator here speaks from a prison cell. Prison—and more broadly the cruelty of the criminal justice system—is a leitmotif in Dylan's work, from "The Ballad of Donald White," through "The Walls of Red Wing," "Hattie Carroll," "Percy's Song" ("He ain't no criminal / And his crime it is none, / What happened to him / Could happen to anyone"), "Seven Curses," "Chimes of Freedom," "Bob Dylan's 115th Dream," "Absolutely Sweet Marie," and beyond. On one level, "I Shall Be Released" is a prisoner's lament. Certainly, many who've found themselves incarcerated have heard it and sung it that way.* But prison here is also, of course, a metaphor—for an oppressive social order or corporeal life itself. It was precisely this kind of flexibility of metaphor than made it possible to turn gospel songs into freedom songs. But here Dylan has taken the hunger for deliverance that fills

---

* "I Shall Be Released" served as an anthem for the campaigns to free the Birmingham Six, Guildford Four, and other victims of miscarriages of justice in Britain in the eighties.

both the gospels and the freedom songs and detached it from religious or political teleology.

> They say ev'ry man needs protection,
> They say ev'ry man must fall.

We are all weak and fallible; we all aspire to some greater freedom, some less oppressive daily existence. In the third and final verse, the prisoner discovers that in his loneliness he is not alone:

> Standing next to me in this lonely crowd,
> Is a man who swears he's not to blame.
> All day long I hear him shout so loud,
> Crying out that he was framed.*

When David Riesman's sociological study of the modern American character, *The Lonely Crowd*, appeared in 1950 it became a bestseller and put its author on the cover of *Time* magazine. The phrase *the lonely crowd* was, in fact, invented by the publishers, and does not appear in the book, but its paradox captured the growing unease about the fate of the individual in a mass society. For Dylan's purposes, all that mattered was the title, not the book. The members of the "lonely crowd" are locked up in individual cells, and yet they share the same grievances and the same aspirations, and live in the same prison. The wistful reaching for the ineffable that animated "Blowin' in the Wind" is very much at the core of "I Shall Be Released," as in other Basement Tapes, but it's been inverted. The indefinitely hopeful has given way to the indefinitely sorrowful. The historical opportunity that could be plucked out of the wind has been spent, and is now a thing of the past—haunting the present. In his earlier guises, Dylan had made ancient modes (folk, blues)

---

* The lyric sung by Dylan and Manuel on the Basement Tapes is different:

> Now yonder stands with me in this lonely crowd
> A man who swears he's not to blame
> All day long I hear his voice shouting so loud
> Crying out that he was framed

sound contemporary; here he made contemporary feelings and experiences sound ancient.

Throughout 1967, Phil Ochs was a familiar figure at antiwar rallies. Three years after "Talking Vietnam," he'd composed a string of songs about the war—"White Boots Marching in a Yellow Land," "We Seek No Wider War," "Cops of the World"—and was more preoccupied than ever by American militarism. Like nearly everyone else in the movement, however, he was touched by the psychedelic moment. That year he released *Pleasures of the Harbor*, using backing musicians, studio effects, and more personal and archly poetic material. "In such an ugly time the true protest is beauty," he wrote in the liner notes. Yet Ochs was impatient with the counterculture. In "Outside Of A Small Circle Of Friends" he jibed at the new self-indulgence.

> Smoking marijuana is more fun than drinking beer,
> But a friend of ours was captured and they gave him thirty years
> Maybe we should raise our voices, ask somebody why
> But demonstrations are a drag, besides we're much too high

The album also included Ochs's newest antiwar composition, "The War Is Over," a song that reflects the febrile mixture of fantasy and despair that characterized the movement in 1967. It was inspired by a suggestion Allen Ginsberg had made to a reporter from the *Los Angeles Free Press*—that the paper should do what he'd done in "Wichita Vortex Sutra:" declare that the war was over. Ochs even staged his own War Is Over rally in New York City's Central Park that autumn. All this irritated the veteran Trotskyist and tireless antiwar organizer, Fred Halstead: "It made me angry at the time because what we all needed in those days was some inspiration to hold on and reach out, not advice on how to put the problem out of mind. There was already too much of that in a variety of forms." [16] Ginsberg defended his chosen tactic. The aim was to "make a magic phrase which will stick in people's consciousnesses like a rock, just as the phrase *domino theory*—another phrase that stuck in people's consciousnesses like a rock—got them all confused. So once somebody gets up and says it, that precipitates the awareness, the same awareness of the same desire to end the war, in lots of other people . . . it's just necessary for me to place my word out there, not to overwhelm but to clarify other people's sane thought . . ."[17]

Ginsberg's aim was to disturb the complacency that he believed allowed Americans to live with the ongoing atrocity of the war, Ochs's song was more ambivalent. It opens with the ghostly image of "silent soldiers on a silver screen" accompanied by fifes and drums and fanfares, the accoutrements of weaponized patriotism. By the time it reaches its end, the martial tempo has been exposed as a death march:

> . . . So do your duty, boys, and join with pride
> Serve your country in her suicide
> Find the flags so you can wave good-bye
> But just before the end even treason might be worth a try
> This country is too young to die . . .

Ochs still cloaked his call for "treason" in the language of social patriotism, but his desperation was growing. The militarized forward motion of the song's musical setting suggests the impersonal relentlessness of the war. It lambastes not only its cruelty and waste, but our own ability to live with it. Even protest has become a ritual:

> Angry artists painting angry signs
> Use their vision just to blind the blind
> Poisoned players of a grizzly game
> One is guilty and the other gets to point the blame
> Pardon me if I refrain

How to break through this sterile charade? If the battle against the warmongers was fought out in our own consciousness, as not only Dylan but many others at the time had suggested, then perhaps it could be won there as well. Marx turned Hegel on his head to found dialectical materialism; in the hallucinatory year of 1967, there seemed plenty of people keen to turn Marx himself on his head, and declare that consciousness determines being. In October, thousands of young people surrounded the Pentagon in a widely publicized collective effort to "levitate" the physical embodiment of the war machine. The final lines of "The War Is Over" indicate that, for Ochs, this is clutching at straws, though he also seems to be saying that all we have to clutch at is straws.

> The gypsy fortune teller told me that we'd been deceived
> You only are what you believe
> I believe the war is over
> It's over, it's over

The refrain is less an exercise in wishful thinking or some Zen mastery of matter by mind than an anguished lament over the widening gulf between desire and reality.*

We penetrate the mystery only to the degree that we recognize it in the everyday world, by virtue of a dialectical optic that perceives the everyday as impenetrable, the impenetrable as everyday.
                    —WALTER BENJAMIN, *SURREALISM*

In October and November 1967 Dylan visited Nashville to record twelve new songs. None of them had been played in the basement. None of them had choruses. And none of them had guitar solos.

When *John Wesley Harding* was released in early 1968, it stood in immediate and stark contrast to current trends. In place of the multi-layered, unabashedly electrified sound that had swept all before it in recent years, Dylan offered an austere, stripped-down alternative, a minimalist ensemble of bass, drums, and acoustic guitar, punctuated by low-key harmonica interludes. Even the monochrome cover seemed

---

* In late 2002, as war against Iraq loomed, Yoko Ono filled commercial billboards in U.S. cities with the message: *War is Over . . . if you want it.* Lennon and Ono's 1969 bed-in for peace owed much to Ginsberg's prophetic politics, though Lennon's relationship with Ginsberg was much less comfortable than Dylan's.

a rebuke to the color-spattered fashions of the day.* In the songwriting, there was a new economy. It was as if Dylan had moved beyond the prolix romanticism of *Blonde on Blonde* into a severe classicism. The imagery was pared back. The florid and extraneous were excised. For the first and only time in his career, Dylan completed most of the lyrics before starting work on the tunes. As he made clear in interviews at the time, he was consciously trying to write with restraint and precision. "There's no hole in any of the stanzas. There's no blank filler. Each line has something." Allen Ginsberg, with whom Dylan discussed the change of style, confirmed, "There was to be no wasted language, no wasted breath. All the imagery was to be functional rather than ornamental." [18]

Like the Basement Tapes, *John Wesley Harding* painted a timeless landscape, saturated in historical suffering. But in place of the Basement Tapes' wealth of personal idiosyncrasy, the figures that occupy this landscape are abstract, universal, isolated. "I put myself out of the songs," Dylan insisted, "I'm not in the songs anymore." [19] He has left the theater of his own consciousness to fashion images and tales that stand on their own, as self-contained vehicles for home truths about the human condition. The songs seem carved in granite. Yet they are also edgy, abrupt, incomplete—and very much enmeshed in the experiences and dilemmas Dylan shared with others on the eve of the world-splitting events of 1968.

In *John Wesley Harding,* social reality seems much more solid than in the kaleidoscopic mid-sixties songs. It also seems less changeable, its features permanent and elemental: poverty, homelessness, loneliness, the arbitrary cruelty of the mob or the state. In some ways, it's a return to the territory of "Hollis Brown" or "North Country Blues"—a territory largely shunned in the psychedelic era. It should have but didn't strike commentators at the time just how political this album was.

---

* The two men standing next to Dylan on the cover are Bengali *baul* musicians who had been visiting Albert Grossman at Woodstock and playing and partying with Dylan and The Band. Their unexplained presence here is one of the very few references in Dylan's work to non-Anglophone musical traditions.

There was no mention of Vietnam or civil rights, but there were immigrants, hobos, drifters, rich and poor people, landlords, outlaws. That this territory did not strike many as "political" is an indication of just how insensitive sections of the American new left had become to the class issues that preoccupied their predecessors. Dylan himself seemed aware of the paradox. When John Cohen said to him, "your songs aren't as socially and politically applicable as they were earlier," Dylan snapped: "As they were earlier? Could it be that they are just as social and political, only that no one cares to . . . let's start that question again." After Cohen repeated the point, Dylan gave a more tight-lipped reply: "Probably that is because no one cares to see it the way I'm seeing it now, whereas before I saw it the way they saw it." [20]

In one respect *John Wesley Harding* was in keeping with musical fashion. It was a concept album, a coherent and distinctive vision, and as such a worthy successor to the string of visions Dylan had etched on vinyl since 1962. But *John Wesley Harding* was also an accident. Initially, Dylan had intended to enrich the Nashville tracks with guitar and organ. Robbie Robertson had dissuaded him, and thus the strikingly bare sound was sent out into the world. Similarly, Dylan left the lyrics of the title track unfinished. He meant to write another stanza but couldn't—there was an ambiguity here he could not resolve. It's not the only song on the album that seems truncated. Dylan himself explained that, despite appearances, these songs were not really ballads; they "lack this traditional sense of time," the narrative patience and scope that Dylan associated with the folk genre.

Woody Guthrie had died in October, shortly before Dylan went to Nashville to record *John Wesley Harding*. He had been Dylan's starting point as a singer-songwriter, stylistically and politically, and Dylan had never wavered in his devotion to Guthrie's music. It's not surprising that the title track, like other songs on the album, revisits a Guthrie archetype. The song begins as a celebration of a modern-day Robin Hood, the outlaw who was "a friend to the poor" and "never known to hurt an honest man," a successor to Guthrie's Pretty Boy Floyd. But in the song's cursory narrative, the notes of ambivalence—the suggestions of violence, guilt, and opportunism—pile up. "All along this country-side, He opened a many a door . . . with a gun in every hand," "he was never known / To make a foolish move." In reality John Wesley Hardin (Dylan added the *g*) was an assassin with some forty killings to his name and at one time a member of an anti-Reconstruction vigilante gang in Texas. He served seventeen years in jail, where he qualified as a lawyer, only to be gunned down by an aggrieved business partner soon after his release. Dylan may or may not have been aware of the historical back-ground (he may just have liked the resoundingly Protestant name) but the evasive formulations of the song certainly undercut any suggestions of noble heroism. "All across the telegraph / His name it did resound." All that's left is the published account, and that could be a lie or it could be the truth—or more likely a compound of the two. There's something of John Ford's ambiguous endorsement of legend over truth here, but with an additional bleakness: history offers no bittersweet vindication.*

Dylan's portrait of the "poor immigrant" is even less heroic. This isn't one of Guthrie's deportees, but a cold and selfish man who lies and cheats. Driven by insecurity and acquisitiveness, he "passionately hates his life / And likewise, fears his death." Lost in an alien land of competitive individuals, the immigrant's very efforts to survive and thrive de-humanize him. He "eats but is not satisfied," "hears but does not see," and "falls in love with wealth itself." It's a form of lifelessness, Dylan's long-standing enemy, but now it is pitied rather than scorned. Like other songs on the album, "I Pity the Poor Immigrant" deromanticizes the oppressed, but also disdains cynicism. The immigrant is a victim of history.

The song also restates Dylan's critique of money-power, the suspi-

---

* *Bonnie and Clyde,* released a few months after *John Wesley Harding,* addresses many of the same themes: the romance and moral ambivalence of the outlaw, the role of the press, the ambiguity of legends. Like Dylan's work of this period, it's also involved in excavating—with the tools of the late sixties—an American past of hard times and stark class divisions.

cion of Mammon that persists through all his metamorphoses. The incompatibility between wealth and human solidarity is made explicit in "I Am a Lonesome Hobo." At first, the hobo presents himself in isolation, an individual cut off from the human family. "Where another man's life might begin, / That's exactly where mine ends." Then he reveals how and why he has fallen from grace:

Well, once I was rather prosperous,
There was nothing I did lack.
I had fourteen-karat gold in my mouth
And silk upon my back.
But I did not trust my brother,
I carried him to blame,
Which led me to my fatal doom,
To wander off in shame.

It seems that the hobo's isolation began not with his loss of wealth but with the effect of wealth upon him in the first place. The last stanza is the hobo's warning, and it's as explicit a statement of values as anything in Dylan's protest phase:

Stay free from petty jealousies,
Live by no man's code,
And hold your judgment for yourself
Lest you wind up on this road.

Some might find this statement of values not only explicit but banal. And at times on *John Wesley Harding* there is a Polonius-like quality in the way "the moral of the story, the moral of this song" is so flatly drawn. However, Dylan routinely undercuts the complacency—frequently, as in the last line of "I Am a Lonesome Hobo," by a brisk reminder that the losses stand unrecouped. And the advice to "hold your judgment for yourself" is more than a world-weary expedient. One respect in which *John Wesley Harding* does break from the Dylan of the mid-sixties is its repudiation of self-righteousness. The need for a more tempered and understanding engagement with a hostile world fills "Dear Landlord," usually read as Dylan's message to Albert Grossman, the manager with whom he had fallen out. The song's marvelous opening salvo—"Please don't put a price on my soul"—is the eternal plea of the artist to the moneyman. Though the artist's "burden is heavy" and his "dreams are beyond control," he vows to "give you all I got to give," but he also knows that he remains dependent on the moneyman's whims:

> And I do hope you receive it well,
> Dependin' on the way you feel that you live.

But Dylan understands that the moneyman himself is a victim of his wealth:

> All of us, at times, we might work too hard
> To have it too fast and too much,
> And anyone can fill his life up
> With things he can see but he just cannot touch.

The plaintive blues moves toward a cautious plea for mutual negotiation based on mutual respect. "Each of us has his own special gift" and therefore: "if you don't underestimate me, / I won't underestimate you." It's one of several songs on the album that end in blank irresolution. In "Dear Landlord" the social nexus is a demanding one. Salvaging a measure of dignity and autonomy requires patient negotiation.

In the compact "Drifter's Escape," Dylan returns to "the courtroom of honor" he'd exposed in "Hattie Carroll." Now it's a broader theater of injustice, and its antics are altogether less dignified. From his dramatic opening cry: "Oh, help me in my weakness," the drifter appears as Everyman, exhausted and bewildered by his fate, persecuted by the state for no reason. The song depicts the public domain as a shameless charade. The judge casts his robe aside and sheds a conspicuous tear:

> Outside, the crowd was stirring,
> You could hear it from the door.
> Inside, the judge was stepping down,
> While the jury cried for more.

For both judge and jury, authority and the mob, justice is nothing but self-indulgent performance and spectacle. The individual is powerless, and can only be delivered by a deus ex machina:

Just then a bolt of lightning
Struck the courthouse out of shape,
And while ev'rybody knelt to pray
The drifter did escape.

The sudden ending is cold comfort. These aren't the chimes of freedom flashing. The rupture between institutions and individuals that had fueled Dylan's work since the first protest songs is here chiseled in granite, presented as an immutable fact of life.

If the drifter is a passive everyman, the Wicked Messenger is a more complicated figure, and his fate is more enigmatic than the drifter's. The song title appears to be derived from Proverbs 13:17: "A wicked messenger falleth into mischief: but a faithful ambassador is health." In Dylan's song, the wicked messenger first appears in public, unbidden, as an obsessive ("a mind that multiplied the smallest matter") with a compulsion to flatter his audience. He makes a bed for himself "behind the assembly hall." One day he brings forth a note to the world reading "The soles of my feet, I swear they're burning." The public response to this personal declaration carries a sting in the tail:

Oh, the leaves began to fallin'
And the seas began to part,
And the people that confronted him were many.
And he was told but these few words,
Which opened up his heart,
"If ye cannot bring good news, then don't bring any."

Dylan explained that this third and final verse "opens it up and then the time schedule takes a jump and soon the song becomes wider." That's a device typical of *John Wesley Harding*'s unfinished parables, as is the abrupt finale.

The wicked messenger is the artist, the prophet, the protest singer, seeking approval but being told clearly by the public what harsh terms that approval carries. As for the "faithful ambassadors," Dylan tells their saga in "I Dreamed I Saw St. Augustine," an adaptation of "Joe Hill," a popular-front favorite, which opens:

> I dreamed I saw Joe Hill last night
> Alive as you and me
> Says I, "But Joe, you're ten years dead,"
> "I never died," says he, "I never died," says he.

Hill, the labor organizer and songwriter executed in Utah in 1915, assures the dreamer that he still lives through the movement he served:

> "From San Diego up to Maine
> In every mine and mill
> Where workers strike and organize,"
> Says he, "You'll find Joe Hill," says he, "You'll find Joe Hill."

The song was composed in the summer of 1936 not by workers or organizers or itinerant balladeers but by two educated leftist intellectuals, Earl Robinson and Alfred Hayes, at the CP-organized Camp Unity in upstate New York, for a campfire program celebrating the legendary singer-martyr. By the end of the year, the new song had spread across the country and was being sung in Spain by members of the Abraham Lincoln Brigade.[21] Dylan would have known the song and associated it with the survivors of the popular front he had met in New York City. He would have known that Joe Hill was a prototype for Woody Guthrie, and indeed for himself in an earlier incarnation. Hill was a full-time agitator and organizer, and Guthrie, though he earned a living (off and on) as a musician and writer, was also in day-to-day contact with working people and their organizations. That experience gave both of them a very different, more immediate relationship to their musical audiences than the one that Dylan enjoyed. This had become deeply problematic for him, and it forms one of the themes of *John Wesley Harding*.

Dylan replaces Joe Hill with St. Augustine. There's no particular significance in the choice; it was enough that it was a saint from long ago. The substitution enabled Dylan to throw his story back into history, and thereby suggest that the tale was eternally recurring. The modern-day secular martyr was being recycled into a type from antiquity. Like Joe Hill, Dylan's St. Augustine "is alive as you or me," but he's not calmly reassuring, he's frantic: "searching for the very souls / who already have been sold." In the second verse, the saint, like Joe Hill, steps forward to address his beloved but debauched democracy ("Come out, ye gifted kings and queens"). However, he does not stir the people to action; he merely asks them to "hear my sad complaint." He then declares, with a lilting finality: *No martyrs are among ye now, whom you can call your own.* This ringing line repeals the substance of the Hayes-Robinson song. A striking statement from an artist who had mourned Medgar Evers and written poems about JFK, who'd lived through the Birmingham church bombing and the murders of Mississippi summer, not to mention the death of Che Guevara, announced weeks before he wrote the song. It seems the public world is now too inauthentic to sustain anything as morally grand as a martyr. The only consolation is to "go on your way accordingly / and know you're not alone." But there's a further twist in this reconsideration of Joe Hill's mission and fate. The singer's dream ends with the realization that he himself is among those who have put the saint to death. (Having declared there are no martyrs, St. Augustine quickly becomes one.) Dylan himself is revealed as one of the distracted mob, one of the persecutors. Paradoxically, that bereaves him of the only consolation St. Augustine has offered, and he finds himself "alone and terrified."

This retelling of the legendary martyr-singer's tale is in part Dylan's reflection on his own democratic-prophetic vocation. The only prophecy the artist can make with confidence is that he and his message will be rejected by a world that values all the wrong things. The movement's reassuring dream of redemption through history has been replaced by a nightmare of unqualified bleakness and failure. The true prophets of freedom (not the charlatans in the media) will always be rejected by those who fear freedom. The pathos of the song, however, lies in the admission of mutual complicity—one of the themes that ties *John Wesley Harding* together. We are all guilty, we all fear the truth, and if any of us were treated as we deserve, we'd all be in trouble. The facile dichotomy between them and us, between the hip and the straight, the in-group and the masses, the leader and the pack has been dissolved by humbling experience.

Prepare the table, watch in the watchtower, eat, drink: arise, ye princes, and anoint the shield. For thus hath the Lord said unto me, Go, set a watchman, let him declare what he seeth. And he saw a chariot with a couple of horsemen, a chariot of asses, and a chariot of camels; and he hearkened diligently with much heed: And he cried, A lion: My lord, I stand continually upon the watchtower in the daytime, and I am set in my ward whole nights: And, behold, here cometh a chariot of men, with a couple of horsemen. And he answered and said, Babylon is fallen, is fallen; and all the graven images of her gods he hath broken unto the ground.

—Isaiah 21: 5–9

The apocalyptic tone is nowhere stronger on *John Wesley Harding* than in "All Along the Watchtower." This startlingly concise and deeply mysterious composition begins in medias res. As Dylan himself noted, it's a case of "the cycle of events working in a rather reverse order." The last verse sets the scene for the first two. And one key to that last verse is the passage in Isaiah quoted above. Here the princes are called to keep watch; the "couple of horsemen" approach from the distance; their message is that a civilization has fallen.

The first two of the three verses that make up "All Along the Watchtower" comprise a dislocated dialogue between the two biblical horsemen, recast by Dylan as the joker and the thief. The joker opens the song with a declaration of the urgent need to escape from a condition of sustained incoherence:

"There must be some way out of here," said the joker to the thief,
"There's too much confusion, I can't get no relief."

Crucially, it's not only "confusion" that the joker complains of but also exploitation—businessmen and ploughmen drink his wine and dig his earth, but have no idea "what any of it is worth."

Where the joker is aggrieved, petulant, panicked, the thief—who replies in the second verse—is calm, "kindly," but also stern. "No reason to get excited" is not the laid-back counsel it may seem. What is needed now, the thief avers, is steely nerves; it's precisely because there is cause for panic that this is no time to panic. Where the joker complains about thieves (those who drink his wine and dig his earth), the thief complains about those "who feel that life is but a joke." It's a caution against cynicism, and a call to find something deeper in this anxious moment. But the thief offers no "way out of here," merely the prophetic injunction:

So let us not talk falsely now, the hour is getting late.

But this command for clarity in extremis is wrapped up in enigma. Communication is urgent and necessary but it remains problematic. At the song's end, apocalypse is imminent. In the Bible, the growl of the wild cat and the howl of the wind are harbingers of the end of times, the fall of Babylon (both can be found in the Book of Revelations, but then, so can almost anything). Critics are right to note the influence of the Bible in Dylan's work of all periods, but it was only later that this interest acquired a mystical or formally religious significance. What grabbed the young Dylan about the Bible was what grabbed him about folk and blues: its archaic and resonant language, the metaphorical power that enabled it to speak of a deeper experience, a more abiding mystery, than the language of newspapers and magazines. A visitor to Woodstock found two books on Dylan's table: a Bible and a volume of Hank Williams's lyrics.

Apocalyptic themes can be found in Dylan's work from the beginning, whether it's the nuclear apocalypse of "Let Me Die in My Footsteps," the egalitarian revolution hymned in "When The Ship Comes In" or the history-galvanized revelation in "Chimes of Freedom." Often the language used to evoke the apocalypse is biblical, but in Dylan's work of the sixties apocalypse is a social category: a response to the bomb, the imminence of social transformation, the impossibility of social transformation, the cataclysm of war. The wind that howls at the end of "All Along the Watchtower" is the same storm of history that blows through "When The Ship Comes In," "Chimes of Freedom," and "Farewell Angelina." But here, history is no longer vindication or revelation or unbearable chaos; it's a universal and inescapable judgment. Its action, however, takes place offstage. Its contents are unspecified. Instead, the song loops back on itself. We're left with the joker and the thief in urgent discussion. The circularity of the song's structure continuously brings us back to the same moment, to the fact that there's no "way out of here." In medias res is not only the song's method but the state it evokes. It gives us history lived on the brink of destruction and revelation. This tautly constructed, self-contained, gnomic song vibrates with impending doom. Soon after the album's release, Hendrix took that vibration and orchestrated into a rock Götterdämmerung. With its slouching vocal and three dramatically crafted guitar solos, his "All Along the Watchtower" may be the most insightful and original of all Dylan covers. (Dylan approved and in the seventies adopted Hendrix's arrangement for his own performances.) Hendrix's single rode high in the charts in late 1968 and was heard far away in Vietnam, where GIs felt they knew exactly what the song was about.

Among Dylan's dramatis personae, jokers and thieves are generally unheroic outcasts, impish misfits, surviving on the margins. Here they are disembodied voices from an interior discussion. And what they are discussing is the appropriate response to an outside world of chaos, injustice, and violence. There's another Old Testament prophecy that may be relevant:

> But if the watchman see the sword come, and blow not the trumpet, and the people be not warned; if the sword come, and take any person from among them, he is taken away in his iniquity; but his blood will I require at the watchman's hand.
>
> —EZEKIEL 3: 6

In the whispered exchange of the joker and the thief, you can hear the dilemmas of those charged with keeping the conscience of the nation—and preserving their own sanity—in a time of war. As elsewhere in *John Wesley Harding,* the democratic-prophetic burden seems a tragic one. "Let us not talk falsely now," but who could possibly do justice to the truth? And if someone could, would anybody listen?

John Wesley Harding gave the impression of an artist who had replaced the teasing glimpses of *Blonde on Blonde* with a clear apprehension of unchanging realities. But it was only an impression. Dylan was, after all, a mere twenty-six years old, and realities were shifting around him at a baffling velocity. The album was not and could not be an old master's final summation. It was, rather, an arrested moment, as Dylan sought to refine the lessons of previous years. Nor, for all its stylistic coherence, is the album entirely sustained. Though "The Ballad of Frankie Lee and Judas Priest" is a favorite with many Dylanologists, it's a contrived allegory that teases and baffles but ultimately bores. (Though the little neighbor boy "with his guilt so well concealed" who mutters "nothing is revealed" is a clue to the rest of the album.) Similarly, "As I Went Out One Morning" fails to satisfy. There is nothing here but allegory, and a not very illuminating one at that. It's an episode revolving around another *belle dame sans merci,* who is encountered when Dylan goes out "to breathe the air around Tom Paine's." If this alludes to the ECLC fiasco of late 1963, then its main point of interest must be that in the last line of the song it is Paine who apologizes to Dylan. (You'd think it would be the other way around). If one discounts this bloodless exercise, the only love songs on *John Wesley Harding* are the two upbeat, pedal-steel–backed country numbers with which the album concludes. They're charming and wonderfully crafted tunes, but utterly without shading. Both songs are simple statements of unconditional submission to love and family. It didn't look like it at the time, but they were portents of artistic decline.

On January 20, 1968, Woody Guthrie's friends and followers gathered in Carnegie Hall to celebrate his legacy and to raise funds to combat the disease that killed him. The benefit concert had been catapulted into the headlines by the announcement that Bob Dylan—who had not appeared in public since his motorcycle accident—would be among the performers.

For Dylan, it was a reunion with old associates from the folk scene: Joan Baez, Pete Seeger, Jack Elliott, Odetta, Judy Collins, Tom Paxton. Interwoven with their performances of Guthrie classics was a prose narrative written by one-time Almanac Singer Millard Lampell and recited by leftist actors Robert Ryan and Will Geer—the latter had worked and traveled with Guthrie in the thirties and forties, and makes an appearance in *Bound for Glory*.* Dylan paid homage to his early role model in his own manner. He brought The Band with him to Carnegie Hall, and together they played three Guthrie numbers in a highly unorthodox style—a rough-edged rockabilly with soulful harmonies and rambunctious guitar solos. It was the ensemble's only public performance in anything like the mode of the Basement Tapes—a dramatic contrast with the confrontational, cutting-edge sound that had characterized their last public appearances. It was still electric and it still rocked, but in place of the immediacy and modernity of 1966 was a package that felt remote, plangent, archaic. Dylan's singing is sometimes shaky, as if he's still in the Catskill basement conducting one of his meandering private meditations on a favorite old tune. But overall, it's a gutsy and original performance, treating the Guthrie originals with dignity but not reverence, and notable, not least, for Dylan's choice of songs.

Having long since mastered Guthrie's wide-ranging repertoire, Dylan could have selected any number of Woody's more playful or personal compositions, but alighted instead on three songs that were explicitly political in intent and rooted in American history. He opened with a raucously upbeat version of "The Grand Coulee Dam," one

---

* Geer was blacklisted throughout the fifties but became a national icon in the seventies when he played Grandpa in the television show *The Waltons*—a liberal but strikingly inauthentic slice of rural Americana.

of the Columbia River songs Guthrie wrote in early 1941, when the Bonneville Power Administration brought him up to the Pacific Northwest to sing the praises of the federally funded hydroelectric project—and counteract the hostile propaganda of the big private power companies. This song celebrates both the American landscape and the intervention of the federal government in that landscape. It evokes the power and majesty of the "that King Columbia River" as it "comes a-roaring down the canyon to meet the salty tide" and the perils humans have faced "In the misty glitter of that wild and windward spray" (which sounds like a phrase from "Mr. Tambourine Man"). Dylan shouts out the lines as if he was trying to be heard above the rush of the great waters. He seems to relish their untameable restlessness. But he throws himself equally into the following verses, explaining how "Uncle Sam took up the notion in the year of thirty three" to harness the river's restless energy for "the factory and the farmer and for all of you and me" (and to help build "a flying fortress to blast for Uncle Sam").

There's no tension here between nature and human society; the singer addresses the Columbia like a brother: "River, while you're rolling you can do some work for me." These days, mega-dams like the Grand Coulee are criticized for their ecological and social costs, and protest singers in the third-world countries where these dams are now built are more likely to condemn than to praise them. Of course, the giant private companies, having found World Bank–sponsored big dam projects highly lucrative, have also changed their tune. What seems to fire Dylan in the Guthrie song is its spirit of celebration, its happy merger of lyrical pantheism and social patriotism. Its New Deal optimism seems worlds apart from Dylan's own political temper at this moment but Dylan refuses to mock or undermine the song; he honors Guthrie by plunging into it with an unsentimental vigor.

Dylan's next choice was "Dear Mrs. Roosevelt," a paean to FDR that Guthrie wrote after the president's death in 1945. It's a one-dimensional eulogy of the rich kid crippled by polio who became the champion of the poor, the enemy of the "money-changin' racket boys," and, fitfully, the great hope of the popular front. Dylan tactfully omitted the telltale verses about the Allies' wartime conferences at Yalta and Tehran:

> He didn't like Churchill very much . . .
> He said he didn't like DeGaulle or Chiang Kai-Shek
> Shook hands with Joseph Stalin, says: "There's a man I like!"

As Dylan and The Band re-created it in 1968, the song is less a tribute to a lost political leader than a mournful memorial of a vanished era and ethos. They drag out the refrain, "This world was lucky to see him born," with a quivering, weary bewilderment, as if facing up to the blank impossibility of such heroes reappearing in their own times.

Dylan finished his set with "I Ain't Got No Home," one of Guthrie's dust-bowl ballads of the late thirties, borrowing the tune from "This World Is Not My Home," a Baptist hymn popularized by the Carter Family. Guthrie, who had been inclined to religious mysticism in his younger days, here turned the consolations of other-worldliness upside down. The result was a grim-minded protest against the earthly dispossession of the poor by the rich.

> I was farmin' on the shares, always I was poor
> My crops I'd lay away into the banker's store
> My wife she took down and died upon the cabin floor
> And I ain't got no home in this world anymore.

Dylan and The Band turn the song into a keening lamentation. "*Po*-lice make it hard wherever I may go," the singer wails, as if the rich man's cops were forever dogging his steps. Guthrie, of course, had considerably more first-hand experience of police cruelty than Dylan. Nonetheless, Guthrie's insistence on the subservience of state agents to economic power haunts the younger man's work, running through "Donald White" and "Hattie Carroll" to "John Wesley Harding" and "The Drifter's Escape." In Dylan's songs of the mid-sixties, the theme is elaborated as a multi-dimensional metaphor. Singing Guthrie's words at Carnegie Hall, as the decade nears it climax and conclusion, Dylan reminds himself and his audience of the metaphor's foundation in an enduring social reality.

"Dylan manifests a profound awareness of the war and how it is affecting all of us," Jon Landau (later Bruce Springsteen's producer) wrote in his review of *John Wesley Harding*. "This doesn't mean that I think any of the particular songs are about the war or that any of the songs are protests over it. All I mean to say is that Dylan has felt the war, that there is an awareness of it contained within the mood of the album as a whole." [22]

By early 1968, the war had claimed nearly 30,000 U.S. lives. South Vietnam had been devastated by four years of brutal counter-insurgency. There were more than half a million U.S. troops in the country. The bombing was relentless. It was hard not to "feel the war."

There is a single direct reference to Vietnam in Dylan's work of this period. It comes in the liner notes for *Bringing It All Back Home* written in early 1965:

a middle-aged druggist
up for district attorney. he starts screaming
at me you're the one. you're the one
that's been causing all them riots over in
vietnam. immediately turns t' a bunch of
people an' says if elected, he'll have me
electrocuted publicly on the next fourth
of july.

When he toured Australia in early 1966, Dylan was quizzed about his views on the war—the Australians had sent troops to back the Americans—but kept ducking the question. When a reporter finally asked if he didn't have any feelings at all on the subject, he said, "Sure I have a feeling about war, about Vietnam. My thoughts lie in the futility of war, not the morality of it." At a press conference later in the tour, he offered a more flippant line.

Q.: What do you think about the Vietnam War?

Dylan: Nothing. It's Australia's war.

Q.: But Americans are there.

Dylan: They're helping the Australians.[23]

In February 1968, as *John Wesley Harding*—sans hype—moved up the album charts, the Vietnamese launched the Tet Offensive. It brought them to the gates of the U.S. embassy in Saigon, but at terrible human cost. Militarily, they were soon dislodged from the cities of the south and thrown back into the countryside. Politically, the gain proved incalculable. Back in the U.S.A. the credibility of the war makers tumbled. Opposition widened and sharpened. Eugene McCarthy's primary challenge to LBJ attracted substantial student support, and his unexpectedly strong showing in New Hampshire hastened the president's decision not to seek reelection. The more radical elements, however, remained convinced that McCarthy and his ilk had little to offer. Even as some young people were taking their first tentative political steps in identifying with McCarthy, others were striding beyond liberalism. Their numbers multiplied in response to the events that toppled over one another during the following months. The assassination of Martin Luther King was followed by a wave of violent rebellion in the inner cities far greater in scale than anything the decade had witnessed. The SDS-led student occupation of Columbia University in April became a foretaste of the events in Paris in May. The assassination of Robert F. Kennedy in June fueled the sense of a society out of control, and also, for the moment, terminated the liberal Democratic option. SDS's ranks now swelled to include 100,000 students nationwide.[24]

By the summer of 1968, black and student unrest in the U.S.A. was clearly seen and felt to be part of a global insurgency. Whether Dylan liked it or not, in many parts of the world he was heard as the voice of dissident America. He was certainly one of the reasons why European youth, overwhelmingly hostile to the U.S. war, did not at any stage repudiate American popular culture. In the U.S.A., no matter how firmly Dylan disclaimed any representative function, his voice was heard more than ever as the voice of and for the social crisis that everyone now agreed was gripping the country by the throat.

As for the man himself, he remained silent as *John Wesley Harding* quickly became his bestselling album yet. In July of 1968, however, he decided to grant an interview, not to the national media, but to *Sing Out!*, the left-wing folk magazine that had championed his early music and passionately debated his development, and was now broke. The interview was conducted by two of Dylan's old friends from the Village, John Cohen of the New Lost City Ramblers and Happy Traum, the banjo and guitar player who was now editing *Sing Out!* and living not far from Dylan in Woodstock. Cohen was deferential and seemed uncritically excited by everything Dylan said. In contrast, Traum was preoccupied with something Dylan hadn't said. He asked his old friend: "Do you foresee a time when you're going to have to take a position?" "No," Dylan replied. That wasn't good enough for Traum, and at several points in the lengthy interview he returns to the subject.

> *Traum:* I think that every day we get closer to having to make a choice.
> *Dylan:* How so?
> *Traum:* I think the events of the world are getting closer to us, they're as close as the nearest ghetto.
> *Dylan:* Where's the nearest ghetto?
> *Traum:* Maybe down the block. Events are moving on a mass scale.
> *Dylan:* What events?
> *Traum:* War, racial problems, violence in the streets.

Dylan remains unresponsive and unimpressed, but Traum reminds him of the Columbia students and their struggle against "the masters of war."

> *Traum:* They're trying to overcome the people ruling them, and they are powerful people who are running the show. They can be called the establishment, and they are the same people who make the wars, that build the missiles, that manufacture the instruments of death.

Dylan: Well, that's just the way the world is going.

Traum: The students are trying to make it go another way.

Dylan: Well I'm for the students, of course, they're going to be taking over the world. The people who they're fighting are old people, old ideas. They don't have to fight, they can sit back and wait.

Traum: The old ideas have the guns, though.

It's when Traum presses on to the specific question of the Vietnam War, and the stand that ought to be taken against it, that Dylan really bridles.

Traum: Probably the most pressing thing going on in a political sense is the war. Now I'm not saying any artist or group of artists can change the course of the war, but they still feel it their responsibility to say something.

Dylan: I know some very good artists who are for the war.

Traum: Well I'm just talking about the ones who are against it.

Dylan: That's like what I'm talking about; it's for or against the war. That really doesn't exist. It's not for or against the war. I'm speaking of a certain painter, and he's all for the war. He's just about ready to go over there himself. And I can comprehend him.

Traum: Why can't you argue with him?

Dylan: I can see what goes into his paintings, and why should I?

Traum: I don't understand how that relates to whether a position should be taken.

Dylan: Well, there's nothing for us to talk about really.

Even that brush-off does not deter Traum, who insists on challenging Dylan's position and finally elicits from him a sharp rebuke:

Traum: My feeling is that with a person who is for the war and ready to go over there, I don't think it would be possible for you and him to share the same values.

Dylan: I've known him a long time, he's a gentleman and I admire him, he's a friend of mine. People just have their views. Anyway, how do you know I'm not, as you say, *for* the war? [25]

And that was the extent of Bob Dylan's contemporary public comment on his government's war in Vietnam, a war that took two million lives and blighted many more.*

In Dylan's nonposition on Vietnam, there's an element of sheer perversity, a desire to tweak and challenge his audience and his followers, a disinclination to give people what they might expect from him. But the wariness of categories here seems more than ever a protective mask, a means of ducking the question. What's frustrating is not that Dylan vacillated or displayed the same confusion felt by millions of others, but that he was so reluctant to work at the problems, so lazily satisfied with facile evasions (in contrast to the demands he placed on himself as an artist). An irascible disposition to pose awkward questions is to be cherished, but those who ask awkward questions must also have the patience to listen to complex answers, and when it came to politics, Dylan, at this stage, did not. He resisted the temptation to swim with the youth tide, to accept voguish answers, but he did not resist the temptation to surrender to answerlessness. In this intellectual retreat, he was not alone, as impatience with the status quo too easily and too often translated into impatience with the intricate and long-term demands of movement building.

If public life is an ongoing test for the artist, then when it came to Vietnam, Dylan failed. He did turn away and pretend that he just didn't see—or rather, he claimed that he saw too much, too far, too deeply, and

* When performing "With God on Our Side" in the late eighties, Dylan sang a new verse:

> In the nineteen sixties came the Vietnam War
> Can somebody tell me what we're fightin' for?
> So many young men died
> So many mothers cried
> Now I ask the question
> Was God on our side?

Dylan inserted the new lyrics—which may have been written by the Neville Brothers for the cover version they recorded about the same time—between the verses on World War II and the nuclear stand-off with the Russians (still ongoing in the late eighties). Though the Vietnam addition lacks the rigor of the original verses, it does fit precisely into the song's revision of U.S. history.

that therefore it was impossible, inauthentic, for him to speak out. That was a posture. Out of his disdain for fashion, for simplistic dualities, out of his anxieties about getting it wrong and finding himself out of his depth, out of his fear of the cost that taking a stand might exact—not least in the public hatred it would unleash upon him—he turned away as surely as one of the citizens in his "Clothes Line Saga."

Nonetheless, in his songs, Dylan had already spoken of Vietnam. "John Brown," "Blowin' in the Wind," "Hard Rain," "Masters of War," "With God on Our Side," "Bob Dylan's 115th Dream," "Tombstone Blues," "All Along the Watchtower": as the decade advanced, these songs sounded more prophetic and pain-ridden.

" 'We're a Winner' is a song with a message," Curtis Mayfield explained in January 1968, "a message to all, and yet basically to the black masses of people . . . things move slowly but with the movement we're a winner." [26] The message made many radio executives uncomfortable. Nor did it sit that easily with the label, ABC, from which Mayfield and the Impressions soon decamped. Mayfield was twenty-six years old. He knew the kind of music he wanted to make, why he wanted to make it, and who he wanted to make it with and for. In the coming years, his black-owned and managed Curtom label would release a series of densely orchestrated socially conscious singles.

"We're a Winner" blended a positive response to the new black nationalism with the optimism of earlier years. "There'll be no more Uncle Tom / at last that blessed day has come." After Martin Luther King's assassination, Mayfield's writing took on a more somber tone, and greater political realism, but remained rooted in the humanistic ideology of the civil rights movement. "This Is My Country," like "This Land Is Your Land," stakes a claim on America. The claim here, however, is staked specifically on behalf of black people, and is infused with an uncompromising urgency:

Too many have died in protecting my pride
For me to go second class

Still, the gentle-souled Mayfield could not resist ending the song with a polite appeal to the fair-minded majority: "And I know you will give consideration / Shall we perish unjust or live equal as a nation?" Curtis, like Martin Luther King, tried to bridge the gap between the moderates and the militants, between a necessary black pride and a more inclusive politics. He was not afraid to lecture the separatists. In 1969 the Impressions released "Mighty, Mighty, Spade and Whitey," an appeal to a movement in crisis:

Your black and white power
Is gonna be a crumbling tower
And we who stand divided
So goddamn undecided
Give this some thought
In stupidness we've all been caught

The harsher mood could also be heard that year in Nina Simone's "Revolution:" "I'm here to tell you about destruction . . ." The album on which this featured also included smoking covers of three Dylan songs: "The Times They Are A-Changin'," "Just Like Tom Thumb's Blues," and "I Shall Be Released." Soon after, Simone wrote "To Be Young, Gifted and Black," ruefully recalling her younger self and the changed circumstances that faced her successors:

Young, gifted and black
How I long to know the truth
There are times when I look back
And I am haunted by my youth
Oh but my joy of today
Is that we can all be proud to say
To be young, gifted and black
Is where it's at

Two years later, Aretha Franklin turned the song into a major hit. Simone, in the meantime, had moved to Europe, following Bob Moses into voluntary exile.

Curtis Mayfield's first solo album, *Curtis,* appeared in 1970. Musically and lyrically it was more adventurous than anything he'd attempted with the Impressions. The richly textured sound was anchored in a deep, funky pulse. And politics were everywhere. The first single from the album was the apocalyptic "If There's a Hell Below We're All Gonna Go." It's an indication of how widespread and deep-going the sense of social crisis had become in these years that it darkened the vision of even a dedicated optimist like Mayfield. Nonetheless, he remained committed to a music of uplift. The solo album also included the alternative anthem, "Miss Black America," "Move On Up," which recapitulates motifs from "Keep On Pushing" and "We're a Winner," and the remarkable "We People Who Are Darker than Blue," a song that ought to be listened to by anyone who thinks that the only true voice of the black power era was one of aggressive nihilism. In "Keep On Keeping On," from his 1971 follow-up album, *Roots,* Mayfield sings: "Everybody gather round and listen to my song, I've only got one. . . ." He wasn't embarrassed to reiterate his core theme—the inspirational gospel politics of "Keep On Pushing" and "People Get Ready," the message of struggle sustained, survived, redeemed, over many years and indeed many generations.

Mayfield's work was part of an efflorescence of social comment in black popular music. After so many years of hesitation and silence among the soul stars, the dam broke. Between 1968 and 1973, James Brown, Marvin Gaye, Aretha Franklin, the Temptations, Bobby Womack, Stevie Wonder, Edwin Starr, and others produced a rich seam of what can only be described as protest music—songs replete with topical references and a partisan appeal—wrought to a degree of musical sophistication undreamt of by the folkies. This was never music for rallies or marches; it was music to dance to.

The hip-hop artists of the nineties ransacked the records of this period; Mayfield is said to be the most sampled of all, a tribute to his fecund musical imagination. Over his grooves, a new generation laid down hard-hitting social comment laced with a revived black nationalism. But they did so in the absence of a mass movement. As a result, authenticity—"keeping it real"—remained highly problematic in the hip-hop world. For some, authenticity was salvaged through gun-toting gangsterism or misogyny. Aggressive postures were certainly more common than active involvement in black communities. But that's what the industry wanted, and it had grown far more ruthlessly expert in appropriating and marketing the authentic than it had been in Dylan's time.

––––––––––

Soon after the *Sing Out!* interview, a national television audience witnessed a Dylanesque nightmare come alive on the streets of Chicago. While the Democratic national convention nominated Vice President Humphrey over antiwar candidate Eugene McCarthy, the riot squad grew restless. Police assaulted and teargassed demonstrators, journalists, delegates and bystanders, apparently at random. McCarthy had advised his own supporters to stay away, and the mobilization for the Chicago demonstration was in the hands of the Yippies, SDS, and others on the far left. The turnout of 10,000 was relatively small, but that did not lessen the symbolic impact of the confrontation between countercultural radicals and Mayor Daley's storm troopers. In an effort to draw young people to the protests, and to up the symbolic stakes, the Yippies spread rumors that Dylan—or the Beatles or the Stones— would be appearing. In the end, Phil Ochs found himself performing "I Ain't Marchin' Anymore" in Grant Park amid flaming draft cards, encircling police, and cries of "off the pigs" from zealots and provocateurs alike. The protesters moved off toward the convention center. There, under the gaze of the television cameras, they were met by a ferocious police attack, to which they responded by chanting "the whole world is watching!" * It was five years to the day since the march for Jobs and Freedom in Washington.[27]

––––––––––

* The protesters also sang "Blowin' in the Wind." To Allen Ginsberg, who was present, the song came into its own that day: "That song could have been any little boy's lyric fancy, but when it was played one afternoon during the convention in Grant Park across from the Hilton, it revealed itself as a prophecy all along, because it described what was going

The events in Chicago were traumatic for Ochs. "Chicago's going to come everywhere in the western hemisphere," he said a few months later. "We'll all get to meet Mayor Daley in person. One way or another, Chicago was very exhilarating at the time and then very sad afterward. Because something very extraordinary died there, which was America." [28] The cover of his next album, *Rehearsals for Retirement,* featured a tombstone with the words *Phil Ochs (American) Born El Paso Texas Died Chicago Illinois.* Commercially, the album was a flop. Harassed by the FBI, appalled at the war and the violence at home, uncertain of his own role as singer and activist, he experienced the first bouts of the depressive illness that drove him to suicide in 1976. "America used to be the melting pot," he said in 1969. "Now the pot is boiling over." Convinced that somehow he had to find a way to speak directly to working-class Americans, he tried to reinvent himself as a Presley-style rock 'n' roller, gold lamé suit and all. The transition was much more artificial than the one Dylan revealed at Newport, and though it led to a similar clash with the expectations of previously devoted fans, it did not succeed in reaching a new audience. The ironically titled *Greatest Hits* album of 1970 made not the slightest dent in the now huge rock 'n' roll market. On one song on the album, "Chords of Fame," Ochs warned his successors:

> I can see you make the music
> 'Cause you carry a guitar
> God help the troubadour
> Who tries to be a star
>
> So play the chords of love, my friend
> Play the chords of pain

---

on right there on the grass. Crowds of strange children with long hair, who weren't afraid to have their bodies hit by police phantoms armed with billy clubs, were demanding reality and truth from business-delegates who were walking around in upstairs Hilton rooms scared of the stink of their own karma. Teargassed! That scene was, literally, blowing in the wind. Was it going to be a police state or a liberation from what had been a police state all along?"

If you want to keep your song,
Don't, don't, don't, don't play the chords of fame

Perhaps the singer-songwriter niche was never the best showcase for Ochs's talents and commitments. He might have flourished in musical theater, if there had been a musical theater sufficiently vibrant and radical to accommodate him.

In August 1968, the Beatles told their fans just what they thought about the latest ideological fashion in "Revolution," a put-down of violent political posturing (with typical sixties volatility, John Lennon would soon recant and recast the message). The underground press cried Judas, but Irwin Silber asked. "Whoever said the Beatles were revolutionaries in the first place? The record companies, the press agents, the promoters, the managers—the whole greedy crew of artful dodgers who figure you can peddle revolution along with soap and cornflakes and ass and anything else that can turn over a dollar." [29]

In November 1968, Columbia Records (Dylan's label) ran a series of full-page advertisements in the underground press—then reaching hundreds of thousands of potential customers—showing long-haired protesters locked up in a police cell, surrounded by placards displaying slogans like *Music is Love, Grab Hold, Wake Up*. Above the image ran the bold strap: But the Man Can't Bust our Music. The small text explained: "the establishment's against adventure and the arousing experience that comes with today's music . . ." but there was no need to worry because "the man can't stop you from listening." [30]

The Columbia campaign assumed that the best way to sell the new music was to emphasize its oppositional nature, as long as one was careful not to mention anything specific that people might be opposed to (notably the war). Other large corporations followed suit. But some six months later, Columbia and the rest cancelled the campaign and withdrew their advertising from the underground press. They claimed that they had been embarrassed by the tasteless and prurient material that often surrounded their ads. They may also have been influenced by an

FBI memo that warned that the ads "appear to be giving active aid and comfort to the enemies of the United States."[31] In any case, they set out to find other means of reaching record-buying kids.

Music From Big Pink, The Band's evocative debut album, was released in mid-1968. Initially, The Band attracted attention because of the link with Dylan: they were his former backing group, their album included three previously unreleased Dylan songs (Basement Tapes masterpieces "I Shall Be Released," "Tears Of Rage," and "This Wheel's On Fire"), and its cover was graced with a charming faux-naif painting by the master himself. But in *Music From Big Pink,* and even more in their second album, titled simply *The Band* (released in October 1969), this ensemble of idiosyncratic talents created a distinctive sound-world that exercised its own powerful appeal.

The Band's special mission was to explore the terrain first glimpsed in the Basement Tapes. In their self-presentation and musical style they were consciously anti-psychedelic; they were counter–countercultural—but never in such a way that anyone would confuse them with the dominant culture itself. They were anything but unhip.

They found authenticity in a lost America of toil and sweat, in the regional, the handmade, the eccentric. Far from rejecting the past, they embraced it, as if it held the only safety and salvation. Their Americana—and it really doesn't matter that four of the five were Canadian—was not the familiar stuff of social patriotism. No national unity, no collective inheritance is celebrated here; instead, we are offered portraits of individuals prey to huge, uncontrollable forces and invocations of fleeting moments of peace and camaraderie.

"King Harvest (Has Surely Come)," from the second album, is one of the very few pop songs of this period even to mention organized labor ("I work for the union . . ."). However, it's a decidedly ambivalent treatment of the subject. The song's story line is obscure, but the meaning, as Greil Marcus said, is in the singing: "just listen to the worry in his voice." What's realized so potently in this song is the rising anxiety of an individual facing impending catastrophe. Despite its promises ("your hard times are about to end"), the union, it seems, cannot tame nature or fate.

The second album also included a song that was to become a standard: "The Night They Drove Old Dixie Down." How strange that this lament for the fall of the Confederacy should touch and stir a white rock 'n' roll audience in 1969—only a few years after television screens had been filled with images from Birmingham and Selma. Stranger still that, in 1971, the song should supply Joan Baez with her biggest commercial success.

Robertson has explained that the song was inspired by a conversation with Levon Helm's father, and his salutation, "the south shall rise again." This unexpected resuscitation of the Confederacy springs from The Band's fascination with the "real America," the America that had not been slicked down and brightly packaged. It reflected their deliberately counter-fashionable sympathy with the redneck nation sneered at by students and intellectuals. But its deeper matter, and its appeal, went beyond that. "The Night They Drove Old Dixie Down" is a lamentation that seems to well up from deep inside a defeated nation. It is a song about the curse of war and especially the price that working-class people always pay for war. It is haunted by that sense of historical loss Greil Marcus speaks of. It resounds with echoes of the Vietnam War.

Chicago and the other dramatic events in America that year were part of a global chain reaction. Just as in the U.S.A., insurgencies had been gestating elsewhere, and now—under the overarching impact of the struggle between the U.S. and Vietnam—they exploded into the open. Britain, Germany, and Japan all witnessed large antiwar demonstrations, student strikes and occupations, and street battles between protesters and police. In France and Italy, there was all that and more—including industrial action on a scale not seen in decades. Student uprisings played a role in changing governments in both Pakistan and Belgium. In Czechoslovakia the Prague Spring was crushed by the Soviet invasion. Maoist youth launched the Naxalite rebellion in India.

And in Mexico City, the Olympic games were preceded by the massacre of 300 student protesters by the police and army.

In that context, revolutionary rhetoric seemed less far-fetched than at any time since before World War II. "The Times They Are A-Changin' " was no longer a wistful prophecy but an accurate description of a global reality. Or was it? In the U.S. presidential election that autumn, the prowar Nixon beat the prowar Humphrey by a narrow margin, with the even more prowar Wallace picking up 13 percent of the popular vote. And most of those who voted for either Humphrey or Nixon agreed with Wallace that the protesters in Chicago didn't get half what they deserved. But while the electoral landscape seemed to defy the left's assumptions of the day, it did not confirm the right's, either. In Arkansas, for example, voters backed Wallace for president, liberal Republican Winthrop Rockefeller for governor, and reelected to the Senate one of the most persistent and high-profile critics of U.S. foreign policy, William Fulbright. People were in motion, and one of the errors of the left was to construct too great a political and cultural gap between the enlightened ones (themselves) and the rest of the population, who were never merely the uniform "silent majority" Nixon and Agnew claimed to champion. Dylan had articulated this "them and us" dichotomy as fiercely as anyone. In *John Wesley Harding,* even as it was becoming the dominant psychology on the left and the counterculture, he had drawn back from it. Others did not.

The whole raison d'être of the New Left had been exposed as a lot of hot air, that was demoralizing. I mean, these kids thought they were going to change the world, they really did. They were profoundly deluded. I used to talk to them, to the hippies, yippies. I understood their mentality as well as anyone could. But things like Altamont, things like Kent State, the election of Richard Nixon, the fact that the war just kept going on and on and on, and nothing they did could stop it.

—DAVE VAN RONK

The SDS national convention held in Chicago in June 1969 was to be the organization's last. Two thousand delegates attended. They had all seen the special issue of *New Left Notes* with its banner headline YOU DON'T NEED A WEATHERMAN TO KNOW WHICH WAY THE WIND BLOWS, a quote from Dylan's "Subterranean Homesick Blues." Underneath the headline was a lengthy statement drawn up by individuals from the SDS national leadership and the Columbia chapter, which had risen to prominence as a result of the previous year's occupation. This statement argued that in the context of the increasingly bloody worldwide struggle against imperialism "white mother country radicals" had to take a new step. If they were really to be of assistance to the Vietnamese and the black liberation struggle—epitomized for SDS by the Black Panthers—they had to become "revolutionaries." And to them being a revolutionary was about engaging in direct physical confrontation with the power of the state and the war machine.

The Weathermen, as the supporters of the statement became known, spurned alliances with "reformists" (anyone to their right) and labor unions, presumed to be irredeemably corrupted by racism and imperialism. Instead, they looked to "youth" as the only constituency within white America that could or would initiate far-reaching change. Youth, even middle-class youth, had little investment in the capitalist system, which was experienced as alien and repressive. The evidence for this was to be found in the manifest radicalization of ever-growing swathes of young people (not only college students) and above all in the phenomenal spread of the counterculture.

For the Weathermen, Dylan was a handy weapon in the factional battle that had preoccupied them for the last year. In early 1968, a small Marxist-Leninist outfit called Progressive Labor had entered SDS—thanks to its antiauthoritarian deletion of the old social democratic proscription of Communists. PL espoused a stridently class-reductionist style of Marxism, opposed the new black nationalism, advocated a "worker-student alliance," disparaged the counterculture, and insisted that its male members keep their hair short and wear "straight" clothes. You wouldn't have thought they would make headway in SDS, with its individualist ethos and ideological agnosticism.

But it was precisely those qualities that made SDS easy prey to PL's organizational discipline and its members' apparent facility—and dauntingly absolute certainty—in deploying Marxist categories.

So the Weathermen used Dylan to show up PL's unhipness, to mock its vanguardism, and to suggest that it was all talk and no action. But they also tried to fight PL with its own weapons—indulging in Leninist jargon in a manner that SDS's first generation and their Prairie Power successors would have found grotesque. Alongside Dylan they quoted Lin Piao ("Long Live the Victory of the People's War"). In coming out for "revolutionary communism" and a strategy of violent confrontation they bid farewell to the Port Huron Statement and indeed to much that had made SDS distinctive and attractive.[32]

Behind the crisis in SDS lay the realities, both heady and harsh, of the growing radicalization of youth and the growing frustration at the movement's inability to stop the war. According to Gallup, in the spring of 1968, 8 percent of students called themselves "radical or far left" (a 100 percent increase over the previous year); 16 percent agreed with the statement "the war in Vietnam is pure imperialism" (a year later, that would rise to an astonishing 41 percent). Sixty-nine percent classified themselves as "doves." *Fortune* revealed that half of all college students thought the U.S.A. was a "sick" society.[33]

In June 1969, SDS seemed to be at the height of its resonance with youth. But as a result of the experiences of the decade now coming to an end, the organization remained unstable. It was two years since the radicals had turned "from protest to resistance." While the former had continued to expand the latter had remained mainly symbolic—because physically stopping the war machine was beyond the capacity of the movement, and way beyond anything organized labor was prepared to contemplate. At the same time, the Nixon administration was harassing dissidents and taking repressive measures that convinced some that "fascism" was at hand. Seven years after Port Huron, the SDS leaders in the Weather faction were still looking for a way to move outside the student ghetto, still looking for a force that could rise to the imminent moral challenge, still uncomfortable with their comfortableness. In battling PL, they saw themselves as the true inheritors of the SDS lineage, and their claim was a reasonable one.

Coupled with the strident but sketchy "anti-imperialist" analysis was the familiar discourse of personal authenticity. The call to direct action and personal transformation (not least rejection of the comforts of middle-class existence), however changed in tone, was an elaboration on the early emphases of the civil rights and peace movements, as was the notion that movements of opposition should somehow prefigure the society they were trying to build. And their belief that where vanguards led others would surely follow derived from the experience of the last nine years, during which, from Greensboro on, small numbers of brave people had been shown to be forerunners of great changes.

Like Dylan at the ECLC dinner, the Weathermen had decided that any investment in the social order disarmed its opponents. They wanted to expose themselves to the dangers from which they were protected—as students, as intellectuals, as putative members of the middle class, as Americans—and to test just how much their beliefs and their politics really meant to them. Nonviolence had been sold to them as both principle and tactic—so they rejected it as both principle and tactic. The power of SNCC's commitment to direct action in the South was transmuted into a worship of action, including violent action, for its on sake, and a sneering insistence that nothing else was authentic. The liberal utopianism of the early sixties had not been abandoned so much as it had turned darkly apocalyptic. The gentle political urgency of "Blowin' in the Wind" had been given a savage twist.

What made Weather and much of the late-sixties left different from their SDS forebears was their adoption of the jargon of Leninism and their uncritical devotion to foreign revolutions. This desperate reaching out to forces and ideas seen to lie beyond America's borders has earned the undying ire and ridicule of many. But even in this, the Weathermen continued to reflect the distinctiveness of the American sixties. America remained exceptional—only now, that exceptionalism was defined as a national barbarism and sickness. Apart from seeking the approval of the Vietnamese and the Cubans, there was little interest in dialogue with the left in other societies. As far as the Weathermen were concerned, no one really had anything to teach them, including the oppressed in whose name they were prepared to destroy and be destroyed. In their anti-intellectualism, the Weathermen were at their most distinctively American, and quite at odds with the global culture of the left, even at that time. Their internationalism could express itself only as a negation, not least of the rhetoric of social patriotism, which, for all of them, still formed an emotional hinterland. In their prostration before the Panthers or the Vietcong, the white radicals professed revolutionary humility and self-abnegation; but there was more than a touch of arrogance and self-promotion in their posturing. They believed they were the youth leaders the media said they were. They accepted the media's narrative of what had been happening in America over the last decade—a narrative comprised of symbolic images, dramatic confrontations, and charismatic leaders. And they devised their strategy accordingly.

For all their folly, the Weathermen—though never numbering more than a few hundred—did embody a more widespread mood, which was why people followed their antics with such fascination, and why many young people identified with them without approving of their actions or having the least intention of following their example. "Weatherman is a vanguard floating free of a mass base," Kopkind observed. "But there's more to it than that. What appeal Weatherman has comes in part from its integration of the two basic streams of the movement of the sixties—political mobilization and personal liberation." [34]

The hippie capitalists who organized the Woodstock Festival of Music and Art in August 1969—those "three days of music and peace" advertised in the underground press—traded heavily on Dylan's cachet. The festival was scheduled to take place not at Woodstock but at Walkill, some forty miles away, before it was moved another twenty miles further afield to Bethel. "The place name *Woodstock*," Kopkind explained, "was meant only to evoke cultural-revolutionary images of Dylan, whose home base is in that Hudson River village. . . ." [35] Some three weeks before the festival, one of the key organizers, Michael Lang, made a pilgrimage to the real Woodstock and appealed to the reclusive master to take the stage that had been set for him. "We met in his house for a couple of hours," Lang recalled. "I told him what we were doing and told him, 'We'd love to have you there.' But he didn't come. I don't know why."

As he made clear to friends, Dylan never had any intention of gracing the festival with his presence. The hippies had already penetrated his rural idyll and he felt himself besieged, physically and psychologically, by the counterculture he'd helped to propagate. "The Woodstock festival," he told *Rolling Stone* in 1984, "was the sum total of all this bullshit. And it seemed to have something to do with me, this Woodstock Nation, and everything it represented. So we couldn't breathe. I couldn't get any space for myself and my family." [36]

Even as it promoted the festival, the underground press baited the entrepreneurs behind it. ROCK IMPERIALISTS MAKE PLANS FOR WOODSTOCK ran the headline of one Liberation News Service dispatch, which argued that "the revolutionary energy of rock 'n' roll is a response to oppression" and warned that the establishment was out to seize that energy. Abbie Hoffman and friends threatened to mount demonstrations against the promoters—until they kicked in $10,000 for food and medical provision and agreed to the construction of a "Movement City" on the festival site. [37]

The argument of the radicals was true as far as it went. Without the movement, there would be no counterculture; without the counterculture, there would be no music and no market for it. Above all, this music made claims to be something more than a commercial product. It belonged not to the record companies but to the constituency that had created it. It was their instrument and if others were going to exploit it, then a tax would be levied—by those people claiming to represent the movement and the generation. Perhaps the most extraordinary thing is simply that the promoters gave in, that the headline-grabbing cultural radicals had sufficient leverage at this moment to extract concessions.

But just how meaningful were those concessions? Movement City was set up about a quarter of a mile from the main stage. There, SDS, Newsreel (an alternative news collective), the Yippies, Hog Farmers, the underground press, and various good causes made camp several days before the festival itself began. Hoffman and Paul Krassner mimeographed thousands of flyers urging festival-goers not to pay the admission charge. They proved redundant. The flimsy barriers were quickly swept aside by the swelling numbers and those who'd purchased tickets in advance need not have bothered. No one who made it to Woodstock was going to be kept out—not least because of the shared sense, invoked by both promoters and radicals, that the music was already owned by the people coming to hear it.*

Despite his irritation, Dylan remained a presiding spirit at Woodstock, potent in absentia, as he had been these last three tumultuous years. Wavy Gravy, Dylan's old comrade from the Village (as Hugh Romney he'd emceed at the folk clubs), was not only master of ceremonies but chief link-man with the Hog Farm Collective, who supplied vital last-minute food, first aid, and security for the 400–500,000-strong encampment. Joan Baez, perceived as a hangover from the first half of the decade, introduced the assembled multitude to Robinson's and Hayes's "Joe Hill," (which she introduced as "an organizing song") and finished her set with "We Shall Overcome," thus bringing a touch of both the popular front and the civil rights movement to the gathering. Country Joe also brought the spirit of protest to Woodstock. That he prefaced his "I-Feel-Like-I'm-Fixin'-To-Die Rag," more grimly pertinent than when it had been released two years previously, with the "Fish cheer"—leading the crowd in chanting the letters *F-U-C-K*—said a great deal about how the mood had changed from earlier periods: the

* In contrast, tickets for the thirtieth anniversary "Woodstock '99" were $180 each, and the pay-per-view telecast $60. Merchandizing was extensive, and strictly licensed. There was a Woodstock platinum credit card with a $100,000 spending limit. Despite its state-of-the-art security system, the concert ended in chaotic scenes that made the original look cozy and tame. Firefighters battled for hours to put out blazes started by concert-goers at the end of the Red Hot Chili Peppers' set. Speaker systems were destroyed, tents burned and trucks looted as revelers danced and drummed their way around the flames. The riot police were called in to restore order.

hopefulness and sobriety of both Newport and the March on Washington had been replaced by bitter despair and ebullient self-indulgence. The same shift in tone could be heard in Arlo Guthrie's performance of his new dope trafficker's epic, "Coming Into Los Angeles."

Among the performers at Woodstock were a string of artists whose work was simply unimaginable without the explorations made by Dylan earlier in the decade: the Incredible String Band, Crosby, Stills and Nash, Creedence Clearwater Revival, the Grateful Dead, Joe Cocker (who sang "I Shall Be Released"), and, of course, The Band, who played "Tears of Rage" and "This Wheel's On Fire." Most of all, wrapping up the festival with an historic performance, there was Jimi Hendrix. His metal-mangled, punk-majestic assault on "The Star Spangled Banner" says more about the festival and the moment than the utopian anthem penned by Joni Mitchell. Hendrix's treatment of the national war song (which might be taken as a coda to his version of "All Along the Watchtower") was rich in aching, exultant ambiguity, and quite indecipherable outside the Sturm und Drang of America in the late sixties. It partook, as surely as the folk revival, in the romance of America, but it was a romance that had turned contentious and bitter. In *Crosstown Traffic,* his masterful study of Hendrix, Charles Shaar Murray writes:

> The ironies were murderous: a black man with a white guitar; a massive, almost exclusively white audience wallowing in a paddy field of its own making; the clear, pure, trumpet-like notes of the familiar melody struggling to pierce through clouds of tear-gas, the explosions of cluster-bombs, the scream of the dying, the crackle of the flames, the heavy palls of smoke stinking with human grease, the hovering chatter of helicopters . . . it depicts, as graphically as a piece of music can possibly do, both what the Americans did to the Vietnamese and what they did to themselves.[38]

Social patriotism had been transmuted into an inescapable nightmare.

As for Movement City, Abe Peck of the *Chicago Seed* described it as "a desperate leftist island amid the rock 'n' roll rabble, full of sterile meetings on how 'we' could organize 'them' . . ." On the second night, after the Who had stormed through "Pinball Wizard," Abbie Hoffman staggered on stage to call for support for John Sinclair, the self-styled White Panther and prophet of "the guitar revolution" who had just been imprisoned for ten years for possession of a couple of joints. An irritated Pete Townshend bumped Hoffman on the head with his Gibson. (Townshend later described the act as "the most political thing I ever did.") Abbie wandered offstage, but if he was perplexed by the nonresponse to his appeal for Sinclair, it didn't stop him celebrating "the birth of the Woodstock Nation" as "the death of the American dinosaur." Hoffman's attempt at a leftist appropriation of the festival (and indeed of the generation, now transformed into a "nation within a nation," just like "the black colony") produced a bestselling book but, in the long run, it was a puny effort compared to the corporate exploitation of the event via record and film, and more recently DVD. In Michael Wadleigh's hugely successful movie, released in 1970 to greater acclaim than the festival itself, all images of and references to Movement City, SDS, Newsreel, and the Yippies were excised.[39]

Like Newport, Woodstock showcased a counterculture defining itself in reaction to the dominant culture—even as the latter sought to exploit and package the former's achievements. The numbers were far greater, as was the money involved, but the old quest for authenticity was still at its heart, though it had become less demanding. Puritanism had been replaced by hedonism; immediacy was preferred to history. Woodstock posed the question that radicals had been debating since the mid-sixties: was the new rock audience—the audience that Dylan helped to fashion—a living community with a political ethic or was it just a new consumer demographic, united by nothing but the music? Was Woodstock itself a moment of collective self-discovery, the self-identification of a new social body, or was it merely the identification by capital of an audience ripe for exploitation?

On the left, there were divided responses. Hoffman and an army of zeitgeist chasers were quick to adopt the festival as a model for a new society, a new America that had miraculously gestated inside the womb of the old. The Weathermen found in Woodstock confirmation of their thesis—that straw they clutched at in their rage and impotence—

that American youth were becoming a revolutionary constituency, shedding their investment in the old world and ready to build the new, without compromise. Others were doubtful. "A ritual consecrated to consumption," sneered a member of the SDS first generation, Todd Gitlin. Irwin Silber was pleased to see how the young people "shed for a few days those hard protective shells which most Americans have created for themselves" but warned that Woodstock was "a 'revolution' the ruling class could live with." [40] Linking the festival experience to the unfolding struggles that had shaped the decade, Kopkind wrote: "For people who had never glimpsed the intense communitarian closeness of a militant struggle . . .Woodstock must always be the model of how good we will all feel after the revolution." [41] But in the meantime, he warned, its impact would be more double-edged:

> The new culture has yet to produce its own institutions on a mass scale; it controls none of the resources to do so. For the moment it must be content—or discontent—to feed the swinging sectors of the old system with new ideas, with rock and dope and love and openness. Then it all comes back, from Columbia Records or Hollywood or Bloomingdale's, in perverted and degraded forms.

The *New York Times* headlined its editorial on Woodstock: NIGHTMARE IN THE CATSKILLS. Tut-tutting about the "colossal mess" of the transient metropole in the mountains, the *Times* conceded that "the great bulk of the freakish-looking intruders behaved astonishingly well. They showed that there is real good under their fantastic exteriors." Like the "Negroes" at the March on Washington, these outsiders had somehow defied a stereotype, and offered reassurance, as well as challenge, to middle-class whites.

Meanwhile, Dylan, lured by a huge fee and the chance to escape the Woodstock mania, flew across the Atlantic to appear at the Isle of Wight festival—an appearance that the *New York Times* deemed worthy of a front-page report. It was his first visit to Britain since the fraught concerts that ended the 1966 tour. Now the audience came not to bait him, but to worship at his feet. His remarks to the press were inoffensive and unrevealing; his set was regarded as spiritless and anticlimactic; he spent nearly all his time with his fellow superstars, and flew back home at the first opportunity.

The disintegration of SNCC and SDS by the end of the 1960s left me with what I consider a genuine posttraumatic disorder.
—STAUGHTON LYND, 1998

As an organization, SDS never recovered from the fractious convention of June 1969. The Weathermen brought in the Panthers to bait PL, but after one Panther made a remark about "pussy power" the lines of contest were chaotically redrawn. Amid PLers waving the *Little Red Book* and chanting Maoist slogans, Bernardine Dohrn led a walkout of the non-PL majority. A day later she returned to pronounce PL's expulsion from SDS—which had been reconstituted under the leadership of the Weathermen and their allies. Needless to say, PL did not accept this fiat. There were now two SDS "national centers," neither of them meeting the needs or even speaking the same language as the bulk of those who had been attracted to the organization in recent years.

The Weathermen called for direct action on the streets of Chicago in the autumn. They hoped to replicate the previous year's dramatic youth-police confrontations—and their radicalizing impact. HOT TIME: SUMMER IN THE CITY, OR I AIN'T GONNA WORK ON MAGGIE'S FARM NO MORE ran the headline in *New Left Notes*. But they couldn't follow up the catchphrases with anything more substantial—intellectually or organizationally. No more than a few hundred joined the Days of Rage in October.[42]

In contrast, less than a month later, three-quarters of a million turned up in Washington to protest against the war, supplemented by another 200,000 in San Francisco. There was no Dylan, of course, but the crowd was happy to listen to John Denver, Mitch Miller, Arlo Guthrie, the cast of *Hair*, and Pete Seeger, who led the protesters in chorus after chorus of Lennon's "Give Peace A Chance." The demonstration was not without tensions. The liberals who had largely eschewed the antiwar movement now sought to place themselves at its head and renewed their efforts to purge it of radicalism. Yippies and others led a militant radical breakaway march to the Justice Department, where they were met by tear gas. Neither the liberals nor the new "revolutionaries" had much to say to the vast crowd that they hadn't heard before, nor did they offer any means of turning this extraordinary outburst of popular protest into something enduring. Nonetheless, the scale and diversity of the marches made it clear, not least to Nixon himself, that the antiwar movement now represented a huge social force. Plans to escalate the conflict—including the deployment of nuclear weapons— were put on hold.[43]

The movement that SDS had helped initiate had now reached truly mass proportions—but the remnants of SDS were not interested. They issued an invitation to select individuals to join a mid-December "war council" in Flint, Michigan. "We have to create chaos and bring about the disintegration of pig order," they declared, and merrily embraced the "vandals" label stuck on them by the media after the Days of Rage, once again quoting "Subterranean Homesick Blues": "the pump don't work cause the vandals took the handles." At Flint, the Weathermen declared themselves for "armed struggle," voted to dissolve SDS and move "underground."[44] It doesn't seem to have occurred to them to take a vote among the 100,000 young people spread across the country who still thought they were SDS members. In the end the message to the rest of the movement was that you did need a weatherman to know which way the wind blows and that they—the SDS vanguard—were the meteorological experts.

On March 6, 1970, three Weather members died when an accidental blast tore apart a lower Manhattan townhouse they had turned into a bomb factory. A decade after students had nonviolently sat-in in Greensboro, the townhouse explosion seemed to suggest that the protest impetus had spent itself in self-destructive madness.* As ever, the critics who prophesize with their pens spoke too soon. When Nixon announced the U.S. "incursion" into Cambodia on April 30, the protests that followed were the most widespread and sustained of the entire war. They touched virtually all sections of society—including GIs—but it was among students that they enjoyed greatest support and were most intense. Sixty percent of the country's college students went on strike, joined by large numbers from high schools and even junior highs. The national guard was sent to twenty-one campuses in sixteen states. Four students were shot dead at Kent State in Ohio and two at Jackson State in Mississippi. In the months to come, Nixon was forced to retreat; Kissinger bemoaned his yielding to "public pressures." [45]

Even as most of the high-profile leaders thrown up during the previous decade stood on the sidelines, disorientated, more people—not least large numbers of working-class people—engaged in political protest. It was in 1969, '70 and '71, after both SDS and SNCC had imploded (and with Dylan wrapped in silence and banality) that antiwar sentiment, coupled with countercultural habits and identities, sank deep into white working-class communities. It was this development, reflected in the swelling mutiny among the GIs, that finally brought the war to an end. [46]

The shaping character of the sixties in the United States was the unevenness of the development of political consciousness. That was true both of the movement itself and of the society it sought to address. Julius Lester wrote in the summer of 1969:

> We refer to "the movement" as if it were a political monolith. But what we now call "the movement" bears little resemblance to what we called "the movement" in 1963. In the early sixties, the "movement" consisted of SNCC, CORE, and SCLC in Afroamerica, SDS, various socialist

---

* Under the impact of feminism, the Weathermen mutated into the Weather Underground; in late 1970, they issued a new manifesto with a somewhat softened tone under the title *New Morning*—after the latest Dylan album.

groups and peace groups in America. . . . Today, "the movement" is no longer an identifiable political entity, but we still refer to it as if it were. It is more a socio-political phenomenon encompassing practically all of Afroamerica and a good segment of the youth of America . . . The political perspective of someone who has been in "the movement" since 1960 (and how many are left?) was, of necessity, going to be different from that of one who entered in 1968 . . . The "movement" veteran had a sense of "movement" history, having lived it. The "movement" neophyte did not. As far as he was concerned, "the movement" began when he became aware of it. . . .[47]

In 1970, in some places, the spirit of "Blowin' in the Wind" and "The Times They Are A-Changin' " was just catching on; for many it was still fresh and even frightening. Meanwhile, bitter GIs gave "Like a Rolling Stone" and "Positively 4th Street" new meanings; disillusioned organizers nodded over "My Back Pages;" stoned kids spaced out to *Blonde on Blonde;* new pastoralists in flight from the cities embraced the Basement Tapes and *John Wesley Harding;* huge numbers continued to get off on the unearthly rock 'n' roll of the mid-sixties masterpieces, whose antiauthoritarian politics now seemed second nature to many. At this moment, in Dylan's music, there was something for (and against) everyone.

Yet Dylan himself had now sunk into silence. Not merely public silence, as in the eighteen months following the motorcycle accident (in fact, one of his most fecund periods); after *John Wesley Harding* he wrote nothing for more than a year. Under contractual pressure to produce an album for Columbia, he returned to the studio in early 1969, with hardly a new song in his head; the result of a series of haphazard sessions was *Nashville Skyline.* For some, this album, with its smooth country style, mellow lyrics and crooning vocals, was Dylan's most attractive to date; certainly it sold better than any of his previous releases. But for all the attempts to find some higher wisdom in the pastiche, the reality was that too much of *Nashville Skyline* was bland, banal, complacent—faults no one would have associated with the Dylan of the previous albums. Perversely, authenticity here seemed to reside in a disavowal of all artistic pretensions and the uncritical embrace of convention. The only challenge in the music was the challenge to sing along to Dylan's cliché odes to private contentment. It was followed by the execrable *Self Portrait*—released in 1970—which demolished the myth of Dylan's artistic infallibility once and for all. Dylan later referred to the late sixties and early seventies as his period of "amnesia," when he forgot how to do what he had once done with such startling facility—write original songs.

Throughout the sixties, Dylan had seen himself as an uncompromising truth-teller, even when he was questioning assumptions about the very nature of truth. But that onerous vocation wavered at the decade's end, and as an artist he was able to rise to its demands only intermittently thereafter. Having confronted the crisis of prophecy in *John Wesley Harding*, it seemed as if Dylan, for many years, could find no way around or through it.

The impetus that had taken Dylan from his first album through to *John Wesley Harding* had come to an end; there would never again be the sense that his albums comprised an unfolding succession of artistic-philosophical visions and revisions. The thread that had bound Dylan to his era and his audience—even when he was castigating both severely—had snapped. "There ain't no use in wonderin' why." What was extraordinary was that an artist and a social eruption should be so persistently, and paradoxically, bound together for so long.

In June 1970, Dylan was awarded an honorary doctorate by Princeton University. David Crosby, who joined Dylan's entourage for the ceremony, recalled the day:

> When we arrived at Princeton they took us straight into a little room and Bob was asked to wear a cap and gown. He refused outright. They said, "We won't give you the degree if you don't wear this." Dylan said, "Fine, I didn't ask for it in the first place." [48]

Eventually, Dylan donned the regalia and accepted his degree. He wrote about the experience in "Day of the Locusts" (the title lifted from Nathanael West's novel of Hollywood corruption).

> I put down my robe, picked up my diploma,
> Took hold of my sweetheart and away we did drive,
> Straight for the hills, the black hills of Dakota,
> Sure was glad to get out of there alive.

Forever uneasy in the role assigned to him, Dylan was still grappling with the authentic, still looking—like Woody Guthrie in the Rainbow Room—for salvation in some distant, imagined America. Only by 1970, that hope seemed little more than a musical gesture.

AFTERWORD: CORRUPTIBLE SEED

The pangs of eternal birth are better than the pangs of eternal death.
—WILLIAM BLAKE

JOHN HAMMOND COMPLETED his generation-spanning run of "discoveries" when he signed the twenty-three-old Bruce Springsteen to Columbia in 1972. In many respects, Springsteen's work over the coming decades adhered much more closely to Hammond's idea of a democratic people's art than Dylan's ever did. At times Bruce seemed like a one-man popular front. He even made "This Land Is Your Land" a staple of his live act.

Initially hailed as the new Dylan, Springsteen showed more resilience than many in living down the tag and overcoming the hype. Though his work is unimaginable without the foundations Dylan laid, its development reflected different times and a different personality. Musically, he remained within the popular idioms fashioned in the sixties; if punk represented the final, self-annihilating outburst of innovation within the white rock tradition, then Springsteen might be seen as the great conservator of that tradition, an artist with a wide appeal but little musical influence.

In the mid-seventies, he was hailed for returning rock to its roots. Not only in his musical style, but in his selection of themes: gang fights, teen tragedies, fast cars, doomed rebellion. "We sweat it out in the streets of a runaway American dream." In a world of glitzy artifice, Springsteen seemed the real thing. But not everyone was convinced. The erstwhile White Panther John Sinclair penned a damning review of *Born To Run*. "Springsteen's are not songs of direct experience . . . they are tales of a mythic urban grease scene . . . a script for a third-rate television treatment of delinquent white youngsters of the slums." The Springsteen boom, Sinclair insisted, rested on carefully propagated illusions. It was "easy to convince well-heeled young college students of today, desperate for an identity separate from that of their despicable parents, that what they are seeing and hearing is the true reflection of the young thugs of the worser parts of town, whose dead-end existence is somehow more exciting than their own." [1]

There's an element in Sinclair's criticism that still rings uncomfortably true. The people in Springsteen's audiences have very rarely been the people he was singing about. His early dramatis personae did owe more to *West Side Story* than to autobiographical realities. But that didn't preclude Springsteen from using these inherited figures to express his own feelings of loneliness and defeat, elation and camaraderie, or his audience from responding to them.

From the beginning Springsteen demonstrated a most un-Dylanlike warmth and capacity for empathy. Like many others, he worked his way through music to politics. It was only after his first flush of big-time success in the mid-seventies that he began to read seriously about his society and its history. In particular, he explored the Vietnam War, during which he'd come of age, and its impact on working-class Americans. On its release in 1984, "Born In The USA" 's bitter, grunt's eye view of the war challenged the morning-in-America jingoism of the Reagan presidency. That didn't stop Reagan trying to claim the song for his crusade. Of course, Reagan's advisers hadn't done their homework; a quick glance at the full lyrics makes it plain that this is a song about how a nation betrayed its own children by sending them off to kill and die in a foreign war. But Reagan's team were able to mistake this national nightmare for a national dream because the rousing rock chorus, heard in isolation, could be interpreted that way. The packaging of the album—stars and stripes to the fore—also facilitated the mishearing. In a nationalist environment, the song's dissonance was lost. And it wasn't just Reagan. For more than a few of Springsteen's fans, the song is a singalong air-punching anthem. Springsteen has tried to reclaim "Born In The USA" by performing it solo with acoustic guitar. His bare-bones presentation of the lyrics is an effort to combat the regressive listening that Adorno claimed would make any real revolt within popular music impossible.

As he's grown older, Springsteen has presented his cast of working-class waifs and strays, hard-drivers, abandoned mothers, small-time criminals, with greater realism and less romance. But throughout his work, he's tended to understand these people not as members of a class spanning nations, not as strugglers within a system, but as an American tribe, indeed, as the real American tribe.

A renewed interest in Woody Guthrie, combined with exploratory, anonymous journeys through the United States, led in 1995 to *The Ghost Of Tom Joad*, a mainly solo and acoustic album. In some ways, it was as bold a shift in tone, and as commercially unpredictable, as any of Dylan's prodigious sixties leaps. These are topical songs and they register an unmistakable protest against the current order. But they are neither strident nor satirical. (Unlike Dylan, Springsteen rarely mixes humor with serious material.) The melodies are delicate and Bruce approaches them gingerly. The massed electric guitars, booming rhythms, and theatrical gestures that filled stadiums all over the world were replaced, for the moment, by a subdued, lone voice that demanded a focus on the words and the tales they told.

These were tales of globalization. The protagonists were migrant laborers and victims of deindustrialization, the multiethnic successors of Guthrie's dust bowl refugees. Springsteen's album was a realistic and humane response to a mighty event: the influx of workers from across the Third World that has transformed U.S. society in recent decades. In his songs these people struggle against a vast, inhuman and often inscrutable economic order. By attending to the details of their survival mechanisms, material and psychic, Springsteen opens up an alien experience to his listeners. He also stresses that xenophobia is a self-defeating reflex. Whether you're born in the U.S.A., in Vietnam, or in Latin America, you're a victim of the same world-embracing system. In *The Ghost Of Tom Joad*, Springsteen aligned himself with the Guthrie of "Deportees" and the Dylan of "Only a Pawn in Their Game." He seemed to be reaching out beyond the confines of social patriotism.

In the title track, the final verse paraphrases Guthrie's "Tom Joad," which was itself a paraphrase of Henry Fonda's valedictory speech in John Ford's movie of Steinbeck's book.

> Wherever there's a cop beatin' a guy
> Wherever a hungry newborn baby cries
> Where there's a fight 'gainst the blood and hatred in the air
> Look for me Mom I'll be there

The Ghost Of Tom Joad seemed a belated vindication of some of the long-standing claims made by Springsteen admirers. He was at last fulfilling his role as a working-class troubadour, a dissenting voice of conscience, honesty, and compassion. In 2000, he made good on his promise to stand witness "wherever there's a cop beatin' a guy" in "(American Skin) Forty-One Shots," whose subject was the fatal shooting of Amadou Diallo, an unarmed African immigrant, by New York City police. The song bravely reminded listeners that no matter how much they'd like to deny it, racism remained a defining quality of American experience. "It ain't no secret my friend / you can get killed just for living in your American skin." The lyrics provoked a degree of hostility to which Springsteen was unaccustomed. Neither the NYPD nor the *New York Post* were pleased. At concerts it became clear that some of Bruce's devoted fans felt the same way.[2] In a letter to a local newspaper, Springsteen responded to the controversy in a half-bewildered tone. To him, the song was just another one of "the questions" he'd been asking throughout his career. "As Americans, who are we? What kind of country do we live in, do we want to live in? I always assume there's an audience out there willing to think deeply about the ideas in the work I do. It's one of the things that keeps me probably closer to the heart of what we're about—we 'Americans.' "[3] Springsteen's decision to place scare-quotes around the national denominator indicated that in the wake of the Diallo killing, and the new globalized world order he'd written about in *Tom Joad,* he felt he was dealing with a problematic category.

This tentative awareness seems to have evaporated in *The Rising,*

Springsteen's rapid response to the atrocity of September 11, 2001. Although this proved to be one of his most commercially successful and critically acclaimed albums, in the long run it may be remembered as one of his weakest. *The Rising* has stirring and tender moments but few songs that amount to more than the sum of their parts. Much of it sounds like a routine run-through of E Street Band moods. Distressingly, it marks a retreat, after *Tom Joad,* to the safe ground of social patriotism. The songs preserve precisely the brief-lived mood of empathy and solidarity that followed the destruction in New York. They evoke the anonymous, unpretentious heroism of the firefighters, the office workers trapped in the collapsing towers, and the friends and loved ones they left behind. Throughout there is a sense that this huge cataclysm has shown the rituals of ordinary life to be both precious and fragile. But there is little indication that this atrocity may carry other meanings and implications. There is no history. The outside world exists solely in a reference to Allah and the singing of Asif Ali Khan in the background of "Worlds Apart." In "Lonesome Day," Springsteen sings: "House is on fire, viper's in the grass, / A little revenge and this too shall pass . . ." but he leaves this territory largely unexplored, settling instead for gestures of affirmation that seem to float away in an insubstantial ether.

The "rising" Springsteen celebrates is not a popular insurrection but an outpouring of community feeling, and by implication an occasion for Americans to unite. As a picture of a people "rising" to a historic challenge, it is more than inadequate. It is untrue. For part of that "rising" was the war on terror and its spawn, the war on Iraq. To the extent that the album is an exercise in lowest common denominator nationalism, it fails to do justice to its immense subject matter, and that is an artistic as well as a political shortcoming.

While Springsteen's *The Rising* was lionized by the American media, Steve Earle's *Jerusalem* was flayed. His "John Walker's Blues" in particular, was denounced as treasonous. But Earle's album was not only more politically challenging, it was less musically predictable than Springsteen's. It showed that there were other, deeper musical responses possible to 9/11. The Alabama Three, best known for supplying the theme song for *The Sopranos*, offered a track called "Woody Guthrie." Despite the outfit's name, there aren't three of them and they come from Brixton in south London, not Alabama. Like British musicians of earlier generations, they put traditional American music to new uses, fusing Delta blues and country twang with techno-funk, enriching the mix with surreal humor and spiky politics. Their love of America's people's music goes hand in hand with a sneering contempt for its political culture. In "Woody Guthrie," they repudiate all nationalisms:

> don't need no country
> don't fly no fag
> cut no slack for the union jack
> stars and stripes have got me jet-lagged

Although the song disavows Guthrie's great social patriotic anthem, it's a tribute to him in a spirit he would appreciate. It hints at the tasks facing his artistic descendants in a world of mass migration and imperial war: "Sing a song for the asylum seeker / for some frightened baby on a foreign beach."

"America" remains a dangerous construct and one that serves the elite better than the majority. In the end, it not only limits but undermines a genuinely radical and uncompromising humanism. Reclamation or reappropriation of "America" has been at the heart of liberal and left strategies in the U.S.A. for many decades, but surely, in light of the rise of an aggressive new American empire, shameless in its claims on global power, rooted in popular xenophobia, the long-running attempt to sugarcoat left-wing dissent by wrapping it in the American flag must be reckoned a failure. After all, "you don't count the dead / When God's on your side."

The day after the U.S. and Britain launched their war against Iraq, I headed for the local high street where our antiwar group had agreed we would rendezvous to make our protest. There I found a group of about twenty adults, all very subdued. The war we had done our best to fore-stall was now a reality. Then from down the street we heard them com-ing. Shouting, chanting, laughing—there must have been 200 of them, children who had walked out from the nearby secondary school, many no more than twelve or thirteen years old. They carried handmade signs saying *Bush and Blair, You Don't Care, No Blood for Oil,* and *Make Love Not War.* They picked up our antiwar banner, swept past the adults and struck off down the busy high street, tying up traffic and pushing leaflets through drivers' windows. Their ranks were soon swelled by groups from other schools. In the end, I'm told the kids marched all the way to Parliament Square—a four-mile hike.

There were similar events all over Britain. Some newspapers de-nounced the schoolkids' protest as the work of outside agitators. Com-mentators questioned whether these children really understood the complex issues. Surely this was merely a passing fad. ("How much do I know / To speak out of turn / you may say that I'm young / You may say I'm unlearned . . .") But the young people pricked the conscience of more than a few adults. We had been told that now the war had started, the debate was over; these kids refused to worship the accomplished fact.

> I don't know if I'm smart but I think I can see
> When someone is pullin' the wool over me

Like the young Dylan, they were claiming the right to speak and to act, to shape the world they would inherit. Tagging along behind their exuberant protest, it struck me that the sixties might someday come to seem merely an early skirmish in a conflict whose real dimensions we have yet to grasp.

This American pride thing, that doesn't mean nothing to me. I'm more locked into what's real forever.

—BOB DYLAN, 1985

In 1974, Dylan and The Band returned to the road. They performed a string of old favorites, including "It's Alright Ma." When Dylan sang the line "even the president of the United States must some time have to stand naked," the crowd roared. Nixon was in the midst of his Watergate ordeal and would resign that summer. It was some kind of vindication for those who had opposed him and his war policies. And the tour was some kind of vindication for Dylan and The Band. In contrast to 1966, they were playing to vast arenas packed with adoring, uncritical fans. But the music was some of the worst either Dylan or The Band ever made. It was the first sixties revival tour, a package dreamed up by businessmen. The tension between audience and performer had gone slack. The confrontation with the new had been replaced by the comforts of the familiar.

Dylan's political interventions in the years since the sixties have been sporadic. In "George Jackson" in 1971 and the epic "Hurricane" of 1976, he once again paid homage to the martyrs of institutional racism. In 1974, he appeared at a benefit organized by Phil Ochs for the victims of the U.S. sponsored coup in Chile. (It was to be Ochs's last political intervention).

The next year Dylan released *Blood On The Tracks,* his most substantial achievement of the seventies and perhaps his most thematically coherent album. After a long silence he had found his voice again—in the pain of a ruptured marriage and the irresolvable conflict between his desire for safety and his hunger for freedom. The album includes recollections of a more hopeful time ("There was music in the cafés at night / And revolution in the air"), but has little to say about the contemporary public sphere, except to imply that it is a morass (with a nod to Woody Guthrie): "Idiot wind, blowing like a circle around my skull, / From the Grand Coulee Dam to the Capitol." Ginsberg called this a "rhyme that took in the whole nation." [4]

In 1979, Dylan embraced a form of Christian fundamentalism. For many fans who'd stuck with him through previous changes, this was the final fall from grace. Nonetheless, Dylan's first Christian album, *Slow Train Coming,* outsold all his previous releases. His writing and singing skills were sharp as ever. The vision they served, however, was bleakly judgmental. In this, of course, the work of the Christian period follows a familiar Dylan vein. The apocalyptic Manichaeism of "Gotta Serve Somebody" can also be heard in "When The Ship Comes In." What's missing is any hint of generosity, any sympathy for human vulnerability. The prophet of freedom had surrendered entirely to dour fatalism, like Wordsworth in his *Sonnets in Praise of Capital Punishment* (to be fair, Dylan's evangelical songs are more palatable than Wordsworth's Tory verse).

Dylan's religious conversion put him once again in the van—of a reactionary backlash. Nineteen-seventy-nine and 1980 ushered in the era of Thatcher and Reagan. On *Slow Train*, Dylan inveighed against "All that foreign oil controlling American soil . . . Sheiks walkin' around like kings, wearing fancy jewels and nose rings / Deciding America's future . . ." But even as right-wing Christian politics became a force in the land, Dylan's visible commitment to Christianity waned. In 1983, he returned to topical song with the overtly social patriotic and protectionist "Union Sundown" and the bewildered Zionist apologia, "Neighborhood Bully," a defense of Israel's airstrike on an Iraqi nuclear facility. He also recorded, but did not release, "Julius and Ethel," a tribute to the Rosenbergs, Communists executed for espionage in 1953 despite the best efforts of the ECLC. Dylan had not forgotten the old left.

> Someone says the fifties was the age of great romance;
> I say that's just a lie, it was when fear had you in a trance

Another, far more remarkable song recorded at those 1983 sessions and not released was "Blind Willie McTell." This is less a tribute to the sweet-toned minstrel who composed "Statesboro Blues" as an invocation of the historical experience behind the blues as a whole—and a meditation on its meaning in our times. It's also a testament to the enduring importance of African American struggle and song in Dylan's inner landscape. In a series of images both compact and multidimensional, Dylan takes us on a journey through history: slavery ships, plantations burning, chain gangs yelling, "charcoal gypsy maidens" who "can strut their feathers well," the poverty-stricken twenties beau with "bootleg whiskey in his hand." In the final verse, Dylan muses bleakly:

Well, God is in heaven
And we all want what's his
But power and greed and corruptible seed
Seem to be all that there is

"Blind Willie McTell" is at once monumental and fragile. It's a summation of Dylan's relationship to a tradition that lay behind his entire career. It also suggests that the only mission left for the artist is to sing the blues—to bear witness to the tragedy of the times.

In 1985, Dylan appeared at the Live Aid concert for Ethiopian famine relief. At the time, pundits were quick to suggest that this event might represent a new outpouring of social consciousness among both pop musicians and their audience. So it seemed natural that Dylan, still more associated with the sprit of protest than any other artist, should feature prominently. Musically, his performance was a shambles. Politically, it was as perverse as his outburst at the ECLC in 1963. He played "Ballad of Hollis Brown," then told the huge global television audience:

I'd just like to say that some of the money that's raised for the people in Africa, maybe they could just take a little bit of it—maybe one or two million maybe—and use it, to pay the mortgages [that] some of the farmers here owe the banks.[5]

Though this remark inspired Willie Nelson to launch Farm Aid, it annoyed nearly everyone else. Bob Geldof, the principal motivator of the event, said Dylan's comment displayed "a complete lack of understanding of the issues raised by Live Aid." Dylan tried to explain his views to Mikal Gilmore:

It's almost like guilt money. Some guy halfway around the world is starving so, okay, put ten bucks in the barrel, then you can feel you don't have to have a guilty conscience about it. Obviously, on some levels it does help, but as far as any sweeping movement to destroy hunger and poverty, I don't see that happening.[6]

The Live Aid fiasco was quintessential Dylan. It was tactless and politically convoluted. It was also symptomatic of his abiding awareness of homegrown poverty. He had always been wary at the ease with which we give to abstract victims in remote parts of the world while ignoring suffering in our own midst. Above all, the Live Aid ramble was a response to his own discomfort about the authenticity or otherwise of this charitable but very glamorous event.

Somehow Dylan's reputation has survived his antics and inconsistencies, as well as the unappeasable hunger of the times for the "new." As the nineties progressed, he enjoyed a revival in esteem and sales. He produced quirky, enjoyable albums and recast himself as a folk and blues fundamentalist, with a voice rendered authentically gritty by decades of alcohol, tobacco, fame, and money. He was Grammied, Clintoned, and Poped. Even his bootlegs became "Official."

But his music of the sixties enjoys a life of its own. It's been packaged and repackaged, along with its era, but it eludes the death grip of academia and the banality of the society of the spectacle. It still exudes the spirit and the pain of human liberation. It still asks demanding questions of anyone who wants to change society. "There must be some way out of here." Dylan never found it, but that doesn't mean he can't help the rest of us on our journey.

SELECT BIBLIOGRAPHY

Aaronovitch, Sam. "The American Threat to British Culture," *Arena: A Magazine of Modern Literature,* June/July 1951, London.

Adorno, Theodor. *The Culture Industry: Selected Essays on Mass Culture,* ed. J. M. Bernstein London: Routledge Classic, 2001.

Adorno, Theodor. *The Jargon of Authenticity,* trans. Knut Tarnowski and Frederic Will. London: Routledge, 2003.

Alterman, Eric. *It Ain't No Sin to Be Glad You're Alive: The Promise of Bruce Springsteen.* Boston: Back Bay Books, 2001.

Anderson, Paul Allen. *Deep River: Music and Memory in Harlem Renaissance Thought.* Durham, NC: Duke University Press, 2001.

Anderson, Terry H. *The Movement and the Sixties: Protest in American from Greensboro to Wounded Knee.* New York: Oxford University Press, 1995.

Auerbach, Erich. *Mimesis: The Representation of Reality in Western Literature,* trans. Willard R. Trask. Princeton, NJ: Princeton University Press, 1953.

Benjamin, Walter. *One-Way Street and Other Writings,* trans. Edmund Jephcott and Kingsley Shorter. London: New Left Books, 1979.

Baez, Joan. *And A Voice to Sing With.* London: Arrow, 1989.

Barker, Derek, ed. *Isis: A Bob Dylan Anthology.* London: Helter Skelter, 2001.

Benson, Carl, ed. *The Bob Dylan Companion: Four Decades of Commentary.* New York: Schirmer Books, 1998.

Bloom, Alexander and Wini Breines, eds. *Takin' It to the Streets: A Sixties Reader.* New York: Oxford University Press, 1995.

Branch, Taylor. *Parting the Waters: America in the King Years, 1954–64.* New York: Touchstone/Simon & Schuster, 1988.

Branch, Taylor. *Pillar of Fire: America in the King Years, 1963–65.* New York: Simon & Schuster, 1998.

Buhle, Mari Jo, Paul Buhle, Dan Georgakas, eds. *Encyclopedia of the American Left.* Chicago: University of Illinois Press, 1992.

Burns, Peter. *Curtis Mayfield: People Never Give Up.* London: Sanctuary, 2003.

Corcoran, Neil, ed. *'Do You Mr. Jones?': Bob Dylan With the Poets and Professors.* London: Chatto and Windus, 2002.

Culter, Dick, ed. *They Should Have Served That Cup of Coffee: Seven Radicals Remember the Sixties.* Boston: South End Press, 1979.

Cunningham, Agnes "Sis" and Gordon Friesen. *Red Dust and Broadsides: A Joint Autobiography,* ed. Ronald D. Cohen. Amherst: University of Massachusetts Press, 1999.

Dylan, Bob. *Lyrics, 1962–1985.* London: Jonathan Cape, 1987.

Dylan, Bob. *Tarantula.* New York: Macmillan, 1971.

Garrow, David J. *Bearing the Cross: Martin Luther King and the Southern Christian Leadership Conference.* London: Jonathan Cape, 1988.

Ginsberg, Allen. *Collected Poems, 1947–1980.* New York: Harper and Row, 1984.

Ginsberg, Allen. *Spontaneous Mind: Selected Interviews, 1958–1996,* ed. David Carter. London: Penguin, 2001.

Gitlin, Todd. *The Sixties: Years of Hope, Days of Rage.* New York: Bantam Books, 1993 (revised edition).

Goodman, Fred. *The Mansion on the Hill: Dylan, Young, Springsteen and the Head-on Collision of Rock and Commerce.* New York: Vintage, 1998.

Gray, Michael. *Song and Dance Man III: The Art of Bob Dylan.* London: Continuum, 2000.

Gray, Michael and John Bauldie, eds. *All Across the Telegraph: A Bob Dylan Handbook.* London, Sidgwick and Jackson, 1987.

Green, Jonathon. *Days in the Life: Voices from the English Underground, 1961–1971.* London: Pimlico, 1998 (first edition 1988).

Guthrie, Woody. *Bound for Glory.* New York: Plume, 1983 (first edition 1943).

Hajdu, David. *Positively 4th Street: the Lives and Times of Joan Baez, Bob Dylan, Mimi Baez Fariña, and Richard Fariña.* New York: Farrar, Straus and Giroux, 2001.

Halstead, Fred. *Out Now: A Participant's Account of the American Movement Against the Vietnam War.* New York: Monad Press, 1978.

Harris, William J., ed. *The Leroi Jones/Amiri Baraka Reader.* New York: Thunder's Mouth Press, 1991.

Heylin, Clinton. *Bob Dylan: Behind the Shades: The Biography—Take Two.* London: Viking, 2000.

Horovitz, Michael, ed. *Children of Albion: Poetry of the "Underground" in Britain.* London: Penguin, 1969.

Jacobs, Ron. *The Way the Wind Blew: A History of the Weather Underground.* London: Verso, 1997.

King, Martin Luther. *A Testament of Hope: Essential Writings of Martin Luther King, Jr.,* ed. James M. Washington. San Francisco: HarperCollins, 1991.

Kopkind, Andrew. *The Thirty Years War: Dispatches and Diversions of a Radical Journalist, 1965–1994.* London: Verso, 1995.

Lee, C. P. *Like the Night: Bob Dylan and the Road to the Manchester Free Trade Hall.* London: Helter Skelter, 1998.

Lewis, John with Michael D'Orso. *Walking with the Wind: A Memoir of the Movement.* New York: Simon & Schuster, 1998.

Lomax, Alan, compiler. *Hard Hitting Songs for Hard-Hit People,* with notes by Woody Guthrie. Lincoln: University of Nebraska Press, 1999 (first edition 1967).

Lomax, Alan. *The Land Where the Blues Began.* New York: The New Press, 2002; (first edition 1993).

Lomax, Alan. *Selected Writings 1934–1997,* ed. Ronald D. Cohen. New York: Routledge, 2003.

Lynd, Staughton. "The Cold War Expulsions and the Movement of the 1960s." Pennsylvania: Labor Solidarity Pamphlet No. 1, 1998.

Marable, Manning. *Race, Reform and Rebellion: The Second Reconstruction in Black America, 1945–1990.* Jackson: University Press of Mississippi, 1991.

Marcus, Greil. *Invisible Republic: Bob Dylan's Basement Tapes.* London: Picador, 1997.

Marcus, Greil. *Mystery Train: Images of America in Rock 'n' Roll Music.* New York: Plume, 1997 (first edition 1974).

McGregor, Craig, ed. *Bob Dylan: The Early Years, a Retrospective*. New York: Da Capo Press, 1990.

Miles, Barry. *Ginsberg: A Biography*. London: Viking, 1990.

Miller, James. *Flowers in the Dustbin: The Rise of Rock and Roll, 1947–1977*. New York: Fireside/Simon & Schuster, 1999.

Murray, Charles Shaar. *Boogie Man: The Adventures of John Lee Hooker in the American Twentieth Century*. London: Viking, 1999.

Murray, Charles Shaar. *Crosstown Traffic: Jimi Hendrix and Post-War Pop*. London: Faber and Faber, 2001.

Neale, Jonathan. *The American War: Vietnam, 1960–1975*. London: Bookmarks, 2001.

Peck, Abe. *Uncovering the Sixties: The Life and Times of the Underground Press*. New York: Citadel Press, 1991.

Reuss, Richard A. with Joanne C. Reuss. *American Folk Music and Left-Wing Politics, 1927–1957*. London: Scarecrow Press, 2000.

Sale, Kirkpatrick. *SDS*. New York: Vintage, 1974.

Samuels, Raphael. *Theatres of Memory*. London: Verso, 1994.

Seale, Bobby. *Seize the Time: The Story of the Black Panther Party and Huey P. Newton*. Baltimore: Black Classic Press, 1991 (first edition 1971).

Shelton, Robert. *No Direction Home: The Life and Music of Bob Dylan*. London: New English Library, 1986.

Sloman, Larry "Ratso." *Reefer Madness: A History of Marijuana*. New York: St. Martin's Griffin, 1998 (first edition 1979).

Sounes, Howard. *Down the Highway: The Life of Bob Dylan*. New York: Doubleday, 2001.

Wald, Elijah. *Josh White: Society Blues*. New York: Routledge, 2002.

Ward, Brian. *Just My Soul Responding: Rhythm and Blues, Black Consciousness and Race Relations*. London: UCL Press, 1998.

Werner, Craig. *A Change Is Gonna Come: Music, Race and the Soul of America*. Edinburgh: Canongate, 2000.

Wolff, Daniel. *You Send Me: The Life and Times of Sam Cooke*. London: Virgin, 1996.

SELECT WEBSITE LISTING

About Bob: www.bjorner.com
Bob Dylan: (official site): www.bobdylan.com
Bob Dylan Roots: www.bobdylanroots.com
Bob Links: www.my.execpc.com/~billp61/boblink.html
Expecting Rain: www.expectingrain.com
Isis: www.bobdylanisis.com

SELECT DISCOGRAPHY

The Band. *Music From Big Pink*. Capitol, 1968.

The Band. *The Band*. Capitol, 1969.

Bob Dylan. *Bob Dylan*. Columbia, 1962.

Bob Dylan. *The Freewheelin' Bob Dylan*. Columbia, 1963.

Bob Dylan. *The Times They Are A-Changin'*. Columbia, 1964.

Bob Dylan. *Another Side of Bob Dylan*. Columbia, 1964.

Bob Dylan. *Bringing It All Back Home*. Columbia, 1965.

Bob Dylan. *Highway 61 Revisited*. Columbia, 1965.

Bob Dylan. *Blonde on Blonde*. Columbia, 1966.

Bob Dylan. *John Wesley Harding*. Columbia, 1968.

Bob Dylan. *Nashville Skyline*. Columbia, 1969.

Bob Dylan. *Self Portrait*. Columbia, 1970.

Bob Dylan. *New Morning*. Columbia, 1970.

Bob Dylan and The Band. *The Basement Tapes*. Columbia, 1975.

Bob Dylan. *Biograph*. Columbia, 1985. (Includes Cameron Crowe's interview with Dylan.)

Bob Dylan. *The Bootleg Series: Volumes 1–3 (rare and unreleased) 1961–1991*. Columbia, 1991.

Bob Dylan. *The Bootleg Series: Volume 4. Live 1966*. Columbia, 1995.

Bob Dylan. *The Bootleg Series Volume 5. Live 1975*. Columbia, 2002.

Woody Guthrie. *Dustbowl Ballads*. BMG, 1998.

Woody Guthrie. *This Land Is Your Land: The Asch Recordings*. Smithsonian/Folkways, 1997.

Jimi Hendrix. *Experience Hendrix: The Best of Jimi Hendrix*. MCA, 1997.

Jimi Hendrix. *Voodoo Child*. MCA, 2002.

The Jimi Hendrix Experience. *BBC Sessions*. MCA, 1998.

John Lee Hooker. *The Real Folk Blues/More Real Folk Blues*. MCA/Chess, 2002.

The Impressions. *Definitive Impressions*. Kent, 2002.

Curtis Mayfield. *Soul Legacy*. Charly, 2001. (Box set includes notes by Clive Anderson and Lawrence Roker.)

Phil Ochs. *All the News That's Fit To Sing*. Elektra, 1964.

Phil Ochs. *Farewells and Fantasies*. Elektra, 1997. (Box set includes notes by Michael Ventura, Mark Kemp, Ben Edmonds.)

Youssou N'Dour. *The Guide (Wommat)*. Columbia, 1994.

Nina Simone. *Essential*. Metro, 2001.

Smithsonian/Folkways reissue, 1997.

Bruce Springsteen. *Chimes of Freedom*. Columbia, 1988.

Bruce Springsteen. *The Ghost Of Tom Joad*. Columbia, 1994.

Bruce Springsteen and the E Street Band. *Live in New York City*. Columbia, 2001.

Bruce Springsteen. *The Rising*. Columbia, 2002.

Dave Van Ronk. *Two Sides of Dave Van Ronk*. Fantasy, 2002.

Various Artists. *The Anthology of American Folk Music*, edited by Harry Smith. Smithsonian/Folkways reissue, 1997.

Various Artists. *Songs for Freedom: The Story of the Civil Rights Movement Through its Songs*. Smithsonian/Folkways, 1990.

Various Artists. *A Tribute to Woody Guthrie*. Warner, 1972.

Various Artists. *May Your Song Always Be Sung: The Songs of Bob Dylan Vol. 2*. BMG, 2001.

Various Artists. *Peace Not War*. Shellshock, 2002.

NOTES

INTRODUCTION

1. Julius Lester. "To Recapture the Dream," *Liberation*, 1969, in *Takin' It to the Streets: A Sixties Reader*, eds. Alexander Bloom and Wini Breines (New York: Oxford University Press, 1995), 632.

CHAPTER ONE: THE WHOLE WIDE WORLD IS WATCHIN'

1. For accounts of the 1963 March on Washington see Taylor Branch, *Parting the Waters: America in the King Years, 1954–64* (New York, Touchstone/Simon & Schuster, 1988), 869–887; Manning Marable, *Race, Reform and Rebellion: The Second Reconstruction in Black America, 1945–1990* (Jackson: University Press of Mississippi, 1991), 213–227; David J. Garrow, *Bearing the Cross: Martin Luther King and the Southern Christian Leadership Conference* (London: Jonathan Cape, 1988), 281–286; John Lewis with Michael D'Orso, *Walking with the Wind: A Memoir of the Movement* (New York: Simon & Schuster, 1998), 213–227.

2. Elijah Wald, *Josh White: Society Blues* (New York: Routledge, 2002), 160.

3. For Dylan at the March on Washington see Robert Shelton, *No Direction Home: The Life and Music of Bob Dylan* (London: New English Library, 1986); Clinton Heylin, *Bob Dylan: Behind the Shades: The Biography—Take Two* (London: Viking, 2000), 125; Howard Sounes, *Down the Highway: The Life of Bob Dylan* (London: Doubleday, 2001), 140; David Hajdu, *Positively 4th Street: The Lives and Times of Joan Baez, Bob Dylan, Mimi Baez Fariña, and Richard Fariña* (New York: Farrar, Straus and Giroux, 2001), 182–183.

4. Branch, 880.

5. George Frazier, "Whose Civil Rights?" *Boston Herald*, August 30, 1963.

6. Hajdu, 182–183.

7. Interviewed by Cameron Crowe in notes for *Bob Dylan: Biograph* (Columbia Records, 1985).

8. Heylin, 73.

9. Malcolm Cowley, *Exile's Return: A Literary Odyssey of the 1920s* (London: Peter Smith, 1983; first edition, 1951).

10. Woody Guthrie, *Bound for Glory* (New York: Plume, 1983; first edition, New York: EP Dutton, 1943), 177–178.

11. Ibid., 287.

12. Ibid., 290–297.

13. Pete Seeger quoted on http://www.woodyguthrie.de/.

14. Woody Guthrie, notes in *Hard Hitting Songs for Hard-Hit People,* compiled by Alan Lomax (Lincoln: University of Nebraska Press, 1999); first edition, New York: Oak Press, 1967), 342.

15. Richard A. Reuss with Joanne C. Reuss, *American Folk Music and Left-Wing Politics, 1927–1957* (London: Scarecrow Press, 2000), 210.

16. Ibid., 138–139.

17. Alan Lomax, *Selected Writings 1934–1997,* ed. Ronald D. Cohen (New York: Routledge, 2003), 57.

18. Ibid.

19. Ibid., 92–93.

20. Guthrie manuscript, February 23, 1940, reproduced on http://www.woody guthrie.de/this11.html.

21. See Charles Shaar Murray, *Boogie Man: The Adventures of John Lee Hooker in the American Twentieth Century* (London: Viking, 1999).

22. Reuss, 159.

23. Lomax, *Selected Writings,* 89.

24. Ibid.

25. For the best account of the Almanac Singers and the politics of the first folk revival, see Reuss, 147–178.

26. Ibid., 150.

27. Ibid., 168.

28. Ibid., 253.

29. Quoted in Paul Allen Anderson, *Deep River: Music and Memory in Harlem Renaissance Thought* (Durham, NC: Duke University Press, 2001), 237. Anderson's chapter, "Jazz Criticism in the Swing Era" considers Hammond's Spirituals to Swing concert in depth.

30. See "A Booklet of Essays, Appreciations and Annotations Pertaining to the *Anthology of American Folk Music,* edited by Harry Smith," included in the reissue of the *Anthology* by Smithsonian Folkways Recordings, Washington, D.C., 1997.

31. Harry Smith, original notes published with the *Anthology of American Folk Music,* included in Smithsonian Folkways reissue, 2.

32. "A Booklet of Essays," 59.

33. Allen Ginsberg, *Collected Poems, 1947–1980* (New York: Harper and Row, 1984).

34. Lomax, *Selected Writings,* 195.

35. Poem reproduced at http://www.bobdylanroots.com/folklore.html.

36. *Biograph* notes, 30–35.

37. Theodor Adorno, *The Jargon of Authenticity,* trans. Knut Tarnowski and Frederic Will (London: Routledge, 2003), 3–6.

38. Alan Lomax, *The Land Where the Blues Began* (New York: The New Press, 2002; original edition, New York: Pantheon, 1993), 12–17.

39. Heylin, 99–100.

40. "A conversation with Dave Van Ronk," David Walsh, May 7, 1998, on World Socialist Website: http://www.wsws.org/arts/1998/may1998/dvr-m7.shtml.

41. *The Bosses' Songbook—Songs to Stifle the Flames of Discontent,* ed. D. Ellington and D. Van Ronk (New York: Richard Ellington, 1959). Quoted in Reuss, 267. See also: http://recollectionbooks.com/bleed/sinners/EllingtonDick.htm.

42. "From 'The Izzy Young Notebooks,' " in *The Bob Dylan Companion: Four Decades of Commentary,* ed. Carl Benson (New York: Schirmer Books, 1998), 4.

43. *Sing Out!* interview reproduced at http://www.culcom.net/~shadow1/interviews. htm#interview2.

44. Lewis, 187.

45. Quoted in Craig Werner, *A Change Is Gonna Come: Music, Race and the Soul of America* (Edinburgh: Canongate, 2000), 12.

46. On freedom songs, see Branch, 290, 531–32; Werner, 11–15; Brian Ward, *Just My Soul Responding: Rhythm and Blues, Black Consciousness and Race Relations* (London: UCL Press, 1998), 202–203, 269–271. Also *Sing for Freedom: The Story of the Civil Rights Movement Through Its Songs* (Smithsonian/Folkways CD SF 40032.)

47. *We Shall Overcome: The Song That Moved a Nation,* video, 1989. Producers: Jim Brown, Ginger Brown, Harold Levanthal, and George Stoney; Director: Jim Brown.

48. Reuss, 98, 100–103.

49. http://photo.ucr.edu/projects/carawan/default.html.

50. Interview in *They Should Have Served That Cup of Coffee: Seven Radicals Remember the Sixties,* ed. Dick Cutler (Boston: South End Press, 1979), 11–31.

51. Heylin, 89–93.

52. Interview in *Sing Out!* October/November 1962, reprinted in Benson, 65.

53. Quoted in Mary Killebrew, " 'I Never Died . . .': The Words, Music and Influence of Joe Hill," http://www.pbs.org/joehill/voices/article.html.

54. Todd Gitlin, *The Sixties: Years of Hope, Days of Rage* (New York: Bantam Books, revised edition, 1993), 86–97; Fred Halstead, *Out Now: A Participant's Account of the American Movement Against the Vietnam War* (New York: Monad Press, 1978), 7–20; Terry H. Anderson, *The Movement and the Sixties: Protest in American from Greensboro to Wounded Knee* (New York: Oxford University Press, 1995); 58–60.

55. Agnes "Sis" Cunningham and Gordon Friesen, *Red Dust and Broadsides: A Joint Autobiography,* ed. Ronald D. Cohen (Amherst: University of Massachusetts Press, 1999), 273–301; Heylin, 90–92.

56. Heylin, 116–117; Sounes, 130–131.

57. Heylin, 93. See also Sounes, 114–115; *Biograph,* 43.

58. Daniel Wolff, *You Send Me: The Life and Times of Sam Cooke* (London: Virgin, 1996), 243.

59. Heylin, 329–330.

60. Gitlin, 111–126; Kirkpatrick Sale, *SDS* (New York: Vintage, 1974), 49–70; Bloom and Breines, 61–74.

61. Heylin, 105.

62. Branch, 662–672.

63. Heylin, 741.

64. Sam Aaronovitch, "The American Threat to British Culture," *Arena: A Magazine of Modern Literature,* June/July 1951, 3–22.

65. Raphael Samuels, *Theatres of Memory* (London: Verso, 1994), 206–207.

66. Lomax, *Selected Writings,* 135–138.

67. Quoted in C. P. Lee, *Like the Night: Bob Dylan and the Road to the Manchester Free Trade Hall* (London: Helter Skelter, 1998), 32–35.

68. Samuels, 305–306.

69. A chat with Martin Carthy by Matthew Zuckerman, in *Isis: A Bob Dylan Anthology,*

ed. Derek Barker (London: Helter Skelter, 2001), 55–62. For Dylan in London 1962–63, see also Derek Barker, "One Time in London," in *Isis,* 49–54; Heylin, 105–111.

70. Ewan MacColl, "Contemporary Song," in *Sing Out!* September 1965; *Bob Dylan: The Early Years, a Retrospective,* ed. Craig McGregor (New York: Da Capo Press, 1990), 91–92.

71. Hajdu, 134.

72. Bloom and Breines, 223.

73. Martin Luther King, Jr., "Letter from a Birmingham City Jail," in *A Testament of Hope, Essential Writings of Martin Luther King, Jr.,* ed. James M. Washington (San Francisco. HarperCollins, 1991).

74. Marable, 70–73.

75. Branch, 813.

76. For an account of the struggle in Greenwood see Branch, 714–725.

77. On Dylan in Greenwood see Shelton, 170–179; Sounes, 133–134; "Northern Folk Singers Help Out at Negro Festival in Mississippi," *New York Times* article, in McGregor, 38.

78. Shelton 179–180; Heylin, 121.

79. Ward, 300–303.

80. See Jim Capaldi's article on *Broadside,* http://ourworld.compuserve.com/homepages/JimCapaldi/Brdsidel.htm.

81. Phil Ochs, "The Art of Bob Dylan's 'Hattie Carroll,' " *Broadside,* July 20, 1964. Available at: http://www.cs.pdx.edu/~trent/ochs/hattie-carroll.html.

82. Michael Olesker, "Charles County Case Prompts Call for Sequel to Song," *Baltimore Sun,* November 21, 1991; see also http://www.expectingrain.com/dok/who/z/zantzingerwilliam.html.

83. *Biograph,* 43.

CHAPTER TWO: NOT MUCH IS REALLY SACRED

1. For Dylan at the ECLC dinner, see Shelton, 200–205. The full transcript of Dylan's speech, Corliss Lamont's letter in defense of Dylan, and Dylan's free-verse apology can be found at http://www.corliss-lamont.org/dylan.htm.

2. See Mike Marqusee, *Redemption Song: Muhammad Ali and the Spirit of the Sixties* (London: Verso, 1999).

3. Sale, 106; Gitlin, 198.

4. Sale, 101.

5. For Dylan's February 1964 road trip see Shelton, 239–251; Heylin, 145–149; Sounes, 146–149.

6. Michael Gray, *Song and Dance Man III: The Art of Bob Dylan* (London: Continuum, 2000), 81.

7. Nat Hentoff, "The Crackin', Shakin', Breakin' Sounds," in McGregor, 47–59.

8. Irwin Silber, "An Open Letter to Bob Dylan," *Sing Out!,* November 1964; McGregor, 66–70; Benson, 26–29.

9. Heylin, 165.

10. Hajdu, 211–212.

11. Lewis, 250.

12. For Mississippi Summer, see Lewis 241–274; Bloom and Breines, 34–39.

13. Bloom and Breines, 42–43.

14. Lewis, 282.

15. Mark Kemp, "Song of a Soldier: The Life and Times of Phil Ochs," in *Farewells and Fantasies* 3 (CD box set), Elektra, 1997. On Ochs and *Broadside* see also: Cunningham and Friesen, *passim.*

16. On Ochs and Dylan see Shelton, 259; Heylin, 234.

17. Quoted in Hajdu, 201–202. An edited version appears in Shelton, 359.

18. Lewis, 262.

19. Peter Burns, *Curtis Mayfield: People Never Give Up* (London: Sanctuary, 2003), 12. On Mayfield see also Clive Anderson, Introduction to notes included with *Curtis Mayfield: Soul Legacy,* compiled by Lawrence Roker (4 CD box set) Charly, 2001; and Ward, 276, 298–299; Werner, 144–151.

20. Leroi Jones, *Black Music,* 1967, excerpt in *The Leroi Jones/Amiri Baraka Reader,* ed. William J. Harris (New York: Thunder's Mouth Press, 1991), 207.

21. Interview in *Soul* magazine, 1969, quoted in Ward, 414.

22. *Biograph,* 50.

23. John Berger, *Ways of Seeing,* 1972.

24. Accounts of Selma march in Lewis, 301–347; Marable, 80–81; Garrow 378–414.

25. Lewis, 340.

26. *Biograph,* 35.

27. For Ginsberg in Prague see Barry Miles, *Ginsberg: A Biography* (London: Viking, 1990), 353–368; "Big Beat," Ginsberg, *Poems,* 349.

28. "Kral Majales," Ginsberg, *Poems,* 353.

29. On the International Poetry Festival at Albert Hall, see Jonathon Green, *Days in the Life: Voices from the English Underground, 1961–1971* (London: Pimlico, 1998; first edition 1988), 63–74. See also Miles, 369–372.

30. Michael Horovitz, "Afterwords," in *Children of Albion: Poetry of the "Underground"in Britain,* ed. Michael Horovitz (London: Penguin, 1968).

31. Ibid, 338.

32. "Who Be Kind To," Ginsberg, *Poems,* 359.

CHAPTER THREE: LITTLE BOY LOST

1. Sale, 185–193; Gitlin, 179–186, 242; Halstead, 24–44.

2. Bloom and Breines, 219.

3. Sale, 221–223, Gitlin 186–187.

4. Gitlin, 178.

5. Heylin, 206. For accounts of Dylan at Newport 1965 see Heylin, 206–216; Sounes 180–184; Shelton 301–304.

6. Sounes, 182.

7. Lomax, 90–91.

8. *Biograph,* 35

9. Dylan interview by Nora Ephron and Susan Edmiston, in McGregor, 89–90.

10. Heylin, 234.

11. Springsteen's induction speech for Dylan at the Rock 'n' Roll Hall of Fame, 1989: http://candysroom.freeservers.com/bruceweb151.html.

12. In D. A. Pennebaker's *Don't Look Back* (1967).

13. *Biograph* notes.

14. Lewis, 350–351.

15. Bloom and Breines, 633–634.

16. Erich Auerbach, *Mimesis: The Representation of Reality in Western Literature,* trans. Willard R. Trask, (Princeton, NJ: Princeton University Press, 1953), 11–12.

17. *Biograph,* 13–14.

18. "Just Like a Woman," Barbara Goscza, can be found on *May Your Song Always Be Sung: The Songs of Bob Dylan, Vol. 2* (CD), BMG, 2001.

19. Theodor Adorno, *The Culture Industry: Selected Essays on Mass Culture,* ed. J. M. Bernstein (London: Routledge Classic, 2001), 32, 37, 40, 46–47, 52, 53, 55.

20. Ibid., 98–99.

21. Ibid., 55.

22. Walter Benjamin, *One-Way Street and Other Writings,* trans. Edmund Jephcott and Kingsley Shorter (London: New Left Books, 1979), 227; Larry "Ratso" Sloman, *Reefer Madness: A History of Marijuana* (New York: St. Martin's Griffin, 1998; original edition 1979), 84–101, 171–186.

23. Miles, 378–381; James Miller, *Flowers in the Dustbin: The Rise of Rock and Roll, 1947–1977* (New York: Fireside/Simon & Schuster, 1999), 235–241.

24. Miles, 385–386, "Wichita Vortex Sutra," Ginsberg, *Poems,* 394–411.

25. Ginsberg, interview, 158.

26. Lee.

27. "Interview with Mickey Jones," in Barker, 96.

28. "Some Great Live Performances—Royal Albert Hall, May 27, 1966: Three Eyewitness Accounts Reconstructed," in Barker, 107–114

29. Marable, 94; Lewis, 371.

30. Garrow, 500.

31. Bloom and Breines, 634.

32. Heylin, 266–269; Shelton, 371–375; Sounes, 216–218.s

CHAPTER FOUR: THE WICKED MESSENGER

1. Quoted in Horovitz, 365.

2. Martin Luther King, *Where Do We Go from Here? Chaos or Community* (London: Penguin, 1969).

3. Andrew Kopkind, *The Thirty Years War: Dispatches and Diversions of a Radical Journalist, 1965–1994* (London: Verso, 1995), 87.

4. Sale, 325.

5. Ibid., 341, 351.

6. Ibid., 352.

7. Ibid., 349–350.

8. Ibid., 344, 349.

9. Jerry Rubin, *Do It!* excerpt in Bloom and Breines, 325.

10. *Biograph,* 18.

11. Bobby Seale, *Seize the Time: The Story of the Black Panther Party and Huey P. Newton* (Baltimore: Black Classic Press, 1991; original edition Random House, 1971), 183–187.

12. Greil Marcus. *Invisible Republic: Bob Dylan's Basement Tapes* (London: Picador, 1997), 124.

13. Ibid., 69.

14. "Conversations with Bob Dylan," interview by John Cohen and Happy Traum, *Sing Out!* October–November 1968, in McGregor, 291.

15. Marcus, 70.

16. Halstead, 204.

17. Interview 1968, in Allen Ginsberg, *Spontaneous Mind: Selected Interviews 1958–1996,* ed. David Carter (London: Penguin, 2001), 143–154.

18. Heylin, 287

19. *Sing Out!* interview in McGregor, 280.

20. Ibid, 291.

21. Reuss, 108.

22. Jon Landau, *John Wesley Harding, Crawdaddy,* 1968, in McGregor, 260.

23. Barker, 104.

24. Sale.

25. *Sing Out!* interview, in McGregor, 265–294.

26. Burns, 44.

27. On the events in Chicago 1968 see Anderson, 214–226; Gitlin 326–336; Abe Peck, *Uncovering the Sixties: The Life and Times of the Underground Press* (New York: Citadel Press, 1991), 111–119. For Ochs at Chicago see Kemp, 42.

28. Kemp, 80.

29. Peck, 169.

30. Ibid., 169–170.

31. Ibid., 176.

32. On the Weathermen see Sale, 557–599; Gitlin, 385–400; Ron Jacobs, *The Way the Wind Blew: A History of the Weather Underground* (London: Verso, 1997).

33. Sale, 480–481; Gitlin, 409.

34. Kopkind, 180.

35. Ibid., 171.

36. Sounes, 249.

37. Kopkind, 171–175; Peck, 177–180.

38. Charles Shaar Murray, *Crosstown Traffic: Jimi Hendrix and Post-War Pop* (London: Faber and Faber, 2001), 32.

39. Peck, 178–180.

40. Ibid., 179.

41. Kopkind, 175.

42. Sale, 600–615; Gitlin, 393–394.

43. Halstead, 491–521; Kopkind, 181–187.

44. Sale, 626–630; Jacobs, 84–89.

45. Halstead, 561.

46. See Jonathan Neale, *The American War: Vietnam, 1960–1975* (London: Bookmarks, 2001).

47. Bloom and Breines, 634.

48. Heylin, 321.

AFTERWORD: CORRUPTIBLE SEED

1. Sinclair quoted in Fred Goodman, *The Mansion on the Hill: Dylan, Young, Springsteen and the Head-on Collision of Rock and Commerce* (New York: Vintage, 1998), 284–285.

2. Eric Alterman, *It Ain't No Sin to Be Glad You're Alive: The Promise of Bruce Springsteen* (Boston: Back Bay Books, 2001), 277–288.

3. Quoted in Alterman, 288.

4. Carter, 391.

5. Sounes, 366–367.

6. Interview with Mikal Gilmore, 1985, in Benson, 181.

INDEX

Album titles are set in italics. Song titles are enclosed in quotations.